CHRISTINE KEELER was a successful model – her portrait astride a chair is iconic – and she now writes and broadcasts. Tried for perjury following the death of Stephen Ward and briefly jailed, the story of her early life was adapted as the film *Scandal*. The truth is far more interesting and intriguing. She has written this book with the author Douglas Thompson.

DOUGLAS THOMPSON is the author of fifteen books. A biographer, broadcaster and international journalist he is a regular contributor to major newspapers and magazines worldwide. His books, published in a dozen languages, include the television-linked anthology *Hollywood People* and bestselling biographies of Madonna, Clint Eastwood, Michelle Pfeiffer, Dudley Moore, John Travolta and Leonardo DiCaprio. Recent successes include collaboration with the entertainer Paul Nicholas, *Behind the Smile*, and with Robson Green and Stephen Tomkinson about their television series, *Grafters*. He lives with his wife and daughter in a farmhouse near Cambridge and commutes regularly to California.

THE TRUTH
AT LAST

– My Story –

CHRISTINE KEELER
with Douglas Thompson

PAN BOOKS

First published 2001 by Sidgwick & Jackson

This edition published with a new chapter 2002 by Pan Books
an imprint of Pan Macmillan Ltd
Pan Macmillan, 20 New Wharf Road, London N1 9RR
Basingstoke and Oxford
Associated companies throughout the world
www.panmacmillan.com

ISBN 0 330 48167 3

1 3 5 7 9 8 6 4 2

A CIP catalogue record for this book is available
from the British Library.

Typeset by SX Composing DTP, Rayleigh, Essex
Printed and bound in Great Britain by
Mackays of Chatham plc, Chatham, Kent

Picture Credits
Unless otherwise stated, photographs are from the Christine Keeler
collection, reproduced by permission of Christine Keeler.
Lewis Morley photographs reproduced by permission
of Christine Keeler and Lewis Morley/the Akehurst Bureau
Adrian Houston photograph reproduced by permission
of Christine Keeler and Adrian Houston
Cottage and main house at Cliveden reproduced
by permission of Robert Smith
Lucky Gordon, Stephen Ward, Stephen Ward with Christine Keeler
and two friends, Jack Profumo, Horace Dibden, Roger Hollis, Eugene Ivanov,
Mandy Rice-Davies and Christine Keeler at the Old Bailey, Lord Denning
reproduced by permission of Hulton Getty Picture Collection

to Desmond Banks

I NOSTALGICISED THE GOVERNMENT BY THE UPPER CLASS, WHICH IS
WHAT I THOUGHT IT WOULD BE – THE WHOLE THING REALLY RUN BY THE
OLD ETONIAN MAFIA – WHEN FIRST I WANTED TO GET IN IN 1964.

Alan Clark, *Diaries*, 1993

AS FOR CHRISTINE KEELER, LET NO ONE JUDGE HER TOO HARSHLY.
SHE WAS NOT YET TWENTY-ONE. AND SINCE THE AGE OF SIXTEEN
SHE HAS BEEN ENMESHED IN A NET OF WICKEDNESS.

Lord Denning, the 'Denning Report', September 1963

CONTENTS

ACKNOWLEDGEMENTS

I thank my son Seymour for being so supportive; Robert Smith for all his hard work, patience and dedication; Douglas Thompson for his keen mind and perceptive nature; Gordon Scott Wise for his vision; Stephanie Williams for her loyalty over the years; and the rest of the girls, Renuka and Sally.

PROLOGUE

GUNSMOKE

I NEVER DID APOLOGISE FOR SHOOTING THROUGH YOUR FRONT DOOR.

Johnnie Edgecombe in a letter to Dr Stephen
Ward written from prison in 1963

London, 1962

I counted out the twenty pounds in single notes and the man carefully handed me the gun. It was a German Luger, an automatic. He also gave me two magazines, one with six cartridges, the other with seven.

I wondered if I could have paid less for just a few bullets. My stepfather had taught me how to shoot and I thought one or two shots would do the job. Looking at the man with the gun, however, it didn't seem worth arguing about. Clearly, for him, the deal was as arranged: automatic and bullets for me, twenty pounds for him.

A cigarette dangling on his lip – it seems silly now but I was worried about the ash falling on the carpet – he slowly counted out the money, note by note, on to the table in the front room of the flat I was sharing with Paula Hamilton-Marshall in Devonshire Street in the West End of London.

The gun-dealer had delivered what I wanted: my chance finally to do away with my tormentor, to kill him.

Though I knew it was for self-protection, I expected to go to gaol, but only for a few years. Yet, because of that damn gun, I have been serving a sentence almost all my life. For nearly forty years I've been branded by events which were turned into a sexual circus to cover up the truth. And I have been jumping through hoops, fearing for my life – and running for it – ever since.

I still believe I could be killed at any moment. Others have been. For I know the truth and it is far more shocking than what the public has been fed through the courts and the press by the British Establishment. Sex was a game; spying was a serious business.

Far better that the Establishment be caught with its pants down than involved in stealing secrets – that was the thinking. Far better for the public to be titillated by aristocratic misdemeanours and laugh at supposedly esteemed public figures begging to be dominated as sex slaves or prancing around in aprons and leather masks and demanding to be whipped for being naughty.

It is important to remember the time, the early 1960s. The difficult days of the 1950s with rationing and shortages were over. People were beginning to feel better: there was a post-war feeling of expectation, almost a euphoria. Harold Macmillan was in residence at 10 Downing Street, telling us: 'You've never had it so good.' He would regret saying that. His 1959 election slogan was to be mercilessly satirized by, amongst others, Trog in *Private Eye*, who drew an exhausted Macmillan staggering away from a hoarding complete with ladder and brush, having just pasted up 'We've never had it so often.'

They said sex began in 1963 with the Pill. Nonsense. It was labels like 'the permissive society' that started being used in the 1960s. There was a boom in psychologists, psychiatrists and psycho-babble as well as the Pill. Suddenly, sex was something people were talking about as well as enjoying – the lace curtains of the 1950s were being pulled back.

It was in this atmosphere – hemlines going up, inhibitions coming down, promiscuity being promoted as mandatory rather than optional – that I innocently wandered into a den of spooks and spies, of men and women on both sides of the Iron Curtain who were operating as much for their own self-interest as for that of the mandarins in Moscow, Washington and London.

I was seventeen years old and warm-hearted in the summer of 1959 when I arrived in London and, unknowingly, into the shadowland Cold-War-era world of those secret armies, the spies. By the late 1950s and early 1960s the focus of British and US intelligence was to fight Soviet subversion in Western Europe. These were the days of names now redolent of espionage: double agent Kim Philby, Royal art surveyor and spy Anthony Blunt, renegades like Guy Burgess and Donald Maclean who had already gone 'over the wall' to Moscow in 1955. There were rumours of dirty deeds, from assassination plots and hazy endeavours to retrieve files detailing the Duke of Windsor's Nazi sympathies to just how many Communist moles comprised the Cambridge spy ring. And how many others were there, scheming and conniving, in unsuspecting corners of society? As we've seen, some are today's grandmothers. There were even said to be agents who truly did have a licence to kill, some of whom had worked on the direct orders of Winston Churchill. And it was so often an alphabetic jungle, a mess of ideals, with MI6, MI5, the CIA and the KGB often taking the same route for different objectives and ideologies.

What happened as a result of my finding myself in the centre of all of this meant I could never escape being Christine Keeler.

I have studied it all for decades, for I have not been able to lead a normal life. And it is now with that scholarship, hindsight and, of course, my day-to-day witnessing of events as they happened, that I feel able, at last, to tell the whole truth. It has not been easy. I do have guilt but now my interests have become secondary to telling the story as it was, as it really happened. I now know that I became a pawn in the Cold War.

Then, the world of espionage was in chaos and there were very real fears that someone might push a button and the world would suddenly stop. But at one time, I was more frightened of being beaten or knifed to death than bombed. Which was why I bought that German Luger. And what happened was the ultimate irony: the gun I had bought to protect myself would be fired – but not by me – and ignite the most lurid *cause célèbre* of the twentieth century.

It seems that even now, in another century, my name is mentioned on the radio or television or in newspapers almost every day. I've been a crossword-puzzle clue, a question on Trivial Pursuit, a 'starter' on *University Challenge*. I have debated the perils of tobacco on the BBC and been approached by British Airways to be a 'twenty-first-century icon' as well as the subject of despicable head-lines and revolting rumours.

It's been suggested that I participated in strange sexual perversions involving the Kennedy White House (if the most powerful man in the Western world did play doctors and nurses in the Oval Office with a redhead dressed up as a nurse, it wasn't me) as well as being some sort of Mata Hari. But, while heavyweight studies are pub-lished around the world and I'm quoted without having actually said a word, in this book I will speak. And at the outset I'll say I was a spy, but never willingly betrayed my country.

History says my story is about sex. It is, of course, but that is just moments of it. I have always been free with my love – it is my nature. I am easily captivated by men and they have always been attracted to me. Maybe I fall in love too easily, trust too quickly, but there never was and never has been anything devious or obscene about my relationships. I liked men and they liked me. Over all the years the sex has taken the searchlights off the spies. Now I am telling for the first time *all* the story.

You might think you know about my life because you lived through it or have seen *Scandal*, the film made about me some years ago, at the cinema or when it is re-run on television. I'm sorry, but that film was just a snapshot of what really went on. Believe me, the truth is stranger than fiction but the whole truth has been too tough to face until now. It is something I have had to do for myself and for history because my story has been distorted.

Am I just crying over spilt milk? Rubbish. That way you just weep yourself to sleep and drown in self pity. You have to fight back, which is why I am about to tell you all this now.

I am revealing things that I have never spoken about before and they do not always reflect well on me. I have to face myself and deal with that. I have always denied being a prostitute and I still do in the sense that most people understand the word. I was set up by the authorities and branded in court as a prostitute but that was to keep me quiet, to stop me telling the truth. I was not the common tart they tried to paint me. It's true that I have had sex for money but only out of desperation and that is still something that I hate to have to admit even to myself. Ironically, it has been sex for love or lust rather than for money that has always caused me more problems.

I was recruited by a clever, charismatic but dangerous man who, when alive, and even after his death, fooled the intelligence services of the West. Stephen Ward has been portrayed in court, in government reports, in film and television as an immoral rascal; he was dismissed as a dilettante Communist sympathizer who was only of harm to himself, a somewhat silly, vain man.

In reality, Stephen Ward was a spymaster who befriended hosts of prominent and powerful people in the British government, aristocracy and even members of the royal family. With associates, he lured many of them into compromising situations. I don't know if he should be called the fourth man or the fifth man or the sixth man but he was in the Top Ten.

Stephen wasn't a mole – he was a badger. He always knew what he was after and, if cornered, he would kill to protect himself. His espionage activities included Moscow's audacious act of putting one of their men at the heart of the British Secret Service during the most difficult period of the Cold War when the paranoia over 'The Bomb' – specifically nuclear missiles – was at its height: who had them and who could use them? Where? And when?

Stephen Ward was in the middle of all this, a spider with a malevolent web that I was, with hindsight, so easily snared into. In turn, his devious plotting against me helped bring about his own downfall and that of the last Conservative grandee government. He had been my mentor, my Svengali, from the time I arrived in London as a teenager. I loved him but we were never lovers. Stephen could only make love to those he despised and even then only in a certain way. Even now it is hard, almost impossible, to explain because it is on a purely emotional rather than factual level that I know Stephen loved me. Nevertheless, he would have killed me as easily as light my cigarette. He stitched me up, stitch after very neat stitch. He was bad and ruthless. Imagine wanting me dead and being quite willing to do it. But I lived through it and survived and I have had four decades to reflect on it.

When I say I 'survived', obviously I have, physically. But I have lived in dread for I know things you just cannot speak about. It's not that I was ashamed of having slept with John Profumo, the Secretary of State for War in Harold Macmillan's cabinet. Or having been manipulated into having sex with a spy from Moscow Centre – in the same week.

Or of attending any of the sex parties which seemed to be part of the Swinging Sixties. Or having sex with President Kennedy's brother-in-law or a threesome with a Hollywood star (where are the pictures he took now?). I was always a most enthusiastic amateur, just as I was when playing bridge with Yehudi Menuhin. But I sensed a threat, which I felt I could not talk openly about. I had concerns for my family, for my two sons. I officially changed my name to escape from a society which would not allow me to live and earn a living legitimately as Christine Keeler. I still dress down as a disguise, hiding in jeans and big woolly jumpers, anoraks and cover-up coats.

I think I might have been one of the most moral women of that particular, frenzied decade. I enjoyed sex and I indulged in it when I fancied the men, but I was no hypocrite. It was others who were disguising their peccadilloes in dinner jackets, diamonds and evening dresses, indulging in weird fantasies. Public probity was just another mask worn by many in the Establishment.

But the world marched on, ignorant of what had really happened. And why not? The official cover-up was titillating enough.

I still find it astonishing that Lord Denning went along with it all. He was the man appointed by Prime Minister Harold Macmillan to lead the inquiry into my involvement with John Profumo and a Soviet spy and what it all meant in terms of British and world security. Lord Denning, the Master of the Rolls, a respected judge, a grand old man of the law, took evidence from me and one hundred and fifty-nine other witnesses over forty-nine days and then published what he wanted.

He never got beyond the hall of mirrors. I had lived in dread of him – this nice, comforting man who took all my evidence and then discarded it. When I complained I was threatened with spending the rest of my life in gaol: Denning quietly but very clearly told me that if I did not behave and stay quiet he would see to it that I did not 'see the light of day for many years'. Instead, he published lies. I had told him everything I am going to tell you but he ignored it, shunned the truth about so much involving Downing Street, the White House and so-called high society. I told him about threats to John Kennedy who would die in Dallas a few months later and about so much else. Denning and the Macmillan government did not want to know about any of that. It was much easier to put the emphasis on other matters and decide that Britain's security was never under threat. What a joke. And Denning knew it. He even showed me a photograph of the man who was one of the twentieth century's cleverest, or maybe luckiest, spies and asked me to identify him; there were other photographs, other double agents.

I suppose the cover-up was not too great a task, for in the secret world, as I so quickly learned, truth and deception wear the same gloves. The Americans, however, were not taken in. And the relations between the British agencies – MI5 and MI6 and Special Branch – and the CIA and FBI in Washington have never re-covered.

I went to Lord Denning looking for a way out of the mess I was in and he juggled with my life and, like a conjurer, made the truth vanish. In the end I was as frightened of what that old man could do as I was of the other dangers I faced. He always smiled at me – and it was a fatherly smile – but all the time it was just to shut me up. The Denning Report published in September 1963, was my downfall. He lied and lied again to make me impotent, to discredit me as a witness, to disguise the truth and destroy my credibility. Denning lived a lie from the summer of 1963 and I don't know how his conscience allowed him to do so, which is another reason I am telling the truth now. I don't want to die and let the lies become history. No one else knows the whole story. I was there. I lived through it. Even now I shake my head and wonder how I survived in view of what I was up against.

But I've been frightened, so frightened to tell everything before. In the mid-1990s I left London to live by the sea and try to find some contentment. I had a family friend in the area and went to visit her. She was living with this man and they seemed to have a pleasant enough life. He knew who I was and paid a lot of attention to me. A few days later, he turned up at my home. I didn't want the attention, I wanted a quiet life but he clearly thought he could have sex with me. He was a pest, another person who heard my name and allowed his imagination to take over. He would not stay away so I asked my friend to talk to him and this awful man told her: 'Christine Keeler? Someone like her usually ends up murdered.'

It was then that I determined to tell my story – all of it – for the first time. I have flirted with some of it before but, as with the film *Scandal*, the surface has barely been rippled.

I used to smile when I was working anonymously in a dry-cleaners or selling advertising space on the telephone about this image people had of me as some grand femme fatale. Yes, I've had my Chanel suits and Bond Street and Harrods accounts but, for many years now I've been more Gap than Gucci, preferring not to draw attention to myself.

Nevertheless, however I dress it up, I was a spy and I am not proud of it. Stephen Ward and Anthony Blunt and the others carried on in front of me as though I was one of them but I wouldn't get involved. I tried to block it out – I was too scared. All these years I hid it from myself, but the truth is that I betrayed my country. Just by admitting that for the first time I have freed myself of an enormously heavy emotional burden. Whenever people have tried to put all the jigsaw together they have been prevented because they didn't have all the pieces. That's why, after years of heart searching, I am finally telling everything. Now, I am at an age when you face, even peacefully, your mortality. If I don't tell it all now, the story in the history books will always be imperfect and that would be wrong.

This thought has finally enabled me to confront what I really did. I have been too ashamed until now to face up to that. I didn't do it for money, I did it for love. But not for a man I ever slept with. On all but a few occasions I have never slept with a man I didn't fancy. But just because I fancied them did not make them good men. Or honest ones. And one I didn't fancy, Aloysius 'Lucky' Gordon, was a vicious man – which is why I bought that Luger. I still wish the bullets had gone in him and nowhere else. Life was never to be normal after that, not after that pistol magazine was emptied at the front door of Stephen Ward's London mews flat. Those seven bullets were fired on 14 December 1962.

They are still ricocheting.

I

NIGHTLIFE

CHRISTINE KEELER EXUDED SEXUALITY, AN ASTONISHINGLY BEAUTIFUL GIRL,
BUT MANDY RICE-DAVIES WAS A BAG OF BONES REALLY, NOT MY TYPE AT ALL.

Peter Bachelor, thirty-year staff veteran of Murray's Cabaret Club

When I take the Tube into central London in this new century I often feel drawn – if it's good walking weather – to some of the old haunts of the Sixties. It's as much to see what's not there any more as to see what has replaced it. The wind of social change? More like a hurricane. I love London for, despite all that happened in the city, I still feel it is my home town. I can drive around without maps, the *A to Z* is in my head. I was one of the first go up in the London Eye which I think is fantastic.

Beak Street is only a short walk up Regent Street from Piccadilly Circus. There's a big British Airways office on the corner and along the street an Italian restaurant and lots of offices full of arty types, people involved in books, magazines and the movies.

Murray's Cabaret Club is no longer there but that's where I first became a sex object. There's nothing much left of it in Soho except the legend and the memories. The basement premises are now the Kabaret club, part of the K-Bar chain, and they have reproduced the oak-panelling, high-backed leather chairs look and the idea of table service.

This story really starts with Murray's, for the club reflected the times and the aspirations and morals of a certain section of society. Downstairs, we star showgirls walked bare-breasted on to the stage, and the hostesses, all cleavage and chat, moved among the wealthy and aristocratic middle-aged male diners and drinkers. However, they could look but could not touch. 'Pops' Murray, as he instructed his 'girls' to call him, ran a sort of visual brothel. There was a pervasive atmosphere of sex, with beautiful young girls all over the place, but customers would always say, if asked, that they only came for the floor show and the food and drink. Indeed it was legend in the West End – again a monument to Pops Murray's perfect sense of public relations – that if anyone 'laid a hand on' any of his girls they would be thrown out, or if any one of us was discovered 'up the lane' after the show with a customer, we would be sacked.

For many men, Murray's provided the venue and the ambience in which to meet beautiful young girls they would not normally have encountered. Some of the girls dreamed of marrying a millionaire and some, indeed, married money and Establishment titles. Pops boasted that the 'crowned heads of Europe' sat at his tables, and many did, but most were the home-grown wealthy, the influential, and especially the aristocracy. If sex had been a social problem Pops Murray – a Scotsman – had found a perfectly English solution to a perfectly English problem.

Percy Murray ended the First World War as a major, but his ambition had always been to dance. A war wound put an end to that so he went into nightclubs, first in Belgium and later in London. The first Murray's Club opened just before the Second World War next door to the Cabaret Club, and when the Cabaret Club went up for sale, Murray bought it and combined the two to open Murray's Cabaret Club. In the austere 1950s, Murray's, with its showgirls and floor show, was a rare West End bright spot.

As the 1960s approached, Pops was already a rich man, with Rolls-Royces and Daimlers, flats in Mayfair and Bournemouth, and a 40-acre estate in Churt in Surrey. He also spent three months of the year in the Majestic Hotel in Cannes. He was a lot older than any of the girls but he had a reputation for running 'the best you've ever had' casting couch. Melanie Carver, who shared her life with Pops, never believed it. She was so young, just sixteen, when she went to work at Murray's that he applied for her to be made his ward of court, to protect her. She lived with him for many years as a member of his family and was close to him until he died in 1979.

He was a careful man. The wages were miserable and we were closely controlled: a hole in your fishnet tights meant a reduction from your wages for a new pair; there were even regular nail-varnish inspections – for cracks or breaks – and the accommodation backstage was cramped. Fines were common for the least offence, waiters had the cost of empty bottles taken from the club deducted from their wages, and whoever else was allowed in, no member of Equity would ever be employed. The club was Pops's life; he had a direct line telephone from his bed to the office.

I came to work there by complete chance. One thing just led to another. My life has always gone in fits and starts punctuated by divine – or often not-so-divine – intervention. I had gone to London in 1959 with my friend from home, Pat, we were sharing rooms and, like many of the young people we met, we were broke and starving hungry. One day I walked into a nearby Greek restaurant in Swiss Cottage. There was a friendly atmosphere about the place and it was alive with young people. Jennifer Harvey was sitting with her Greek boyfriend Andreas who ran the place. Jenny was the beautiful feathered dancer featured in Murray's velvet-covered brochure. We're still good friends, Jenny and I, part of that past. That day things were so desperate I approached Andreas nervously and asked if he could let me have some bread and milk and I would pay him as soon as I could. They both looked a little startled. Jenny was a natural blonde with blue eyes and a perfect figure. She spoke straight and to the point: 'Give it to her, Andreas, and I'll pay you the money if she doesn't come back.'

Andreas had a neat, trimmed moustache and beard. He was hand-some with sharp features and he wore a hand-made tailored suit. He ordered the waiter to get the bread and milk and asked me if I wanted a cup of coffee, but I refused as I had to get back to Pat with the food.

After I left I later learned that Jenny and Andreas bet on whether I'd be back or not, Jenny betting that I would. I did return the following evening as Pat had managed to get a few pounds together. When I arrived Andreas was sitting with some friends; he offered me a cup of coffee and invited me to join them, telling me that

Jenny had just left to go to work at the Pigalle Club where she was a dancer. I told him that I was looking for a job and he suggested I try another Greek restaurant, Angelo's, where a job was going as a cloakroom girl and also serving behind the bar. I was lucky and managed to get it. That way I met a Greek called Harry Avoletis who was a regular at the restaurant. He was a student of philosophy, very quietly spoken, a lover of concert music and Indian food. He was huge and powerfully built with tight, curly black hair. He looked like a Greek god, very athletic, and hoped to run the marathon for Cyprus in the Olympic Games. I even think I was a little in love with him; he certainly fascinated me for a time. But life wasn't exactly exciting; I hardly went out because money was so short, so I just dreamed that one day something would happen to change my life. That chance arrived in the shape of a beautiful woman, Maureen O'Connor, girlfriend of a friend of Harry's.

She walked into the restaurant one night in a glamorous dress, her hair shimmering. She was amazing; all eyes turned as she walked past. The waiters, even the manager, were attentive. I had never seen anything like her before; she looked like someone from the pages of *Vogue*, impossibly elegant and well groomed, confident and graceful.

I was mesmerized. While I was clearing her table she started talking to me, laughing and chatting so easily. Then she asked if I was interested in trying for another job.

'Why don't you come and work at the Cabaret Club? That's where I work. The money's much better and it would be much more fun. Mr Murray, the owner, is always looking for new talent and you've got just the right kind of looks.'

I did not react particularly coolly. In fact, I squealed: 'Me?'

'Yes, why not? I'll arrange for you to meet him,' she said. 'I know you'll do fine.'

'What do you have to do?'

'Dance on stage.'

I went along to the interview in a state – I had stage fright before I even had the job, being the kind of person who got butterflies before even getting near the stage. But when I arrived, I thought the club was such a let-down, really shabby. Faded red lamps stood on the tables and in the revealing daylight you could see the flaking paint and tarnished fittings. Where were the glittering costumes? Upstairs, being patched by the girls? Where were the soft lights, the music, the romance?

But eight pounds, ten shillings a week was still a dream and it eliminated the nightmare of worrying about the rent or money for the gas meter. Maybe it was even a chance to become someone in this world.

Pops was as much of a shock as the crumbling grandeur of the club. I don't know what my image of an entertainment mogul was – like Lew Grade, I suppose: the big cigar and lots of showmanship. Pops, who styled himself on the club brochure as 'Percival Murray, Founder, Creator and Active President', had a big, naughty grin and heavy-rimmed spectacles dominating his face. He looked too jolly to be the boss. But that, indeed, was what he was. He was right down to business without any fanfare: 'OK. Let's see if you can do anything. Put on a costume and just see if you can follow the routine.'

I was terrified and my heart thumped as I moved with the music. I just wanted to disappear before they chucked me out.

'Right. Enough,' screamed Pops.

I froze. I was shocked and then he shouted:

'You're hired. '

It was a wonderful moment. Blissfully ignorant of the disastrous chain of events that was to follow, I giggled with nervous excitement, thrilled and happy to be given this opportunity.

I loved it when I first started work, really loved it. I began as an understudy and had to work with all the other girls to learn the steps. There were plenty of rules so it took a little while, but at last I felt that I belonged. Most of the customers were pampered old men, but we had a few parties with some of the Arab boys who came to the club. They were young and looking for fun. After we finished work, they'd be waiting outside to take us out for a cup of coffee. Then we could relax and giggle and stop pretending to be nice to clients. It wasn't long before the money improved; the girl

I had been understudying left, and once onstage I soon got a starring part in the show. When we weren't onstage, we were allowed to sit out with the audience for a hostess fee of five pounds. That way I was soon making about thirty pounds a week.

There was always some gossip going on at the club about one or another of the girls' clients or their boyfriends. A girl who had important clients was looked up to by the others. The dressing-room was a radio station for gossip. And there was always one of the girls in trouble and in need of an abortion, which was illegal until the Abortion Act of 1967. There were many backstairs 'doctors' making a good living from performing abortions; one would even host sex parties and then abort girls who got into trouble.

Most of the men at Murray's were older and, on the surface, respectable businessmen. But there were others, like Etonian Michael Lambton, a cousin of Lord Lambton, and a former Guards officer, who took me out to the cinema and to dinner. He didn't like me working at Murray's as it wasn't quite the right place for an aspiring publishing executive's girlfriend to work. He often asked me to leave, but I took no notice. Michael loved to drink and was even banned from the club at one stage. It was New Year's Eve and we had been fooling around together. I ended up pouring a bottle of champagne over his head and he tipped the contents of the ice bucket over mine. It didn't go down well with the management. Nice ex-public schoolboys weren't supposed to do things like that, and they threw him out. It was a shame for he was young, good-looking and good fun. He liked horse racing though he wasn't a gambler and told me there was a curse on his family name. Michael wanted me to move in with him from the beginning but, although I did land up in bed with him, I didn't love him.

Instead, I moved from the double room I'd shared with Pat into a single attic room in the same boarding house as another Greek I had made friends with, Andreas Diamond, who played piano at Angelo's. Andreas had been married to a beautiful Greek actress and was destined to be a concert pianist until he had a dreadful accident with one of his hands. His wife then left him and he emigrated to England. He was a sharp card player and we spent a lot of time together in his room playing. Harry was beginning to bore me; all he though about was getting ready for the Olympics. He'd walk up the five flights to my room with me on his back – in training. I was young and lively and attracted to men and I could always enjoy relationships without long-term commitments. At the club there was a handsome waiter, so good-looking that all the girls eyed him. I took him back to my attic room and I remember Harry coming in early in the morning. The waiter and I lay motionless pretending to be asleep. Harry came over to the bed and lifted the blanket, but we still did not stir. Then he walked quietly away downstairs.

Pops found out and he sacked the waiter. The club rules said that staff were not to mix, but he kept me on after giving me a ticking off. It might have been his conscience; Pops didn't always stick to the non-fraternizing rules himself and was more than a father-figure to some of the girls. I suppose he couldn't help himself with all those naked bums running around. He liked Maureen and me and we got away with a lot more than some of the other girls. I was young and wild then – life was all about having fun and enjoying yourself and I was certainly doing that.

I was still not comfortable onstage at Murray's so I'd pop into Angelo's on my way to the club for a drink which gave me the Dutch courage to appear half-naked. Pops considered that he had the best floor show in the world and it certainly was impressive. There were two shows a night and they each had three different numbers with two stage acts in between. It was all very lavish and the individual costumes cost a fortune. One number was changed each year so we were forever having costume fittings or rehearsals. There were two different bands, one playing Latin American, the other more traditional music. When the band played 'That's Why the Lady is a Tramp', it was time for us to get ready for the show.

During the show there were two raised orchestra areas each side of the stage where the band stood. Three of the girls were singers only. Then there were some hostesses who were not part of the show. The dressing-rooms were beautifully panelled and the main dressing-room for the girls upstairs was huge and expensively decorated. Half of the wall area was covered with mirrors surrounded by lights and it was always warm and comfortable. Our dresses hung along a rail in the middle of the room, all cocktail dresses. After I left, Pops changed the rules and the girls were only allowed to wear long evening dresses which he considered more elegant.

One of the many rules of the club was that we had to wear silver or gold shoes or shoes that matched your dress. As a star turn, I earned ten pounds a week, but ten shillings was deducted for the hairdresser as we had to have our hair done at least once a week. In the early 1960s this was a 'high-class club' – the only one of its type in London which was not a pick-up place.

Members (there were nearly twenty thousand files kept) could bring their wives and many married Murray's girls. Some of the girls used the club to launch show-business careers. Kay Kendall, for instance, had started out there before making movies like *Genevieve* and marrying Rex Harrison. Some of the girls did not sit out with the customers because they were married or Pops wouldn't allow them to if he thought it would ruin their mystique as a star. People said that some of the girls went to bed with the clients and that some didn't. I certainly did not go to bed with any client but I did go off with one or two whom I liked and trusted.

Maureen O'Connor sat with Huntington Hartford, an American millionaire. He had pots of money and liked the good life. Maureen gave him this long story about wanting to stop working at the club to become a writer, a novelist. It's a marvellous story, I really adore it. He told her he would help and she was delighted, thinking that he was going to set her up in a flat where she could enjoy the solitude to compose her best-selling plots. All Huntington did was buy her a typewriter. And plenty of drinks.

The name for the number of fruit cups you could persuade the customers to buy you – and bottles of champagne for themselves – was 'scalps'. We earned points based on how many bottles of champagne the client bought and you could make more by bringing someone in for dinner. We had to have one fruit cup too, which was eighteen shillings, the champagne was ten pounds a bottle and the food was excellent. The head waiter was Toni and Peter Bachelor would carefully watch the guests. Lesley Crispin was the doorman and for years he occupied what was one of the West End's most influential jobs, on first-name terms with the Fifties and Sixties glitterati. It was strictly for members only. Once Lord Lyle of Tate & Lyle sugar was turned away at the door as he was not a member.

One of my friends at Murray's was Lynette Warwick. She had been a dancer and was married to a man who looked the double of Lord Montgomery. After I left the club she had an affair with David Murray, the old man's son who also worked at the club. They ran away together and got a chicken farm in the country.

Princess Margaret visited and Princess Muna, who was Toni Gardener an Ipswich telephonist before she married King Hussein of Jordan, brought many Arabs to the club. King Hussein was a regular. John Hurt's long-time companion, Lyse Denise, also worked at Murray's before I got there. She was killed while out riding with John who, in this small world, would play Stephen Ward in *Scandal*. It was Lyse's face that was on the programme book. The mother of Sara Brightman who married Andrew Lloyd-Webber also started out at Murray's.

With all these connections, when my affair with Profumo became headlines, Pops thought it would be the end of the club but the demand for membership grew and it even became a stop for tourists visiting London. Lesley Crispin had to deal with an endless queue of overseas visitors, especially Japanese, wanting to come in and see me, even though I was long gone by then. As is the club now, as I walk along Beak Street, Soho, watching the tourists trying to find Carnaby Street, another landmark of the Sixties.

But the memories have not gone. Working at Murray's left you in an unreal world: at night-time you entered this fantasy place, where the rich and famous queued for your attention; the days were an endless series of dinner and party invitations, and the social life was truly amazing. It was only after I left Murray's and returned to the real world that I realized the strange underground fantasy life I had been leading.

Pops and his 'family', the one he created, also enjoyed a lifestyle that was the stuff of fantasy: every year they would set off for the

French Riviera. He paid for everything but everyone worked hard, even on holiday: finding new ideas for costumes, scanning the shops for new materials and ideas, changing the flowers in his suite every two days and all dining together in the evening. At the beginning of the Seventies, Pops and his son David fell out and parted professionally. Mr Murray's health grew worse and the club began to suffer – a situation which his expensive lifestyle didn't help – and it closed in the autumn of 1979. Pops had sold all his cars and other assets to try and keep Murray's going but it was no use. All that was left was the membership list – thirty-five years of London high-life. Peter Bachelor put that history into black plastic bags to be collected with the rubbish and that was the end of Murray's.

But not, of course, in my memory.

It was where I met Stephen Ward. And it was where John Profumo took me long after our affair was meant to be over. I had to smuggle him into Murray's because he was not a member, not on that illustrious list. It was the night we made furtive love in his car and he got me pregnant.

2

FAST TRACKS

SEXUAL INTERCOURSE BEGAN IN NINETEEN SIXTY-THREE.

Philip Larkin, *Annus Mirabilis*

In one of those twenty-first century space-filling columns in the *Sunday Times* they posed the question: 'Who would be shocked by Christine Keeler now, when slapperhood is such a prerequisite of modern celebrity?'

Who indeed? But for millions of people it was me who invented sex. Today I find it difficult to have relationships – sexual or otherwise – with men. I am close to my second son and we spend a lot of time together. But I don't even get a Christmas card from my other son. He was brought up by my mother.

Losing him and losing contact with my family is the most hurtful thing that has happened in my life. My father is dead, my mother does not speak to me and one son disowns me. So much, so much has happened since I remember being three years old and waving goodbye to my father. I can see it now: it was an air-raid shelter at our home in Hayes in Middlesex. The next time I saw him was eighteen years later. I was in the dock of London's Marylebone Court accused of perjury; he was in the public gallery. I sensed him there, saw him looking at me, saw my own features in him. My sons don't have any of my looks but I have his, especially the silly nose.

My father was adopted and took the name Keeler from his adoptive family. Later, in 1954, he became Colin King and worked as a photographer at Butlin's Holiday Camp in Clacton, Essex. He met my mother, Julie Payne, at the start of the Second World War.

My mother was brought up in a convent and the nuns had taken the East End out of her voice but not removed it from her spirit, her attitude. My father was in the RAF at Uxbridge when they married in 1939. He always blamed himself for it not working out; he thought my mother was a wonderful woman.

I was born on 22 February 1942 and my parents' marriage was dissolved in 1948, but they had separated before that and my mother and I lived with my grandparents. Then Edward Huish turned up as my 'stepfather', whom I was always told to call Dad. Perhaps I thought he was coming between me and my mother. I never really felt comfortable with him.

I was about four years old when we all began living in a converted railway carriage at Wraysbury in Berkshire. The railway carriage was on wheels and I felt like a character from the American television series about the legendary Wild West train-driver Casey Jones. I had my own room for the first time, instead of sharing with mum. Our house was situated on a back river to the Thames. It was never heated and there was no hot water; I slept with my knitted lamb for comfort. Mum cooked on a fire for the first few years until we got electricity.

My new Dad had a very Presbyterian work ethic. He was always working at something even if he didn't feel well. He never lived on credit; he didn't believe in such things.

I was thirty-four before he married my mother. That they were living together would upset her – it was considered not proper to live with someone in those days. He had been married before and left a wife and son in Wales; perhaps that's why he brought me up like a boy. I was a bit of a sniveller behind my mother's apron but he made me work, fixing up the trailer and keeping the garden up to scratch. The worst job was stuffing the roof rafters with glass fibre; I was small enough to reach in there and I got fine pieces of glass all over my body. It seems that my body was always going to get me into some kind of trouble.

I made friends with the neighbours' children, including a girl called Anne, who was a year and a half older than I was and lived in a proper house two doors away. One day when I was five, I fell into the river and Anne jumped in and saved me. Anne was the only other girl of my age in the area, so most of the time I played with the boys, usually down by the river. Once we found an unexploded wartime bomb and carried it all the way back to one of the boys' homes. Every time we dropped it, we ran away and waited for the explosion. Eventually we hauled it up before the boy's dad. The boy stood there, his hands on his hips, grinning, and announced: 'Look what we've found, Dad.' His father went white. The RAF evacuated the whole area and took the bomb away, but we got our names in the local paper for digging it out of the mud and slime. It was my first headline.

Dad was strict. He gave me the worst patch of garden to work at and I hated it but he was determined to bring me up tough and never let me get away with being just a girl. There was a time Anne hit me; she often did, and I didn't do anything about it because she was older and bigger than me. I used to run back indoors to my mum, crying, 'Mum, Mum, Anne's hit me. She hit me.' And of course I'd get all Mum's sympathy and attention. But this time Dad was at home and he wasn't going to let me off that easily. 'Shut your face crying,' he told me, 'and just get straight along outside and hit her back, or you'll find yourself in worse trouble with a good hiding from me.'

I did exactly as he said, and after that Anne never dared to hit me again. It was a lesson I took too long to learn properly. I was always wanting to compromise and not to confront situations, running away from problems rather than dealing with them properly as I am now. I wasn't naïve; I was frightened.

Mum used to worry if no one was playing with me, and she bribed the boys with sweets to play round at our place. When the sweets were finished, the boys left. Men, I would learn, were not much different.

Dad was prone to pneumonia and in 1947 when the valley flooded and water filled our house he got sick with a fever. We were one of the last families to be evacuated but by the time we were, Dad had started frothing at the mouth and rushed around throwing and ripping the furniture, hysterical with the fever. He ran out of the house and waded thigh deep through the flood water. When the rescuers finally got to us Dad was rushed into hospital. He was back to his old self when he came out, and immediately set about teaching me how to drive and how to shoot.

'Take the car up the road,' he ordered. 'But if you hit anything, I'll hit you.' I never did hit anything, although my feet hardly reached the pedals. I also learned to shoot better than him. We lived in the country and he had a small calibre rifle for hunting rabbits. He let me use it and I discovered I had an 'eye'. He also had an old handgun some crony had given him and I learned to aim and fire that.

It was always Dad who gave me orders and told me how to help around the house. Mum just carried on waiting on me hand and foot, cooking and serving food, washing and ironing and making the bed. Dad was the law. When I was nine, the school health inspector said that I was too skinny, and that I was suffering from malnutrition. He arranged for me to be sent to a holiday home in Littlehampton to be fattened up for a month. It was run by nuns, and when I arrived there were sixteen boys staying, but no girls. We were all skinny as rakes. We bathed and played ping-pong and one of the older boys taught me how to play chess. It was the first time I felt myself aware of a boy.

Dad was not always difficult. I think he was fond of me because he put together my first bike with bits and pieces from scrapyards. I think only the inner-tubes of the wheels were new. It was not long after Dad made that bike, that I was in the headlines once more. Anne and I got into the papers for saving a man's life. We had been sliding on the ice that winter and when we slipped into the bushes by the garage for a pee, we found a man lying unconscious. We ran for help and the man was resuscitated; he had been suffocating from car fumes. When Mum heard about it, she was annoyed that the man never bothered to come and thank us.

As soon as I got my bike, I stopped seeing so much of Anne. She wasn't the tomboy I was, and with my bike I was away with the boys after school. Throughout the summer we swung across the river on ropes, climbed trees and fought.

There was Tommy Jones with dark, short, curly hair, Keith, Alan the timid one, and Christopher, who was my age and always wanted to fight me. Christopher was the crazy one; he had been shell-shocked during the war and sometimes went off his head. He used to cut the heads off birds.

Dad was brutal too. He drowned our dog's puppies. He put them all in a sack and shut me in my room because I had asked for one to be saved and wouldn't stop whining about it. He just walked down to the river and dumped them in, keeping them under until they were dead. Once I brought a field mouse home. I held it out in my cupped hands, very pleased to have such a warm, living thing to play with. But he took it away from me, threw it on the floor and crushed it with his foot. I remember it squeaking.

When the school inspection came, I hid my bike in the fields because, though it was a good bike, it didn't have any brakes. I started doing a paper-round when I was twelve, and did it for two years on that bike. It meant getting up at six in the morning and riding six miles to fetch the papers, deliver them, and then get to school on time. I was happy to get out, to make fast tracks from that converted railway carriage.

What happens in such an enclosed space is everyone's property – even when you're supposed to be asleep. All the rows, all the decisions – you hear everything. And if you don't understand what's going on, you make up your own explanations for why people do such hurtful things to each other. But it doesn't stop you being hurt.

I was chosen by Wraysbury School to throw the discus and javelin in competitions with other schools but I just didn't want to. Mum and Dad didn't care what happened to me at school. They didn't bother with parents' day and because they didn't care, I decided not to care. I felt isolated.

The headmaster called me into his study to try and force me to compete against the other schools. I was far better than anyone else in the school, but I wouldn't be persuaded. He tried to reason with me, but nothing would change my mind. That stubborn streak stayed with me and I believe to this day that it kept me alive.

Then my friend Anne moved into the class above me and made friends with another girl, which really upset me and I refused to talk to her. Once when I passed her on my bike, she was walking with a boy and wearing a bit of lipstick. That was the end of our friendship; I felt betrayed.

And I was no longer a tomboy. On television there was a blonde called Sabrina who appeared on the Arthur Askey Show. Her talent was all in her chest and because of my development in that area I was nicknamed Sabrina. The days when I had helped Dad take his car to bits, taken my bike apart and painted it, made go-carts and climbed trees, were over. We were changing; the boys too. But I wore jeans longer than the other girls at school, who rushed into wearing skirts.

I could not understand what was happening to me and whether it was because of that, or just my family circumstances, I started feeling out of place. Everyone I knew seemed to fit in, to have a role. I was different. I felt awkward, as if I was beneath them all. Instead of passing off, the feeling grew and I felt even lonelier.

Mrs Dreen up the lane had a granddaughter called Veronica Briggs who I was supposed to be going to the pictures with. I went round to Veronica's house wearing a skirt – it must have been one of the first occasions I had worn one – but all of a sudden Mrs Briggs decided that Veronica wasn't allowed to go, and wouldn't tell me why. I knew there must be a reason and I wouldn't leave until she told me. When Mrs Briggs went to the lavatory, I locked her in and forced Veronica to tell me.

They didn't think I was the right kind of friend for Veronica: I wasn't nice, I lived in a shabby railway carriage. I suppose I had sensed it all along, but hearing it out loud like that shattered me. I was branded a 'bad' girl before I knew how bad that bad could be. Was it me? I earned fourteen shillings a week from my newspaper round and I got more by babysitting. But the fathers, if they got me alone, would try to kiss and fondle me. I hated it. I had seen my mother and dad making love and it had upset me – I didn't want the fathers of these little kids I had been looking after pressing and rubbing themselves against me. I was terrified that what went on between men and women might happen to me. I was no Lolita – but everyone wanted me to be. It was years before I was to read Nabokov, anyway.

At fifteen, on my birthday, Mum took me to the employment agency and they found me an office typing job. After that, I had another five jobs, one after the other, and I hated them all.

'Well, if you're not happy at work, Christine, you come home,' said Mum.

So, I stayed at home and did the cleaning, cooking and washing up, and she went to work instead. All this time, I wasn't speaking to Dad. I was terrified of him; I avoided and ignored him totally. This went on for over a year and eventually produced a rash of spots all over my body. Mum took me to the doctor who said it was a nervous disorder and sent me to a woman psychiatrist. It was Mum who cried in the consulting room.

'It's dreadful. I can't go on,' she told the psychiatrist. 'Christine won't speak to her father, and he won't speak to her.' 'Why not?' the psychiatrist asked me. 'I hate him. I hate him,' I cried. I couldn't say why, or explain it any more than that. All I knew was that I hated him. 'She'll have to go away from him until she calms down and sees reason,' the psychiatrist said.

Mum and I went to Redhill to stay with my uncle and aunt. They had only just got married and didn't really want a fifteen-year-old girl in their house but they helped. Mum cried every day and spent every evening on the phone to Dad. After four days she couldn't take it any longer and went home, leaving me behind. I got a job in a tie factory, stencilling pictures of girls on to the ties. I only worked there a short while. The spots went and, soon after, so did I. I had to go home but I still wouldn't speak to Dad and I started going out with a nice local boy and staying out late at night to keep out of his way. This just made him jealous. I didn't know what the problem was at the time but he warned me when I was going out: 'The door will be locked at ten sharp. In or out.'

So I got locked out, and Mum cried and made a scene until he let me in. But he was furious that boys, men, were interested in me. It sent him into rages, crazy rages. It seems astonishing to me now, even with all the knowledge I have gained since of how men can become possessive and obsessive. 'She's a bad lot and there's no controlling her,' Dad would yell at my mother, and end with his usual chorus: 'She'll end up no good.'

I had to get out of the house. The employment people got me an interview in London for a job as a model in a showroom. My job entailed some stock-taking as well as parading the dresses in front of the customers. London was an adventure land. It was such a small town in 1957, you could criss-cross the city in no time. Everyone seemed to know everyone and everywhere. It was a village compared to today but for me it was heaven. I'd go to see foreign films – Ingmar Bergman was my favourite – but I always had to catch the last train home as I was commuting every day to the showroom. I would daydream on the train, romantic dreams of meeting the right man in the right place. Instead, a bad habit began: I fell madly in love with the son of the boss of the showroom. Wrong man. Wrong place. He ignored me.

But others did not. Somebody who did seem to care about me was a student from Ghana who was paying for his studies by cleaning the shop where I worked. He was always kind and smiled at me. I felt superior to him; a lot of people did in those days. Stephen Ward could describe black people as 'primitive' in 1963 and the newspapers would print his remarks without fear of criticism, never mind reprisal.

For me, to feel better than some other human being was uplifting. Today I believe that we should all share the world equally. Then, as a young girl, it was good to believe I had something better going: which made a change from the way I'd felt in Wraysbury. One day the student, Dennis, asked me whether I would come up to London at the weekend and help him with his studies. I didn't see why not. When I got there, he seemed less keen on his studies and more keen on chatting to me. We talked quite a bit; I told him about myself and what life was like in the converted railway carriage. He told me how lonely he was in London, that he had no real friends.

'But it makes me happy to have you here,' he added, leaning forward to kiss me. I let him, but when he wanted to move on to the bed, I panicked and got up to go. 'Don't worry, honey, we won't do it properly. We'll just play a bit, that can't do any harm. I'll show you.' I was very curious. I had often wondered what it would be like, and since he had promised not to go the whole way, I agreed and hopped on the bed. But an erect penis has no conscience. Once he started there was no stopping. I can't say I was stimulated by losing my virginity; I wondered what all the fuss was about. It didn't hit me until I was sitting on the train on the way home. Then I felt terribly ashamed of what I had done, and every time I thought about it I felt sick and unable to contain my dark, dreadful secret. I never saw him again.

I left the job and went to work at Caroline Dresses around the corner but everything had changed. London was not paradise any more. I was still living at home and found a job as a receptionist in Wraysbury. I had met a nice boy called Peter Lewin who I still keep in touch with today. He wanted to marry me but his parents objected. How life – the world – might have been different if there had been some fairy-tale romance. And a happy ending.

Peter's father was the local Conservative councillor. The family's big boast was that his mother had once danced with Fred Astaire. In our small world, she had met Peter's father while she was working at Murray's Cabaret Club. Peter took me to my first show at the London Palladium where we saw Bruce Forsyth.

Peter also took me to my first dance, in Hammersmith. Mum had bought me a pink second-hand dress for the occasion but Dad told him to 'Fuck off'. I was surprised when Peter told me as Dad normally did not swear. Of course, I understand now, he was mad with jealousy. Peter and I would take his friends with us to dances in Wimbledon and Hammersmith, usually Bob, Bill and Clive who we called 'the boys'. They were his drinking friends, his mates. I wanted to marry Peter and get away from Dad but Peter's family thought that he was too good for me.

I always wanted a man around. I thought life was all about couples, being together; it was the way everybody was and I wanted to be the same as everyone else. The sex side of the relationship seemed part of that. After Peter I went out with an older man,

Danny, a drummer, but again Dad wouldn't have it. I tried to kill myself by taking a whole bottle of aspirins but I only went deaf and was very sick.

I then met Jim Calfie, a soldier from the nearby US Army base who lived close to Wraysbury in digs with two other GIs. He was a white man, older than me by a couple of decades but the loving was good. I often stayed the night with Jim and let him make love to me. It was warm and comfortable lying in his arms. My mother thought I was staying with Jackie White, a local girl who I had met with Peter Lewin. When Jim returned to America, I'd stay at Jackie's and we travelled to Kingston and London in search of Americans because we preferred them.

But it was a local boy, Jeff Perry, who first got me pregnant. When I told my mother, it was the excuse that my father had been waiting for. He told me that I was no longer allowed to go out and had to stay in my room for the next few months, so I got a pen and tried to abort myself. If I died so be it. I was sixteen and desperate. Where else could I turn?

Abortion was the only answer for me then. Castor oil, gin, whisky. Hot baths and steam until you think you're passing into nothingness. All is black and your body floats above you, way above. Your body doesn't function. You feel weak and lifeless. But the life within you is still there, growing, beginning to show.

What will the neighbours think? They'll say what they think. They're the kind of neighbours who make sure they know exactly what's going on the whole time. You feel bad, you are bad. You've got yourself pregnant and the neighbours really will have something to talk about – unless you get rid of it.

Get rid of it. I can't do it. I have to. It's down there and it's got to go. Push in a knitting needle. That's what they say works. Probing and poking with a needle until you know you've broken it. You must bear the agony until the pain makes you crazy. You can no longer think, 'Why?' You just poke and probe, knowing you'll die a worse death if you don't go on. So you do. 'Mum! Mum!' I cried out. Thank God. She came and saw the state of me and rode off on her bicycle to get the doctor. My child was born.

Naked, withered and premature. A half-dead screaming infant leaving me with a gaping wound. They took him to hospital and he died. I called him Peter before he died. I couldn't sleep. There was no sleep for me, no peace, just the pain and the shame. They wrapped my breasts up, to flatten them, for they were full of milk which my aborted infant did not need. I never liked my breasts after that. I hated them, I suppose, for what I had done. They were a daily reminder of baby Peter.

I was just seventeen, I did not have many illusions left and the ones that did remain were soon to vanish. I don't think I was ever innocent. Yet, I was so young that I still had hope, hope of happiness and a 'normal' life. After that abortion, I began my search for a guardian angel – someone to love and someone to guide me. When I think of it now I don't know if I was consciously looking for someone; it was, I think, something born in me. I was a bright kid at school; I could do the work and get decent grades in most subjects. Often, I reflect on how I would grade my life. Differently, if not for Murray's.

I had only been working for Pops for a couple of months when one night a rich Arab, Ahmed Kenu, who I had sat out with before, asked me to come and join him and his friends, a middle-aged man and a starlet, for a drink. As soon as I sat down Stephen Ward leaned over and said softly: 'I saw you in the show. You were delightful. Will you dance with me now?'

To me he was an old man, but I accepted. He danced rather close and squeezed me and asked what my plans were for later. I thought he wanted sex and said, 'I'm going home.' I pulled away from him. He offered to take me home but I told him that was impossible, I had to go home alone. I was going to see Harry after work and it would be late anyway as I'd been sitting out with Ahmed. There was something about Stephen and even in those first few moments I sensed that he wasn't going away – not easily, anyway. And there was something magnetic about him, a spider and fly manner. But I didn't want to get caught by this old fellow. He persisted and the implication was obvious: 'Do men take you home sometimes?'

I was silent. He changed tactic: 'You know, I really must have your phone number, Christine,' he whispered as I led him back to Ahmed's table. 'You are a very sweet person. I think you and I are going to be friends for a very long time.'

I didn't pay any attention to what he said but he continued chatting to me and ignoring the starlet, which annoyed Ahmed. Sensing the ill-feeling, Stephen stood up. 'I must have your phone number before I leave,' he insisted. Ahmed and I realized that he wasn't going to go until he'd got it. I made some nonsense up.

'SW1 0256, room 5,' I gabbled, so he wouldn't catch it, but Stephen had a notebook and pen at the ready and made me repeat the number until he'd got it. Then, wishing Ahmed a pleasant evening, he and his companion were gone. Stephen called the next day – three times. I refused his invitations, but he kept on ringing and I discovered that he was an osteopath with a fashionable clientele. We had a telephone romance and eventually I got used to the calls and even looked forward to them, for Stephen had great charm: 'I'm in my consulting room, Christine, just waiting for my next patient, so I thought I'd see what you were up to . . .'

I kept putting off another meeting, though, until he found out where my parents lived; I had told him that I was going to my mother's for the weekend, to put him off, but immediately he had to know where – and, of course, he knew Wraysbury and even the street next to our little lane. I saw his car pull up outside our cottage, watched him stroll up to the door and heard his knock. I opened the door. 'Christine!' He sounded surprised to see me. 'I was passing right by your door so – I've got a little cottage not far from here. Why don't you come and see it? I thought you'd enjoy the drive.'

'Well, I don't think I can,' I began and, since I could hardly close the door, I invited him in for tea. Mum had never met any of my London friends, and she was surprised and pleased to see Stephen. He immediately dominated the room: 'I'm Stephen Ward. What a charming little place you have here. Absolutely charming.' He walked over to the window. 'And what a lovely view.'

'Yes, everyone likes it,' said Dad, who chatted to Stephen while

Mum fussed around making tea. Dad told him: 'We have a river running along the back.'

Stephen played the game: 'But how absolutely marvellous. My cottage is beside the river too. I was hoping to take Christine to see it this afternoon . . .'

3

UPSTAIRS, DOWNSTAIRS

MR BILLY WAS FRIGHTENED OF HER –
HE WOULD TURN WHITE WHEN SHE CAME IN THE ROOM.

Rose Harrison, maid to Nancy Astor, Britain's first woman MP,
on her employer's effect on her son Bill Astor

When I first went to Cliveden, I had none of the foreboding of the second Mrs de Winter when she first sees Manderley in Daphne du Maurier's *Rebecca*. I should have done. I too was going to be haunted by a place.

This grand Buckinghamshire house, ruled over in dynamic fashion by Nancy Astor for most of the last century, and converted for this one into a grand hotel with five-star prices but poor service, was to become the symbol for all that would go wrong: for the blackmail and treachery and the dirty secret world that would shadow my life. When I went back in 1999 it was my first time at that cottage on the Cliveden estate in more than thirty-five years. In a way, I was pleased to see it again. But it was no dream for me; it was another part of the exorcism of the lies of the past. The place didn't frighten me as much as the memories.

It all started so innocently. Cliveden, on the banks of the Thames near Maidenhead, is an idyllic backwater away from London. There are 400 acres of land, owned by the National Trust, and lots of history, created by an eclectic, eccentric cast of characters. Oswald Mosley stayed there and so did Von Ribbentrop, Germany's ambassador to Britain. Nancy Astor had rubbished Hitler during lunch with Ribbentrop, something about how could people take seriously a politician with a Charlie Chaplin moustache. That got her on a Nazi hit-list that was discovered after the war.

Her eldest son Bill never had her gumption. He became a patient and friend of Stephen Ward in 1950, a couple of years before he inherited the title and became Lord Astor. I never knew of him nor can think of him other than as Bill. With Stephen at Cliveden it would be 'Bill this' and 'Bill that'. The Astor family, through Bill, were Stephen's greatest conquest. It appealed to him on a snobbery level and was perfect for his espionage activities. At Cliveden, where he had had the use of the cottage since 1956, he had access to the people who really mattered.

When Stephen had arrived at my home that June afternoon in 1959, Dad took him out to look at the view. I was still wondering what to do about him when my mother started asking questions about him and saying what a 'catch' he was. I said I could not get rid of him and she said I should be trying to hang on to him. I said he wanted to take me for a run out to see his cottage at Cliveden and my mother encouraged me to go. She was flabbergasted that I might say no. It was getting a little heated but we were interrupted by Stephen, who came running up the back steps laughing. 'I nearly fell in the water.'

Over tea Stephen put the charm in overdrive for my parents saying how wonderful he thought I was at Murray's. She told me how lucky I was to have such a man as a fan. Stephen pretended to blush at that, to be flattered but coy about it. He had won. How he must have smirked inside as he said: 'London is a dreadful place, and for a girl with Christine's looks it can be even more difficult to survive. There are so many undesirable types trying to exploit girls . . . a dreadful, dreadful place. Frightful, unless you know the kind of people who can help you.'

My mother kept nodding her approval. Yet, all I saw was this old man — at forty-seven he was thirty years my senior — who was saying: 'I don't know why you don't come for a drive, Christine.'

My mother almost forced us into Stephen's car and we took off, Stephen talking non-stop as usual. He told me that Lord Astor, one of his patients, had allowed him to use the cottage for eight years. 'Isn't it a simply marvellous day? I'm so glad you could come,

Christine. I've been longing to show you my cottage and meet you again ever since I saw you dance – isn't that just simply marvellous?'

I laughed, caught up in Stephen's enthusiasm. He had begun to spin the web. We were at Cliveden before I knew and drove through the park with Stephen keeping up a running commentary: 'Bill Astor is a very old friend and Cliveden is still a power to be reckoned with. Famous people have always come here and still do – politicians, royalty, diplomats – and Bill entertains much as they did in the old days. There's always people around at weekends and during Ascot week and things like that. Always people, always fun. There are shooting parties – any excuse for a gathering. The costs are huge, you know; you need thousands of pounds to keep a place like this running. He's married again now – the third time.'

In March 2000, a biography of Lady Astor, the former model Bronwen Pugh, was published and in it she painted Bill as an innocent who never strayed anywhere near the girls that Stephen took to Cliveden. That wasn't how I saw it. He was chasing me around the room trying to pinch my bottom from the moment I met him. Bill was always interested in his own satisfaction, especially then, when Bronwen was pregnant. Bronwen also said in the book she helped to be written that Stephen had an 'aura of evil' about him. Goodness knows what she would have said if she could have heard Stephen talking about her that day, my first at Cliveden. He chuckled as he talked of Bronwen who was tall for a model: 'You wouldn't believe it if you had seen her on the catwalk. I know that all models must have their own style but really Bronwen always looked like a clown.'

As he was talking I noticed a house ahead. Remember, I was used to a converted railway carriage, to tiny flats, to sharing. I had thought it would be one of those chocolate box, English country cottages with roses climbing up the walls. In front of me was a mansion by comparison. A fairy-tale castle. We walked into a magnificent reception room, which was quite empty. 'I never use this room,' Stephen explained. 'I really must get some furniture for it.' In all the time I knew him the furniture never arrived.

The kitchen was like a palace to me. It was stocked with everything, enough for a big family. Stephen was like a rabbit with food during the week but every weekend was a feast, it was part of his escape from London, he said. His escape from the madness. The first thing he wanted was to draw me. He pulled out his sketch-pad. This, as always with Stephen, was the final flattery.

And I was flattered. I kept as still as possible, trying to be the professional model. As he drew he told me about his life but he mainly talked about the people he knew. He was a name-dropper: he had sketched most of the members of the royal family. People like Prince Philip and Winston Churchill used to visit him for treatment. I was amazed that he knew all these people, let alone that they actually came to see him. I was terribly impressed by it all. He had not only drawn Prince Philip but also Princess Margaret and Lord Snowdon, the Duke and Duchess of Kent, Princess Alexandra, the Duke and Duchess of Gloucester and Princess Marina. There were lots of others including foreign leaders like Archbishop Makarios. Colin Coote, the editor of the *Daily Telegraph*, sent him to Israel to do sketches for the newspaper of the trial in Jerusalem of the Nazi, Adolf Eichmann. Colin Coote would also introduce Stephen into very different circumstances. He died, as Sir Colin, in 1979 never knowing the true measure of his involvement in the Profumo affair. I certainly like to believe that he was not knowingly involved but so many were. I was beginning to meet them.

And the cottage? Stephen paid Bill Astor only one pound a year in nominal rent. In return, Bill got the talent of Stephen's hands which had first cured him after a hunting accident in 1950. It was a hands-on arrangement.

There seemed at the time no ulterior motive for Stephen's interest in me. Did he really just like me? I was used to men liking me but I'd learned that there was always a subtext which usually involved me getting my clothes off. The difference with Stephen was that he wanted me to get naked with other people. Powerful people.

That day at the cottage at Cliveden he talked and sketched and the time flew by. We were there for two or three hours and then Stephen drove me home. He dropped me off and did not stay. I was so excited by the afternoon's events I was giggly, like a little girl. I raved on to my mother about the cottage, the size of it, the setting. It was all money, money, money. My mother kept saying I had to hold on to Stephen: I was lucky, he would be good for me. As it turned out, as Mae West said, goodness had nothing to do with it.

Stephen phoned me in London the next day and asked if I would go out for a coffee. I said I was too busy, but he insisted and I felt I could hardly refuse. I said I could be picked up at three and Stephen came to fetch me at three o'clock on the dot and we drove to the West End.

He told me more about the famous people he knew and promised that I would soon be introduced to them. It seemed like such good news to me: an opportunity being offered by a man who did not seem to want to use me. But I was still worried about him. It seemed too good to be true and there was something of the night about Stephen.

He moaned about Murray's, saying I never had free evenings. I said I enjoyed it, the fun, the money, the people I worked with. But he was already able to 'read' me: 'Why don't you try modelling instead? You'd have your evenings free then, and I think you'd be very successful. I could introduce you to someone who could help.'

I told him I had tried modelling in the clothes shop but the manager kept trying to get me into corners and press himself on me.

'The dirty devil. Men are such bastards.'

'Only dirty old men,' I said, looking at him, wondering if he could be one – just with stranger tastes. I decided he wasn't.

I left to go to work at Murray's hoping that would end it but Stephen insisted we go out again the next day. I asked him to telephone thinking that would give me time to make up an excuse. The persuasive Stephen went to work sweet-talking about how wonderful, how beautiful I was. All women like to hear that – especially seventeen-year-olds – but I was still cautious. Was he looking for a bit on the side? Was he married? 'Good heavens, no! Marriage is certainly not for me.' He drove me home and said I was the first girl he had liked so much in such a long, long time. It sounds like syrup now but with his voice and manner he made it seem so true, so safe. I quizzed Michael Lambton at Murray's. I thought he would have heard of Stephen but he hadn't. Michael thought he was a new boyfriend but I said he was an old man, but apparently well connected. I decided to wind Michael up. It was never difficult: I said I thought Stephen was looking for company because he was lonely, and Michael retorted: 'Well, he sounds a bit of a crank to me.' I didn't take any notice because Michael was rude about people as a matter of course, although he was more instinctive than either of us knew.

The next day the phone went: Stephen, right on cue. Another drive, he offered, and somehow I didn't have it in me to turn him down. I pleaded work, visiting a boyfriend, but he kept saying it was a lovely day for a drive, that I had to have some life of my own.

I had been thinking about what he said. Truthfully, I had been thinking a lot about Stephen and what the modelling opportunities could be. Murray's was fine but not a future. I was young and the customers were fat, older men who talked about stock prices as they tried to touch you up. They would never understand why you were not interested. Stephen wasn't talking business – not that I knew – and he had not put a hand near me. He treated me like a human being, as an equal. He didn't look down on me, or leer like so many others.

I agreed to see him again. He had me, hook, line and sinker.

We went to the same coffee bar and we were on our second cup – Stephen on his fourth or fifth cigarette – when he suddenly propositioned me. Or so I thought. He wanted me to live with him, but he quickly explained it was a platonic undertaking. We wouldn't get in each other's way. I was working at night, he during the day. It seemed to make sense but I still needed persuading. I had my room. But he made it sound like a lark to go and see his place. He never put a lot of pressure on you, but his enthusiasm made you feel you were being silly and letting him down if you didn't accept.

We drove round to Orme Court in Bayswater, which wasn't a very good area. His flat was tiny and on the top floor but there was a lift. There was a bed-sitting room with two single beds pushed close together, and an adjoining bathroom. We would share the bed but only as brother and sister; there were never to be any sexual goings-on between us.

The flat was clean and that, along with the bathroom, convinced me. I longed to have a bath in it. We had had a bathroom in the caravan but no running water, and the bathroom at my lodgings was shared by all sorts of people, and always filthy. Compared to this flat, the boarding house was dark and dirty and very depressing. There was no carpet on the stairs and the building smelled. It was Dickensian. This was modern living. Stephen, amazingly, wanted more coffee. On went the kettle. I automatically reached for the cups. I had made up my mind. By the autumn I had moved in with him. There we were, a team. Not a couple. A team. But at that moment I had no idea what a deadly game we were playing.

Stephen seemed to work when he wanted. He went on about his modelling contacts. Being a showgirl took up most of my time. In the afternoons we went to West End coffee bars. I was bored with Harry and his exercising and with all the posing in the mirror that he did. That was another reason I moved in with Stephen. He was perverse but he was also persuasive. He charmed me, the usual treatment: soft, cultured voice and compliments. He told me he decided I was to be his 'little baby' from the moment he saw me onstage at Murray's.

By then, I also trusted and respected him. I was in the web. I started going AWOL from Murray's at the weekends and I would go to the Cliveden cottage with him. We often took long walks over the grounds. It was an amazing place, hills, caves and macabre statues here and there. Just above the cottage in the wood, there was a witch circle, the real thing, about ten feet in diameter. He tried to scare me by wailing like a ghost but I was not superstitious, not easily frightened by that sort of thing. It was real-life bogeymen who were to terrify me.

I forgot Harry and Andreas but Peter Lewin and his friends visited the cottage often. Stephen never minded as long as they brought their own steaks. His favourite Sunday lunch was roast lamb with mint sauce. It was winter and we sat in front of a huge coal fire. He loved to get away from everything at the weekends: 'I believe one would go crazy if they couldn't get away at the weekends.'

There was no telephone, radio or television at the cottage. It was completely cut off. Jon Pertwee, who become most famous as a popular Dr Who – and remained a loyal friend to Stephen throughout everything – had a cottage about 500 yards away. He was the nearest neighbour.

When Stephen went to the big house to massage Bill, I normally waited for him at the cottage. Literally, Stephen had his fingers on the pulse of the Establishment.

4

HANDS ON

WHEN HE CAME TO CLIVEDEN HE WOULD OFFER TO MANIPULATE
ANYONE'S BACK. HE OFTEN DID MINE. HE WAS VERY GOOD, BUT THERE
WAS SOMETHING PSYCHOLOGICALLY WRONG WITH HIM.

Pamela Cooper, mother of Lord Gowrie, former
Minister of the Arts, on Stephen Ward, 1993

Stephen had rather bulging eyes under his glasses as he was very
short-sighted. Apart from that patrician, hooked nose he was rather
attractive with thick, brown hair, a handsome jaw-line and an
excellent body. When he smiled the whole of his face lit up and he
had the most mesmerizing voice that I had ever heard which he used
to make you feel important. It was deep and cultured. It was also
deceptive. At first, he always allowed me to be myself. I was sensitive
about men pawing me but there was never the slightest move
towards me in that way. I was surprised at first – everyone else was
always so quick to grab. Then I just began to accept it; I didn't think
him 'queer' in any sense. As well as using women, Stephen liked their
company. He was a gossip, always wanting to be an 'insider', the first
with the news. He talked a lot which suited me as I was a listener.

Stephen found out all about you in a long, slow way. It was over
cigarettes and cups of coffee, lots of both. He would occasionally
have a glass of white wine but coffee, always with two sugars, was
his addiction. He never rushed; he found out the facts gradually but
was also expert at reading your emotions. Later, he could be almost
certain how I would react to any particular set of circumstances. As
an osteopath he was remarkably skilled with his hands but he could
manipulate people's minds almost as easily.

He seemed proud of being an outsider, a maverick, which I found strange for all the time he also wanted to be part of the in-crowd, especially the high and the mighty. He was a snob in the way a certain type was then: it wasn't about money but the way you wore your hat, who your tailor was. He drove a Jaguar: second-hand but a Jaguar, which in those days meant a great deal.

Position in society meant much to Stephen, even if he helped along people's perception of himself. His father, Prebendary Arthur Evelyn Ward, had gained first-class honours at Balliol College, Oxford and was the vicar at Hatfield in Hertfordshire when Stephen was born. He became Prebendary of Exeter Cathedral in 1934. Stephen's mother, Eileen, had strong Irish connections and Stephen would go on about his 'Irishness' and connections on St Patrick's Day.

He seemed to feel it important that I thought of him as a superbly complex man. He would go on about his public-school education at a place called Canford in Dorset and then he would sound let down by it. He didn't do very well and went off to Germany work-ing as a translator but he never knew much German. Stephen said that as a young man he hung around the embassy crowd and had dates with some of the girls who worked there. He was also mixing with the working girls in Hamburg. He was fascinated by them and I think that's where he got his taste for the darker side of life. He was going out with nice young things one evening and then slumming it along the Reeperbahn the next. He would always say that he found ordinary, working-class girls nicer, kinder and more genuine, than society women. He liked young girls in Hamburg – and kept on liking them as he got older; if anything the girls got younger.

When I remember what he told me about his life in Germany between the wars – he also had a spell in Paris – I can see the clues to why he became what he did. He was still only in his late teens, early twenties: that's when you are in love with love. Stephen loved the thought of a brand new world where there were no rich and no poor, where everyone was the same.

After that he went off to America to study to become an osteopath. It was seen as a fad but Stephen, as he did with everything he was involved with, took it very seriously. He told me it was his passport to advancement.

But at first it didn't do him much good when the war started. He wanted to be in the Medical Corps but they wouldn't have him; he might as well have been a witch doctor as an osteopath. He became a bombardier with the Royal Armoured Corps but one of the officers allowed him to use a Nissen hut as 'consulting rooms'. Stephen treated soldiers and officers but he upset the Royal Army Medical Corps (RAMC) doctors. The compromise was that he was allowed to join the RAMC – as a stretcher-bearing medic. He said he continued to learn about osteopathy during the war as he went on treating people in his unit.

When he got back to London he went legitimate. He couldn't afford Harley Street but found consulting offices and a flat nearby, in Cavendish Square near Marylebone. He would boast about going to treat Winston Churchill and talk about patients like Frank Sinatra and Elizabeth Taylor. He said when he started work he was getting paid less than ten pounds a week – about what I got at Murray's.

They said later that he suffered from 'acute emotional frustration' but I never saw that with Stephen; all I found was a determined man. He taught me to play bridge – I am a good card player – another of the skills he used to get on in society, like his sketching. He was a very talented artist; he would do pictures of me in seconds – as if by magic. He had instant recall of a look, a moment in time.

Stephen liked to be out and about enjoying himself. Sometimes there would be no patients and he would be hanging around for hours at a time. He was paid five guineas for each session, each consultation; he also earned money from his sketches and there was some family money. He didn't need to earn money off women to finance his lifestyle; that was all part of the cover-up. He paid a lot of rent, drove a fancy car and liked good restaurants because that's how he met the people he wanted. 'Style,' he would say, 'it's all about style.'

He never talked much about his only marriage. Patricia Baines was younger, twenty-two, and he was thirty-six when they married in 1949. She was also stunning looking, a model and beauty queen. I think she was Stephen's first 'arm candy'. She was there to show off, like a new car. He said they went off to France for a mad, passionate honeymoon but even by then, from what he said, the passion seemed to be over. He said there some 'instability' and the marriage was finished by the end of 1950. That 'instability' was Stephen wandering around London picking up girls.

Almost everything that has been written before about Stephen suggests that he only started attracting and chasing girls around the time that I met him. He was born a ladies' man, I can assure you. During and after his marriage, there were girls, girls, girls. Some vanished. Some, like Vicki Martin, died.

Through Stephen Vicki became a close friend of the Maharaja of Cooch Behar but she was killed in a car crash in 1956. She was alone in the car and it seems that the brakes failed. It was a terrible shock for many people and made worse because there were never any real details of her death. Stephen said that some of the most famous men in the country were upset by Vicki's death. David, the Marquess of Milford Haven, the cousin of the Duke of Edinburgh, was at the funeral. Stephen told me how he and the Marquess and Prince Philip had all visited nightclubs together in the 1940s. They were quite wild times and it was all thought to be a little delicate for Prince Philip when Elizabeth became Queen, according to Stephen. He had no time for Philip and would always put him down in conversation for he hated the Establishment. He thought the House of Lords was full of idiots: 'Through inheritance alone these people have been set up in the House of Lords to make judgements on our account, let me tell you.' He would get more and more heated and red in the face: 'It's like a thoroughbred animal; they marry their cousins and land up retarded and deformed with the interbreeding.'

Nevertheless, despite those views, Stephen was a huge success as a social climber, with the help of some of his past girlfriends. Stephen's girlfriends – and he had many – came to him for help and advice. Whatever their personal story the advice was the same: 'Follow your instincts and desires' was his mantra. And he knew who to deliver it to; his closest friends were mostly young girls who had had a raw deal, been abused by men. The line he spun to me and the other women he was involved with was that we were better than men, more clever more sharp whereas men were 'dirty little bastards, following their pricks'.

Stephen liked glamorous woman around him but not pushy or pretentious girls. Maggie Brown was a big-time model when Stephen knew her. She later married the composer Jule Styne but she was happy to take up a paint brush and help him decorate the Cliveden cottage. Another was Eunice Bailey, who married the son of the millionaire Sir Harry Oakes. Stephen did not like to say too much about her – she was one that got away, escaped from him, and he didn't like to lose. He believed all these girls owed everything they did in the world to him.

He was like Peter Pan in Never-Never Land except that he was a magnet for lost girls not lost boys, of course. Stephen's *métier* was to search out lost causes and, like a little boy, enjoy getting them to join his game. I suppose he never really grew up, which is why he could see everything as black and white. There were no grey areas: Stephen was always right. I found that out time after time after time.

He didn't like women like Bronwen Pugh – and he didn't believe that class distinction should stop attractive and intelligent girls from appearing in society. He preferred girls like Pat Marlowe, whom he recreated. She was an Essex girl, Anita Wimble, and had the most amazing breasts; she went without a bra long before the Sixties got going. Pat wanted to become rich and famous so she went out with rich and famous men.

She was involved with Bill Astor and Stephen said they used the cottage. She went on the international circuit and knew the Hollywood producer Mike Todd before he married Elizabeth Taylor. She was always in Monte Carlo or Paris but for all that she was an unhappy woman, dying from an overdose in 1962. I think it was suicide but, like her idol Marilyn Monroe, you can never be sure about that sort of death, especially in the fast crowd she was with.

When I first arrived in London the nation was just 'going continental'. Sexually, Stephen complained about the British attitude which was still too slow for him. He went on about the hypocrisy with sex being banned from the streets but orgies going on behind the grand front doors of society. Everybody, he said, should be free to do as they wished. That was the world he wanted. Secrets were high currency for Stephen. He liked to whisper in company, appear to know more than he did. He told me about the titled gentleman, a friend of Bill Astor, who liked to be naked and harnessed to a cart like a horse. His wife would sit in the driver's seat and whip him until he was happy. And satisfied.

I might have been a teenager when I met Stephen but I was not innocent; nevertheless the sex stories still shocked me. Stephen kept insisting it was all 'normal'. People, he said, were more forthcoming when they were naked. The inhibitions were down – and they were then more likely to trust you even when they had their clothes back on. This is where some of his female connections helped. Later, Lord Denning made sure that many of the girls' names were kept out of his report – especially Mariella Novotny who was used by British law enforcement agencies, including the security services, as an inform-ant. She was married to a much older, intriguing character called Horace Chapman–Dibben. He was short but full of old-style charm, an antiques dealer known to everyone as 'Hod'. Mariella's father was born in Czechoslovakia but the exotic continental connection ended there. She herself was born in London, in the East End, and her birth name was Stella Capes, but Mariella Novotny had a more whiplash ring to it as far as she was concerned. Lord Denning, however, did not find all her connections and the subterfuge intriguing – he was intent on keeping the spotlight on me as much as possible. It was not in his interests to highlight Mariella although she was Miss Kinky. She had a tiny waist that exaggerated her ample figure. She was a siren, a sexual athlete of Olympian proportions – she could do it *all*. I know. I saw her in action. She knew all the strange pleasures that were wanted and could deliver them.

For me, it was a strange but exciting life. I had the glamour and excitement of Murray's and, from Stephen, a daily education in how the other half – especially the kinky half – lived. He often met them through quite legitimate contacts who were patients or friends of patients.

One of Stephen's friends was the glass company owner Robert Pilkington and he took me to one of Robert's parties in Mayfair. Stephen was always so polite at parties, so polished, and he usually knew the guest list and planned his questions in advance. 'How do you do, sir. I'm Dr Ward and whom do I have the pleasure of meeting?' Having a pretty girl at his side helped him to gain men's confidence – men, no matter how hard they try, cannot stop themselves showing off in front of a pretty girl. They also brag and Stephen was always ready to listen.

He would sit up waiting for me to get home in the early hours from Murray's and I would tell him the latest gossip: who had come in and who had sat with who, important information in the world of compromise and blackmail. Most evenings he would drop me off at Murray's and sometimes he would pick me up in the early hours and we would go to the Saddle Room, a nightclub run by Peter Davies, a former Grenadier Guard, and owned by Helene Cordet. He introduced me to Peter and Helene. Helene died in Switzerland in 1996. Stephen was friendly with her – he said he knew her well because of the Duke of Edinburgh; they all had mutual contacts in social circles. He said the Duke had 'another family' with Helene, a piece of gossip that was not nearly as widespread then as it would become over the years. But it was typical of Stephen that he knew all about it at that time.

He found out so much through the Thursday Club, a group of heavy-drinking males who met most weeks; the Duke of Edinburgh was a member, along with lots of 1950s 'faces' like Gilbert Harding from television's *What's My Line?* and the actor James Robertson Justice. It was the photographer known as Baron – he was a friend of Stephen's and with the help of Lord Mountbatten photographed the royal family – who came up with the idea of the club. They met at Wheeler's in Soho and drank vast quantities of champagne. Stephen told me all about the rules; one being that they always had to have oysters – good for the libido. Michael Eddowes who was to play a great part in my future was a member, as was the MP Iain Macleod who was Leader of the House of Commons during the hysteria surrounding my affair with John Profumo.

Baron – his second name was Nahum but he never used it professionally or privately – had a place in Piccadilly and Stephen said that was where some raucous, champagne-fuelled parties were held. There were lots of girls at the gatherings, he said, and they played games like 'Chase the Bitch'. It often involved degradation with the women and also the men being made to beg or clean floors or indulge in some perversion that turned them on.

Stephen could always sense people's sexual tastes – and egg them on, make them go further than they might have otherwise. It gave him control because people would sometimes be shocked at just how far they would go. Others simply enjoyed it, loved rough sex and all the bondage and whips. Stephen knew all the Masonic handshakes and he said that at some of the parties the girls would just wear leather Masonic aprons. 'They would be flicked up and down like a sporran,' he would laugh.

Some of the women Stephen was involved with were heavily into sadistic sex and there were 'black magic' parties which were really just an excuse for group sex sessions. There would be phallic totem poles around which all these women would bow and scrape. It was just to get them all going – especially the men. Two-way mirrors were commonplace – as much part of the sex games as big, plastic penises. Stephen said these people liked to suffer for their sex as well as their sins. He said they were just people enjoying themselves and saw nothing wrong with it. He would take part and whip girls – he whipped me. But only once.

Great discretion was necessary over any homosexual goings-on for these were illegal, even between consenting adults, until 1967 and Stephen knew all about the Lords and prominent clergy who were 'fruity', as he said, with one another. Stephen often had dinner with Godfrey Winn who was a Fleet Street star writer and a dreadful old poof and poseur. He was a user, not a friend. But Stephen made use of him for gossip from the homosexual world, about men like Anthony Blunt. Blunt's long-time lover was Peter Montgomery, the brother of Hugh Montgomery who was the Very Reverend Monsignor Montgomery.

But there was nothing spiritual about the gay set. There were what we now call rent boys on the circuit. Lord Boothby, who was mixed up with the Kray twins, was known to be a habitual user of these young lads. His penchant was for rubbing himself, while naked, up against their private parts. He was a close associate of the Krays, who procured young men for his sexual amusement and then blackmailed him. When aspects of this 'secret' life were published in the *Daily Mirror*, Boothby sued and won damages. Later the *Daily Mirror* was vindicated when the total truth was revealed. The newspaper was also proved correct in the case of the entertainer Liberace who also won a lawsuit denying he was a homosexual, something that became emphatically clear in later years even before he died from AIDS. As if that weren't enough, Boothby had a long affair with the Prime Minister's wife, Lady Dorothy Macmillan. It was a strange circle to be connected with: Boothby was with rent boys one moment and then with Dorothy Macmillan another. A peer of the realm? It still seems weird to me.

And there was the well-known actress and entertainer, something of a show-stopper on stage, who always went around with a group of theatre boys. She liked to bugger them and, other than that, I will have to leave it to your imagination. But that was what she enjoyed.

Stephen strolled though all of this; these people were his power. His main weapon were his connections. He would wink at me beneath those hooded eyes and whisper when he talked about Helene Cordet who seemed a perfectly pleasant woman. The Saddle Room was the first discotheque in London, a magnet for 'deb's delights' whose cars used to roar up Piccadilly. You could never park in Hamilton Place. The club was decorated to match its name with posters from the Burghley Horse Trials and portraits of riders in hunting pink.

It ran on loud music and lots of whisky but the overwhelming rule was discretion. No matter who you were – however famous or infamous – if you wanted to be left alone you were, even under the 'witch ball' near the tiny dance floor. Crown Prince Harald of Norway would be treated the same way as a young man about town. You could smooch with whomever you wanted. There were showbusiness types and smart young men from the army.

The Saddle Club got a lot of attention on the premise that Helene Cordet and the Duke of Edinburgh had been lovers. They had known one another since they were children, she was six and he was half her age. His parents, Prince Andrew and Princess Alice of Greece, were in exile when they met as kids. But later he often visited Helene's mother's home in Marseilles. Stephen said he was the father of Helene's son Max. Helene happily admitted that Max was illegitimate and that the Duke had helped with his school fees at Gordonstoun where both he and Prince Charles were educated. Helene's daughter Louise, in turn, sent her children to Gordonstoun.

It astonished me, having known the story for years, that Max made a public statement in 1989 denying that the Duke was his father. What was the point? It only stirred it up again. Thirty years earlier, Stephen had told me all about it.

But I learned, first hand, from another of the Duke of Edinburgh's lovers about another child. I was with her when she was pregnant.

5

UNDRESSING FOR DINNER

STEPHEN WARD DID NOT CONFINE HIS ATTENTION TO PROMISCUITY –
HE CATERED ALSO FOR HIS FRIENDS WHO HAD PERVERTED TASTES.

Lord Denning, 1963

Even with all these sex games going on around me and Stephen gossiping about it, I was still not clear what he had planned for me. I was always comfortable with him, relaxed and able to put my feet up. Metaphorically – not on the furniture. He didn't allow that. I must have told him my very short life-story a dozen times but he kept asking for details, especially about boys. He would look at me and I would wonder what he really, really wanted. When I brought up sex and suggested I wasn't that interested he waved me away as though the thought was preposterous.

His enthusiasm for everything overcame any concerns I had – I thought I had landed on my feet. He seemed upset if I got into a mood. He would tickle me, ask for a smile, and then we would be chatting away again. Stephen was never guarded around me. I once walked in on him talking angrily on the phone but he didn't fuss about it. He obviously didn't care that I could hear what he was saying. He wanted another cup of coffee. After all that had happened in a short time, I was pleased to have someone to talk to; he was a father-figure but also a friend. There was no need for secrets. I could tell Stephen anything. He never seemed to worry if he was on the phone when I came into the room, or if he was studying documents and I dumped a cup of coffee down beside him. I suppose we think of spies with TOP SECRET stamped on their foreheads. It is much more mundane than that.

For days I would not see Stephen at all. He would be gone by the time I got out of bed – the only evidence of him, a sketch left for me. There were a couple of times when I think he was challenging me sexually but he never got me in a corner. We got into a routine after that, always talking about the men I met at Murray's. I never really had any friends, just Stephen. He was my companion, my confidant. He would tell me stories about his nocturnal escapades with prostitutes. At first, they thought he was strange because he simply wanted to hear about their tricks, their antics. He was fascinated by that underbelly of London.

At Murray's my career was not advancing. I was getting fed up and my attitude led to fines so my weekly pay packet would shrink. As we were walking around stage half-naked it was a fine if you had any marks on your body, love bites or bruises. I had picked up some bruises – and fines.

The bruises were part of the sex games Stephen finally got me involved in. He had told me that they all began in a very respectable way. There would be drinks, civilized conversation, dinner – and then, from what he said, everyone was at it like rabbits. Astonishingly, that was about right. What I found more ludicrous than anything was Stephen sitting around with a lot of naked men talking politics after they had all enjoyed themselves. Some of these people seemed insatiable, they could go at it for ages and come and come and come. And after all of that, it was casual chat about government policy on this and that. That's civilization for you – I suppose the Romans started it.

One dinner party is emblazoned on my mind. Stephen was adamant that before I went to the club, we should go to this house in Mayfair for an early evening meal. He said they enjoyed being watched having sex. It sparked up their marriage without any risks. I was intrigued.

After all the stories, here was the action. Stephen said this same group had gone to the cottage at Cliveden for a session. He said one of the men, called Bill but not Bill Astor, had got into bed with a girl while his wife had it off with another man. Bill had finished quite quickly and then cheered his wife on. All he was interested in, according to Stephen, was that his wife had a terrific time. They were, he said, the sort of people who would never need marriage counsellors. Stephen had, as always, intrigued me. He made it sound a jolly jape, a bit of fun. Well, it was an eye-opener.

There were six of us including Stephen and myself: our hosts Bill and Mary, and another couple, John and Carol. (Of course, these are not their real names!) It was just as I had been told: drinks and polite conversation in elegant surroundings. Everyone was dressed up – they might have been going to the theatre or the opera. We wandered through the drawing room and into the dining room. The highly polished oak table was set with Georgian silver. Then, I did a double-take. The table centrepiece was not a floral arrangement or an ornamental display. It was a huge plastic penis.

It pointed to the ceiling from the middle of the table and did not match the Georgian silver. Stephen was quick to point it out, to praise it. Bill explained they had smuggled it in from Germany: 'They've got them in all sorts of shapes and sizes. And some of them are hairy. And one had dragon's spines. We were simply terrified coming through customs!'

'What on earth would you say if they caught you with that in your case?' wondered Stephen.

'Mine was shot off in the war. Be a good chap, that's for my wife's convenience,' laughed Bill. 'They're jolly useful, aren't they? You use them on different girls all the time, don't you, darling?'

Mary's smile broke into a big grin and she said: 'Oh, yes.'

And looked at me.

A couple of glasses of wine had made me giggly – and brave. Stephen looked at me with a raised eyebrow and asked me what I thought of it. I whispered a compliment and took another gulp of wine. Stephen kept going on about the size of it and I didn't know where to look. You know what happens – when you try to avoid eye contact that's exactly what you start staring at. All I could see was this big prick and I was thinking that's just what Stephen was to get me into this.

I smiled, thinking this was the way to behave. I said I had to leave by 9.30 pm to get to the club on time. I thought I could escape.

Mary stopped that: 'Well, in that case, my dear, we'll finish dinner a little earlier than usual.'

Dinner over, Mary vanished. But not to get the coffee. She returned swishing in wearing nothing but a straw skirt. There wasn't a lot of straw. The other three started undressing and so did Stephen who helped Bill open up a sofa bed. I was the only one with any clothes left on. I didn't feel at all sexy. Sex to me was something you did with one other person, quietly and with the lights off. Stephen laughed: 'Off with your clothes.'

Well, what could I do? I took them off. Bill was making love to Carol and he reached up and took one of my breasts and started kneading it. He was loving it and it was different. When Bill had finished with Carol, he leaned towards me. I could see Stephen watching, not participating, while all the others were at it as hard as they could. Mary then jumped up and got a whip from the coffee table and handed it to Stephen. He looked at me with a strange glare in his eye and called me a naughty girl, his naughty little baby, and then let me have it with the whip.

It welted across my stomach. 'You naughty little baby,' laughed Stephen while Mary kept going down on me. The whip hurt. It was no fun and I started to fumble for my clothes. The others paid no attention to me. I dressed and announced I had to leave for work. All Mary said was 'See you again, soon.' I might have just had after-dinner drinks, they were so casual. And that was how they treated each other at these parties. Stephen showed no concern at all. He was totally naked but escorted me to the door telling me not to be upset with him.

The people and the bodies, all shapes and sizes, would change but the protocol stayed much the same. Drinks, usually lots of them, food and wine and sex in every which way. It was always a posh crowd who would arrived in chauffeur-driven Bentleys or Rolls-Royces. It seemed to me then that having money dictated that you had group sex as often as you possibly could.

When I told Stephen that I was not interested in orgies he accused me of being too self-conscious. His line was that we all have bodies and there was nothing to be ashamed of. He said the orgies did not arouse him but he found them amusing to watch. But I had seen the cruel streak when he raised the whip to me – it was not something even a personality chameleon like him could disguise.

Later, Stephen met Valeria who worked in a circus. Sitting on elephants had given her strong thighs; she was a tough, naughty girl who liked her fun. He got very fond of Valeria who rather liked his sadistic tendencies. One day at the cottage at Cliveden as I was going to bed Stephen told me he had tied Valeria up to his bed. They had been playing some bondage games. He told me not to free her. She was screaming one moment and then laughing hysterically the next. I was a little jealous of Valeria but she got her revenge on Stephen.

She was the first person I knew who ran away *from* the circus. Stephen had introduced her to an eminent barrister and she fell madly in love with him. It could have been the wigs and cloaks. Stephen was furious and took a risk by phoning the police to tip them off as Valeria was under age. He was fuming when he talked to the police. I heard all the call and he was bitchy, like a nasty old woman. I was pleased Valeria had gone for she had intruded on our companionship.

After the orgy, I gave him a look as we sat drinking coffee in the early hours of the morning. He must have thought he had gone too far with me. He asked me if I still wanted to share the flat and I said I did, provided there were no orgies. Then, the conversation seemed to drift in a different direction. Stephen started talking about a bigger flat and I thought he was going to say we would host orgies. He said all he was thinking of was card evenings, bridge games. His mind seemed to wander and then focus and he said, 'We could get married.'

I was nonplussed by that but he rattled on about sharing his home with me. It would be the perfect no-sex marriage. It would be ideal, an open arrangement with no jealousies or questions but almost constant companionship. He didn't like sharing with men – they were too untidy. Years later sharing a flat with my son Seymour I understand what he meant. Stephen was clean, spotless – he scrubbed and scrubbed his fingernails and hands. His fastidiousness was a foible. Marriage? It seemed pointless. I never thought it would work and Stephen did not push. He knew I would make up my own mind and strangely it was his determination to get a bigger flat, not his marriage proposal, which brought about the opposite – I left him. For the first time. For one of the most infamous men in Britain.

I don't know how evil Peter Rachman really was but his name was a dark shadow over London in the late 1950s and early 1960s. R-A-C-H-M-A-N spelt notoriety. Part of his legacy was to the English language. The *Concise Oxford Dictionary* defines Rachmanism as: 'Exploitation of slum tenants by unscrupulous landlords. From P. Rachman, London landlord of the early 1960s.'

I liked him. Very much.

He died young, aged forty-two, in November 1962 and is buried in the Jewish Cemetery at Bushey, Hertfordshire. He lent me some money the week he died. We were fond of each other and things were difficult for me at the time – I was running for my life and Peter helped. He had been an escape for me when I felt Stephen was taking too much control over my mind. I always felt I *owed* Peter. It was a naïve and very provincial attitude for the times.

What I hadn't realized then but see now was how much people were used in the village that was London in the late Fifties and Sixties. People like me who came on the scene were there for the good of others – people didn't help you or love you for yourself but for what they could achieve through you or from you.

It is part of life, part of the cycle – it happens every day. I wasn't innocent but I was still wide-eyed about what life could offer and what people could do for me. And of all of them it was, amazingly – given his reputation and history's perception of him – Peter Rachman who helped me while he was dying.

I had no idea at the time that he was at death's door. He was clearly not well but then he never was. He was all silk suits and Havana cigars – he had that portly, powerful Churchillian look. His squeaky voice diluted that image, that gravitas, but Peter was a single-minded man. Given his history that is hardly surprising.

He was born in Lvov in south-eastern Poland where Hitler

placed many of his concentration camps. Peter's parents perished in one of them in 1940 but he was allowed to live by working as a labourer for the Nazis. He never said much about it but he told me they worked you until you collapsed and died. Peter knew this and went on the run – into Russia. He survived the Russian winter fighting and foraging for everything, for his life.

He told me about eating a barrel of caviar in one go and I know seeing caviar on a Mayfair menu would make him feel ill. His minders told me he had eaten human waste to survive but he insisted: 'I never ate German shit.' The fear of starvation never left him. Even when he was making thousands of pounds a week he still hoarded stale chunks of bread; he kept them under a mattress, like cigarette dog-ends, with rolls and rolls of twenty-pound notes.

As the war went on Peter bounced around and ended up fighting with the Polish Second Corps. When he finally arrived in Britain he was put in another camp and did not become 'free' until 1948. He worked in all kinds, but mainly with other Polish refugees. In the 1950s he was working for a Soho tailor – and screwing as many girls as he could. He knew all the working girls where he lived in Bayswater. He was not a man to want strong, emotional entanglements. Sex to him was like making a telephone call.

And he was on the telephone most of the time. All the time I was with him we had sex at least once a day – after lunch. He called it his 'afternoon nap'. One of the girls Peter had met turned him on to the London property market. Girls wanted flats and the respectable-looking Peter could rent them and then sub-let them to the girls. Immigration from the West Indies was high and landlords did not want to rent to black people. But they would to Peter who turned the properties into lucrative sub-let properties – he was making tens of thousands of pounds a year by the time I met him.

I never knew about the terror tactics with tenants who didn't pay rent or were difficult. I knew there were 'assistants' for I fell in love with one of them. Peter charged enormous rents for the properties and if there were problems the utilities would be switched off or the drains blocked. He had contacts in the Tory government including one minister, Ernest Marples, who tipped him off about property –

Peter owned land on which sections of the M6 motorway now run. When I was with him I didn't know the extent of his empire or exactly how he ran it. Michael de Freitas – who would become the notorious Michael X who was strung up for murdering his English lover in the Caribbean – was one of his enforcers, his minders.

Michael de Freitas modelled himself on Malcolm X in America. He was typical of the nastier of Peter's men; he would carry out orders without question. I wasn't surprised when he was convicted of murdering Gale Benson who was just twenty-seven and the daughter of the millionaire former Tory MP Leonard Plugge. Gale was a twin and there were always stories that she was also Jacqueline Kennedy's half-sister. Michael was a nasty piece of work, a real head case. He could intimidate you just by being in the same street. He didn't need to be armed but some of the men had guns, others had Alsatians, when they went rent collecting. And all the time Peter was this lovely, always-laughing little roly-poly man. Great fun.

Which is what I thought when I first met him with Stephen. I had soon learned that Stephen paced the room puffing a cigarette when he was planning something. Before I knew it we were off to Bryanston Mews, to a flat behind Marble Arch, to visit Stephen's contact who would find us a bigger place.

Peter couldn't keep his eyes off me. I felt them looking at me as soon as I walked into the room. This was an infamous apartment. Peter had arranged to have it after the death of Dennis Hamilton who had been married to Diana Dors. Hamilton supplied girls and was into sex orgies at his house in Maidenhead. He took movies and recorded, on a system linked to loudspeakers, famous names at play. Peter went to lots of the parties and to Hamilton's high-stakes gambling sessions.

A reckless voyeur, Dennis Hamilton had a two-way mirror at his and Diana's house at Maidenhead. It was installed in the ceiling above a double bed in what they called the Penthouse so that you could look down on the action. It was, supposedly, more of a kick from that angle. Hamilton died shortly after his divorce from Diana, from complications brought on by venereal disease, the Al Capone curse.

Diana had sued for divorce citing the actress Shirley-Ann Field as co-respondent. When he moved out, Hamilton moved the mirror to Bryanston Place. It was very ornate and had pride of place up on the sitting-room wall. And here we all were sitting in the room. Who knew who might be looking in? It was not until later I found out the mirror had a crack in it – Diana, apparently, had broken it and it didn't work anymore. Sherry Danton was with Peter. I liked her from the minute I met her. She was down to earth and I knew she was honest. She liked people and trusted them, maybe a little too much as it would turn out. She was gentle and kind.

Peter and Stephen talked like the old friends they were. They both knew Dennis Hamilton and his 'little black book' of girls. They also had lots of other shared contacts in the twilight world of London. Peter invited us to dinner at the El Condor Club which was very 'in', like the Saddle Room. Princess Margaret and the Duke of Kent were regulars. It was Stephen's sort of place and he spent longer than usual getting ready that evening, shaving and scrubbing himself for ages.

Sherry and I got on well. She was wonderfully made up with the latest look and she had such long eyelashes. They were stick-ons: I went and bought some the next day. We talked about fashion – and about how nice Peter was. She explained that she did not live with Peter. Her 'friend' was Raymond Nash, one of Peter's partners, a Lebanese whose real name was Naccacciah. He was a moneyman involved with gambling. He was also married, said Sherry, so she didn't see enough of him which drove her to despair. She saw him once a week if she was lucky and that was often just for a few hours. He and Peter shared the profits from the El Condor Club. Raymond filled out a dinner suit with style and although he adored Sherry she was never going to be the only other girl in his life. I felt sad for her – it was obvious it was not going to work out for her. When I look at her picture now, all these years later, it does give me a shudder; her blonde hair and bright eyes look out at me with so much hope. She was a darling. She just fell in love with the wrong man. I know that story, only too well.

But our friendship began with a wonderful evening. I had found a girlfriend. To me, they were beautiful people, grown-up and stylish. It was a world I was attracted to. Sherry asked me around the next day. Of course, Peter had put her up to it. While Sherry and I were having tea at Bryanston Mews, he turned up and was full of humour and chat. He wanted to play chess – so we did. It was really the beginning of my relationship with him. When I said I had to leave for work at Murray's, he was aghast. He wanted us all to have dinner. Why was I working if I lived with Stephen? I tried to explain my situation but Peter could not understand our arrangement: I wasn't providing sex for Stephen and he wasn't keeping me. That was a puzzle for Peter who saw all things in black and white. You paid for what you had in some way or another.

Peter was a card player and he played his cards well with me. Nightclubs would just age me quickly, he said, and if I wanted to work in them I should be sharing a flat with a girl, not with a man who wasn't even looking after me. My situation was not good, not good at all, he said, with raised eyebrows and his voice at high pitch. He was almost squeaking as he went on about Stephen's meanness. Then the hook went in: Sherry models. Why don't you? Sherry will help. Sherry, on cue, played her part saying she would love some company in the flat which was absolutely big enough for the two of us. It would be fun. I think I would have gone ahead even without their persuasion.

Stephen had been making all sorts of promises to me about modelling work but had never followed through. Here was a chance. But I felt guilty about Stephen and Peter sensed it. He urged me to stay with Sherry, give up Murray's and he would help me out financially until I was earning well as a model. I had the figure for it he said. It sounded quite logical for that was what I wanted to hear.

And so I ran away from Stephen. Unable to confront him, I waited until he was at the cottage at Cliveden and got my things from Orme Court. I was moving into a brash, materialistic world. Peter loved diamonds – cuff-links, tie pins, expensive baubles. He bought me custom-made suits and sent me off to hairdressers all the time. He bought me perfumes. He liked to dress me up in nightgowns and jewels and then undress me in the afternoon.

As I said, sex to Peter was part of his daily life. He took it like a vitamin pill, for his health, he said, and he popped me every day. It was clinical . . . strange. Peter would come round to the flat in the afternoons during the week and we would have sex. He would be gone by early evening; he could have been keeping a dental appointment. He could never make love face-to-face – I had to sit facing away from him. There was no romance, no foreplay. He would push me into the bedroom or grab my arm and lead me in. It was like clockwork. I was in love with the idea of Black Magic chocolates and pink champagne and frilly lingerie – I was happily indoctrinated by the advertising world's view of sex – but there was none of that in the bedroom with Peter Rachman.

There was something deeply hurt in him from the beatings in the concentration camps and he would never ever get over it. He had survived but as a very damaged man who nevertheless tried all he could to help the people he liked. Like Stephen, he was also a Jekyll and Hyde.

I became his and he showed me off. He would take Sherry and me out and parade us around town and into his clubs. He would only eat at his own places or where he knew the management and staff. Even then he would have me or whoever was with him wipe glasses and cutlery with a clean napkin or handkerchief. He had a morbid fear of being poisoned and liked me to taste his food.

But Sherry and I got on. When Raymond Nash came around I would sleep on the sofa for we normally shared the double bed in the flat. Sherry taught me all she had learned. In return for this lifestyle I was always to be available for Peter. Nothing was said. It was understood.

And Sherry helped with my modelling aspirations. She had once been the hostess on *Play Your Hunch*, the British version hosted by Alan 'Fluff' Freeman of an American television game show. Her family had paid for her to attend the Lucy Clayton School which was the best modelling school in London.

She taught me all she had learned from Lucy Clayton and introduced me to her agent, Pat Glover. Peter paid for my photographic portfolio which was taken by Edgar Brind the same photographer who had taken Sherry's model pictures.

Pat Glover got me a job on *Play Your Hunch*. I was one of three contestants on the show pretending to be professional puzzle-makers and the celebrity panel asked questions to guess which of us was genuine. It was a laugh. I had to pretend to tear paper into doll shapes. This sort of life seemed easy and I liked the idea of being on television. Peter was pulling the strings and paying the bills but to me I seemed to be in charge of my destiny. Life looked to be on the right track but my own impetuous nature was soon to get in the way of that. And a man, a gorgeous man with thick dark hair and mesmerizing brown eyes. Unhappily, he was also Peter Rachman's protégé, a man he looked upon as a son. I turned him into a prodigal son.

Sherry and I were enjoying ourselves. We never knew Peter terrorized his tenants as he always showed us his good side. He talked about the old white people who he didn't charge rent and the young, derailed, aristocrat type who he also helped as he liked mixing with them. He never brought anyone back to the house except Raymond, but he only arrived with him occasionally.

I still felt guilty about leaving Stephen. I look back now and try to fathom what the hold was that he had and although it was intangible it was very real for me. I felt I had to contact him.

It didn't work out the way I imagined. The reunion was not happy. I telephoned Stephen and went to visit him at the Kenco Coffee Bar which was round the corner from his practice where he normally had lunch. He did not bother with conversational niceties. He was wearing a dark suit and a severe look and went straight for me: 'You're a very silly girl going round with a man like that – why you could be a duchess yet you have thrown yourself away on a man like Rachman.'

I was in no mood for a lecture. I was already getting bored by having to be around for Peter all the time and I didn't want a lesson in human behaviour from Stephen. Anyway, I thought he was just being bitchy so I said so and didn't stay long. Whether Peter knew about the meeting I don't know but the next day he offered to drive me to my mother's. Dad liked Peter and because of that he and I got on better than we had in years. Before that he had gone out into the garden every time I visited my mum. Peter had tried to keep me sweet by giving me an MG sports car and I told Mum and Dad about it. Dad had given me driving lessons when I was just a kid – I happily drove around London and the countryside without a licence – and he was quite proud of me.

But Peter was not so happy or proud when he found out about my affair with Serge Paplinski, his right-hand man and protégé. It was one of Serge's cars that Peter had given me to run around in. Serge was in charge of Peter's office in Westbourne Grove, London, and also something of a bodyguard. He was a tough guy and had a group of helpers who were all big, fit men. Serge also had Alsatians . . . and he was gorgeous. I was only a young girl and just to look at Serge made me want to swoon, to collapse in his arms. He could tell that but he tried to stay away from me because of Peter. The more he resisted the more I kept tempting him. I just wouldn't give up.

As a kid during the war, Serge had fought with the Resistance in Poland. At the age of thirteen, he was ordered to go and kill an informer who turned out to be a woman. She offered herself to him but he refused and shot her. I didn't find out about this until many years later. After the war he was put in a Polish internment camp in England. No one knew what else to do with him. He had grown up in the wild, in the woods. He hunted deer for food. He got out of the camp but had no money, no way to live – he couldn't kill his food in London. Peter found him on the streets just wandering around and he adopted him, civilized him.

Serge was not the brightest man in the world but he was loyal to Peter. He tried to ignore me but I wouldn't leave him alone. He became a challenge, a big, hunky challenge. It wasn't Serge's fault because I pursued him relentlessly. I drove around London late at night tracking him down and waiting for him till early morning until eventually he took me home. It was wonderful. He was young and strong and virile. It was proper, passionate love-making. I decided, a silly young girl, that I was madly in love with Serge.

I had been rather fed-up without boyfriends of my own age, but the car made up for that, although Peter didn't like me disappearing in it. Serge, when I got my hooks into him, supplied the romance. Peter 'knew' I was seeing someone – it must have been my love-struck manner – and, predictably, he did what he always did when anyone upset him: he put his boys, his trained thugs, on me. It was just a small taste of what I now know his tenants must have endured.

I was driving through London at night, trying to clear my head, when a big Vauxhall cut me up and then forced me into the curb. I just sat there as I watched a minder I did not know walk across to the car. He was big, fat and ugly. Terrifying. *Mister* Rachman, he said, was concerned about my welfare being out on my own in the early hours. I had better go back to the flat. *Mister* Rachman was waiting. The warning went no further than that. I felt relieved that nothing more was said or done to me. Peter could be dangerous but probably did not want to destroy me as I was a possession, albeit a difficult one. Naturally, I took no notice of this very clear warning, this threat.

I spent as much time with Serge as I could but I had to share him with Peter who relied more and more on him to run the business. I couldn't have cared less about Peter's business, I just wanted to be with Serge. Peter still came around for his sex visits most days but at night I went out with or looking for Serge.

Then, one night, I went looking for him in a casino he ran on the Cromwell Road and Peter was sitting there playing cards with a group of men. He looked up and his eyes frisked me. I could tell by the hurt look on his face that he knew for certain what was going on between his 'boy' and me.

I decided to keep a low profile as far as Peter was concerned. I was trying to get as much work modelling as possible but when I wasn't working I spent more time with my mother, extending weekend visits. I also saw Peter Lewin and his friends. Back in London the atmosphere with the other Peter got worse and worse as he did not believe I was just visiting my mother. At times, he got violent and would punch the wall next to me. It was the bad side of Peter Rachman that I had not witnessed before, but his tantrums would vanish as quickly as they boiled up.

One weekend he turned up at my parents with one of his minders and just burst in on us. He demanded the keys to the MG and, smiling, said I could have them back if I was a 'good girl'. He did not say anything about Serge but that's what he meant. He didn't want to hurt Serge – but he did want to guard his property and that included me. I didn't like the feeling, being someone's chattel.

Of course, stupid, stupid, stupid, when I went back to London I immediately stayed with Serge for a few days. Peter had his other minders watching the place. He knew enough about me to predict what I would do, that I would rebel. I always have and I suppose I always will, as I did then with Serge.

Peter was very angry, furious, when his boys told him where I was staying and Serge and I thought he was about to send in his troops of minders. I decided then that they both had to end there – my relationship with Peter Rachman and my love affair with Serge. I think at that point Peter would have set the dogs on both of us, murdered us, he was so furious.

I couldn't even collect my belongings from Bryanston Mews because Sherry, my great friend, had a bigger obligation to Peter. She was in love, madly in love, with Ray Nash and when Peter told her to lock me out, she did. I understand now but at the time I was terrified. However, after some terribly heated exchanges, Serge managed to calm Peter down and retrieved my suitcases. Later, Peter, who had never heard of a platonic relationship, was able to shrug it off. It was like losing diamond cufflinks: he could always get others.

Stephen Ward had fallen out with Peter over my affair with him. Peter told me that his friend had cursed him out on the phone and said that Stephen was just jealous. Both of them believed I belonged to them. With Peter, as with Stephen, I had no life of my own. Or rather, I had no mind of my own. It was always being made up for me.

It had been an easy trap to fall into. I soon stopped thinking for myself and whenever I had any doubts, it didn't take Peter long to make me see things the way he did. His way of life seemed good to me; it was brash but, as far as I knew, this was the high life. I always had as much cash as I needed; Peter usually carried a bulging roll of two or three hundred pounds with him, and paid cash as he swept through London with his entourage and me. It was his parade, *his* cavalcade of self-acclaim. But I no longer wanted to be part of it. Instead, I fled Peter's world and exchanged it for one with far more deadly characters.

6

CHAMPAGNE MODELS

DID HE LEAVE A WILL?

Mandy Rice-Davies on the news of the death of her
lover Peter Rachman, November, 1962

I thought Mandy Rice-Davies was a true tart. There was always
shock on her face whenever she thought she might have to do more
than lie on her back to make a living.

Or swing from chandeliers. In the years since we first met I feel
she has misrepresented events and put me down. She must have
liked my style though – for she impersonated it in her fantasies,
taking over my life.

Mandy handed out quotes as readily as her sexual services. I hope
the sex was better value. However unwittingly, she contributed
through her silly stories to the official cover-up of the political
upheaval of the early Sixties. Yes she was young and heedless but,
still, she caused serious trouble to me and others by her antics.

She had just turned sixteen when I first met her in September
1960. She had lost her virginity and any illusions a year earlier. Her
heavy make-up added a few years but she *was* bubbly. There was
that fun about her – she was the other side of the coin from Sherry
who was no free spirit.

Policeman's daughter Marilyn Rice-Davies from Solihull, Bir-
mingham, was, as Mandy Rice-Davies, up for anything. Sex or larks
and a laugh. She called herself a model but that was more in hope
than in her c.v. Everything about her said 'I Want to Marry a
Millionaire'; she might as well have carried a placard.

I had returned to Murray's. Pops had sent me a threatening letter about my broken contract in June that year, while I was still living with Sherry at Bryanston Mews. I had stuffed it in a wallet and forgotten about it.

When I ran out on Peter Rachman, I turned once again for help to Jenny Harvey who had believed in me over the milk and bread, had trusted me. She had a bedsit with a large, separate kitchen which had a bed in it. The set-up was not perfect but it was an escape route. I moved in. Jenny was still involved with Andreas and it didn't take long before I was seeing Harry again. He was still obsessed with keep-fit and weight-lifting. I was quite happy to clamber up on his shoulders again. I might not have been ecstatic with any of the arrangements but I felt safe.

It seemed natural to go back to Murray's for I also felt safe there. Pops was fine about the contract; he played at being angry, staged it up, but he knew that the customers liked me and I was good for business. He had photographs taken of me to advertise the club and it was as though I had never been away. All the regulars were around including Michael Lambton who was as in love with me as ever and the champagne flowed. Michael said his life would be perfect if he could quaff champagne from my high-heeled shoes all day, every day. That was his ambition.

Mandy entered my Murray's dressing room and upset the balance of my life: nothing was ever the same afterwards though it was not all her fault. Nevertheless, I was not happy to be sharing my dressing-room with anyone, especially this girl. She had the odour of aspiration about her. She seemed gauche to me for I was the expert, or so I thought. Mandy watched and listened – she had imitated the other girls' dance steps to get her job at Murray's and now she learned from me.

What we both wanted was 'proper' work as models. And fun. We found that getting on was easier than being nasty to each other and after work we started going to parties with a group of Arab boys. They loved Mandy and the parties got wilder and wilder. We both started going out with Arab lads and staying overnight with them. Then we got into the habit of shopping and going around together.

As I said, Mandy was bubbly: she lived a lark, not life. I was only eighteen and I wanted a lark too. I felt I deserved it after living with Stephen and Peter Rachman, both control freaks. It was more fun to stay in town than to go out to visit my mother, and Mandy and I would roam around Chelsea and Belgravia and the West End. We had no money and neither of us could cook so we were always hungry, looking for someone to buy us lunch or dinner.

Michael Lambton lived for a good time. He was besotted with me and I admit I took advantage of that. I asked him for the deposit – a month's rent – on a flat in Comeragh Road which was way out on the District Line at Baron's Court. It was West London but it seemed so far out it might have been the American Wild West. I promised Michael that I would see him more often, be nicer to him. We grew very attached and were quite ardent lovers but I never truly loved him. It would have been better if I had. For a time we were engaged; Michael bought me a beautiful diamond-and-sapphire ring.

It was a cruel thing to do to Michael but I so badly wanted a place of my own. Or at least, somewhere that I could live my own life, be in control. Pops had taken me back once so I thought I could return again, if necessary, and I had some security there, so I decided to try modelling full-time. Mandy too was fed up with the club – she hadn't found her millionaire although she did have a fling with a fabulously rich American. But he made the mistake of wanting her to be a good girl and that was that. She was also involved with a US industrialist, but that didn't last. Men never took Mandy very seriously. I was always the one the boys were serious about but, typically, I didn't want that kind of relationship.

When I left Murray's for the second time, Mandy came along. We were fed up with work and fed up with Arabs. We felt underpaid and overtired. The flat would mean fun, having parties, going out rather than working at night, having a good time. We began sharing the flat – after she did a moonlight flit. Or tried to.

Mandy owed her landlady a month's rent, so we decided to move her and her things out in the middle of the night. Mandy had a lot of stuff, so I rang Michael at midnight and asked if he could bring his car round to help. 'Can you park round the corner?' I asked him to make sure that we didn't alert the landlady. Michael was immediately suspicious: 'What are you up to? It's a funny time to move, isn't it?'

'Nothing, Michael, honestly. Please come round.'

'But why on earth do you want to move now? It's the middle of the night.'

'We just want to move to Comeragh Road as soon as possible.'

Michael finally agreed to help. We looked out for him and when we saw the car we crept downstairs, our arms full of clothes. Of course, the stairs creaked. Then Mandy had to drop a teddy bear, which bumped all the way down. The landlady's door opened and she rushed out to see what all the noise was.

'And what do you think you are doing at this time of night, Miss Davies?'

The minute I saw her, I ran out of the house to the car and leapt into the passenger seat. Michael and I waited for ages, but Mandy didn't appear.

'Go and see what's happened,' I ordered Michael.

'It's nothing to do with me.'

He was acting annoyed with me that I'd involved him in the escapade but I was enjoying every minute of it. We waited another half-hour, then I decided to telephone Mandy, who was in tears. 'She won't let me go. She's threatened to call the police if I don't pay.' I told Michael what had happened and he laid out another forty pounds. We were off, legally, officially, all-paid-up to Comeragh Road, which was wonderful.

It was the first place I'd ever felt was really mine and I was so proud of my flat. We had some great times there – I was determined to make up for all the evenings I had lost working at the club. One evening we put on our best dresses and went to an expensive restaurant. We ordered champagne and acted like duchesses; everyone wondered who we were. The bill came to thirteen pounds – a fortune then – so Mandy grabbed the sweet trolley on the way out, to make sure we got our money's worth, and we jumped into a taxi. We stuffed our faces with the goodies from the dessert trolley, giggling madly from all the champagne.

The next morning brought reality. We were broke and still had no jobs, so we devised a wonderful plan to fool Michael. Mandy rang to tell him to come round quickly – I was ill. I hadn't actually seen him once since moving in, so I wasn't greatly in favour, but he was our only hope.

'You must come round, Michael, Christine's very ill. The doctor came, and he said she'll have to have an operation. Just please come round, Michael, she's been asking for you. But you won't be able to stay long (we had invited our two Persian boyfriends round later) because the doctor says she's supposed to rest.'

I covered my red face with white powder and waited in bed for Michael. He didn't believe I was as ill as I made out, and when I asked him if he could lend me seventy pounds for a private operation he refused: 'I've given you enough money already and I can't carry on just handing it out like this.'

'Oh, please, Michael,' I pleaded. 'You're the only person in the world who will help me. I promise, the minute I'm better, we'll go out together.'

Eventually he agreed, which saved the moment for us. He had only just left when our boyfriends turned up. Poor Michael, I really had him on a string, but I was far too young ever to be able to take him seriously. Or much else. Looking back, I wish so badly that I had. Instead, our 'engagement' over, he met and married someone else. At the time it didn't bother me at all; my Persian boy, Manu Jahambin, was the one I wanted. I truly liked him.

However, Manu had gone off to Persia to visit his relatives and I was lonely so I decided just to pop into the Kenco where I knew I would find Stephen. It was November 1960 and he did not want to chat that day. He was taking coffee with Colin Coote, the editor of the *Daily Telegraph*, who had commissioned him to sketch the Eichmann trials, and a Russian called Eugene Ivanov, a Naval Attaché.

I walked out of the Kenco and went back to the flat, brooding, but it had been nice to see Stephen again. I sat smoking cigarettes and then decided to telephone him. He sounded delighted and was full of questions. Soon he started to visit the flat and met Mandy, who thought he was gay because of his bitchy way of talking about people. Stephen, in turn, was not sure of her; they were like cat and mouse around the flat.

Stephen kept making casual suggestions to me that I did not understand at first but then it became clear that he would like me to leave Mandy and move in with him at Wimpole Mews. He kept raving about the place, the facilities, how clean it was, what a good location but I just shrugged it off. One night he said, 'Let's all go to the cottage.'

I liked the idea. It would be a change and Cliveden was somewhere I enjoyed. Grudgingly, Mandy was invited too. Stephen said he would bring his cousin, a pilot called Tim Vigors, to make up the numbers. Whether it was to annoy me or show what control he had over women, Stephen slept with Mandy the first night although he didn't like her and he was off-hand with her after they had been to bed. I don't know if the sex had been difficult – maybe Mandy had been cheeky – but Stephen was not a happy or satisfied man. He then got angry with me. I had jumped on to the sofa for some reason and he yelled at me to get off. He had never yelled at me that way before and it upset me very much. Mandy was upset too with his attitude towards her. So when Stephen went off to the big house to treat Bill Astor, taking Tim with him, Mandy and I took off – we were getting good at this – and hitchhiked back to London.

But Stephen got over his snit and it was only about a week before he dropped in to see me at Comeragh Road bringing Bill Astor with him. Mandy was there too. Bill Astor was no matinée idol but he was a charming man, with impeccable manners and good humour – more gallant than gorgeous.

The moment Stephen introduced Bill to Mandy and me, the good Lord Astor was chasing us around the flat trying to pinch our bottoms. He thought it was all good fun and gave Mandy a proper touching up, but it was all a bit of a game and went no further than that – for the moment. Bill was just placing his marker with Mandy and he would collect. Stephen knew our rent was overdue and Bill gave him a cheque which he handed to me. Stephen and Bill had an arrangement which involved Bill getting the sort of sexual adventures he did not have at home. Stephen wasn't around Cliveden just to treat Bill's aches and pains; there were other regions to be looked after.

And the arrangement suited Stephen because of Bill's close connections with the powerful in politics and his access in word – and documents – to vital government areas.

Stephen also knew the value of celebrities. He was not starstruck but he knew that others were and that having famous friends was an entrée. Douglas Fairbanks Junior was Stephen's movie swashbuckler. He had made dozens of movies including *The Prisoner of Zenda*, *Gunga Din* and *Sinbad the Sailor* and was as much a swordsman off-camera as on. Mandy and I met him at the Twenty-one Room in the West End, a glorified knocking shop with overpriced drinks and rooms to rent upstairs.

Mandy and I went upstairs with Fairbanks, who was twirling his moustache like one of those frock-coated silent-film villains. And he *was* a bit of a villain. He wanted the lot – from both of us. Mandy and I got into this big bed with him and we had a threesome. He loved it – and he paid us.

He also wanted to take pictures of me and Mandy afterwards – we were having a giggle and didn't hide a thing. Goodness knows where those pictures are now that he's dead. I suppose they might be in a vault somewhere to this day. The sexy old rogue was ninety when he died in May 2000. He just liked to take photographic evidence of his conquests and the action. He wasn't worried about it – he kept saying this was the best way to enjoy sex; the more the merrier. Because of his movies and what he said, I always think of him as a sexy Robin Hood.

Meanwhile Stephen's cousin Tim Vigors had developed a crush on me. He was a Battle of Britain pilot, a real gentleman and different from the other men I was meeting. Schoolgirlishly, for a while I really thought I loved him. He was terribly romantic, and loved holding hands. To me he seemed the perfect gallant hero, although far too old for me, so he had a key to the flat and was practically living with me.

One day he told me that his divorce was finally through. He was terribly excited and planned to move in with me permanently. Everything was arranged, but when the day came, I couldn't do it. I'd completely changed my mind and wrote a note telling him so and asking him to leave his key. When I heard him coming, I left the note out on the hall table and hid under the bed in the next room. Poor man, he left without a word, leaving his key behind.

Mandy and I were still going to the Twenty-one Room and it was there that I met Major Jim Eynan. We liked each other from the start. He was a fine-looking man who enjoyed going to the cinema and restaurants. He also wanted to go to bed with me in the afternoons and, for nearly two years, he often did. Ours was a commercial situation for Jim always advanced me some money for rent or helped out financially in other ways. He was to meet some interesting people because of me.

As was Mandy. It was the Twenty-one Room where I met Nina Gadd, who was a fun sort of girl – or so I thought at first. One evening Nina asked Mandy and me to dinner with some men, purely on a sex-for-money arrangement. Neither Mandy nor I had had much success at modelling, probably because we hadn't taken it seriously enough. I had got hold of my agent, Pat Glover, and introduced Mandy to her. However, Mandy did not have the figure or posture to be a model though she did get one job much later where she and three others skated past the model girl who advertised Pepsodent toothpaste. All you saw of Mandy was a quick shot of her back.

At that point, we were grateful for what money we could get, to pay for food and rent, so we went to a few of Nina's 'dinner parties'. Where I lacked courage, Mandy didn't. It never bothered her to get money out of men; she was very level-headed about that sort of thing. The trouble was that money became too easy to get and my modelling went out of the window.

We were with a couple of Americans one evening at the Savoy in the Strand. We had been in the ladies' room near the Grill and when we came out I walked straight into Peter Rachman. He was with a cold-looking blonde. I threw my arms around him and introduced him to Mandy.

Peter looked the picture of a Hollywood tycoon and Mandy's jaw dropped. I thought she was going to shout: 'Millionaire!' She just gaped. We all arranged to meet later at Comeragh Road. We dumped the Yanks – after dinner – and went home to meet Peter. He brought the blonde with him and she hung on to him but I wasn't interested. He was still rather fed up with me, but was delighted by Mandy. She was just the type of girl he needed: a pretty face and happy to be just that and no more. I gave Peter our telephone number and, true to form, he acted fast. He arrived in his coffee-and-chocolate-coloured Rolls-Royce the next day and that was the beginning of a long, off-on affair. I was happy for Peter. He had a girl he could rely on and I think Mandy was fond of him in her eccentric way. I thought: good luck to her.

Peter dumped her on a couple of occasions but then took her back to Bryanston Mews. At the start Mandy got eighty pounds a week from Peter and that's when her airs and graces began. He bought her an Arab horse and she trotted around on it, quite the little lady. But her association with Peter also got her involved with the Kray twins, men I would also meet. Peter was having a lot of success with the El Condor Club where Michael Caine and Terence Stamp were regulars, so later he opened La Discotheque. By then he was paying protection to the Krays.

One night Mandy was behind the bar at La Discotheque cleaning a glass for Peter because of his hygiene obsession. She was just seventeen, remember, two years younger than me. One of the twins – Peter could never tell me which one – came in and saw her behind the bar and demanded a drink. She told him she was not the barmaid; he said to get the drink anyway. She said he should get lost. Peter went white. Ronnie or Reggie went purple and grabbed her and she bashed him on the face. Peter intervened and after a lot of talk and thousands of pounds being paid over the incident was closed. Officially. But Peter, a man infamous for terrorizing much of London, was always concerned the Krays would take revenge.

That Christmas 1960, Mandy came back to Comeragh Road and we, two teenagers, spent the holiday together. We went out shopping using dodgy cheques up and down Knightsbridge and bought a proper turkey for Christmas dinner. We cooked it without taking out the giblets. What did we know? I was reading *Lady Chatterly's Lover* which had just been allowed in the shops. It cost me three shillings and sixpence and I was interested because of all the fuss during the Old Bailey trial over whether it was or was not obscene. What it was, was boring. Most people just wanted to read the naughty bits.

I suppose what I was looking for was fun. John Kennedy was in the papers having just been elected President in America but my life seemed to revolve around finding enough shillings for the gas meter which was insatiable; my handbag seemed like a suitcase with all the coins. And America seemed so far away, France was much nearer.

So with cheques bouncing all over the place Mandy and I took off for Paris. Also, Manu was seeing other girls – he was treating me the way I treated men and I didn't like the tables being turned on me. However, in a way it made him strong and that attracted me. But I was serious about getting modelling work and I managed to get a job in Paris with Chanel for teenage wear. The problem was I had to wait around until the season began in March. It was a crazy time in Paris and we stayed in lodgings and conned men into buying us dinner.

Sometimes the men got out of hand. I really had to run for my life when I was cornered by four men – I can see them now in identical white roll-neck pullovers – threatening to kidnap me. It was then that I thought I would be safer back in London. But Mandy wanted to go to the south of France. She was mad for the Riviera – in those days it was the Cote d'Azur not Malibu and Hollywood where young girls wanted to go. It was the capital of indiscreet liaisons where everybody seemed to be a duke or a prince. For Mandy that was heaven. She had heard that that was where all the action was – and there were plenty of rich old men. To please her I stole a car which we dumped after I'd driven it into the ground – it had been a hell of a journey. We had to pass a police convoy but all the policemen did was stare and wolf-whistle at us. Mandy met her old men and I met Leo Lux, a French film producer.

But I wasn't comfortable in the south of France and I wanted out.

Rich old men, even with bad coughs, were not my scene; I missed London. I liked the sunshine in Nice but it didn't compare for me with London, so when Leo helped me with the money for the fare I was on the next plane. Driving along the Cromwell Road, I happily watched the rain pour down and down on the shiny streets.

But there was a big price to pay for running off to France: I had lost the flat. I had realized that Mandy would never be my soulmate but the flat had been fun. At first I moved in with Manu which was a bit awkward as his lodgings were for male students only. Finally, when Mandy came back she went to stay with Nina Gadd.

Manu had a distinctly sadistic streak in him, and I must admit I quite enjoyed it when he threatened to hit me for disobeying him, although I cried when he did. During the day he used to study and in the evenings he went out with different girls. I just couldn't accept that. I could do it but not him. I was little Miss Double Standards.

I hated waiting up for him, but refused to go to bed before he got home. Sometimes I used to chase round the West End looking for him in clubs. But if I eventually found him, laughing and talking with his friends, he just ignored me. I took it all because I was crazy about him, but it really hurt. I would get quite desperate and clutch at his sleeve and make a terrible scene, anything to get my own way, but he only enjoyed me when he had me pleading and cringing. He used to keep a whip on top of the wardrobe as a constant threat. The relationship couldn't go on but it was Manu who ended it. One day he just told me to get out. I couldn't understand it; I had done everything for him and yet he didn't want me. Michael Lambton would have given me the world but . . . it's the classic story. I never liked *Gone With the Wind* but I should have paid more attention.

I thought I was going to be putting shillings in gas meters for the rest of my life. Where was I going to stay? I hadn't seen my mother for ages but I wanted to stay in the city. I thought I might get Manu back. The only person I could think of was Stephen. I telephoned him and he came to collect me straight away. 'Stephen, it's all been so dreadful,' I sobbed.

'Don't worry any more, little baby. It's like we always planned and you will have your own bedroom – now let's hurry, *Panorama* is on TV.' It was Stephen's favourite programme and I sat back in the car happy and feeling safe at last. I had grown up. This time I thought I would stay with Stephen for ever. Later, he drove me back to collect my clothes and when we got to the lodgings, he waited for me in the car. Upstairs I found Manu on the bed, showing photographs to another girl. I wasn't as grown up as I thought: I screamed and rushed at him, giving him a good thumping. I had my tough side too. But I was tearful as I stumbled and ran out to the car with all my clothes.

My real lessons in life were about to begin. I get goose-bumps at the back of my shoulders thinking about it even now. Life had been complicated but it had all been an adventure, a lark. In February 1961 BBC Radio cancelled *Children's Hour*, a show I and thousands of other kids had grown up with. It was an omen. I wasn't going to be playing kids' games any more. For me, it was *the* time of sex, lies and spies.

7

TRAITORS' MEWS

IT IS IMPOSSIBLE TO PROVE THE NEGATIVE.

Prime Minister Margaret Thatcher to the
Commons in 1981 on the suggestion that Sir Roger Hollis
was secretly working for 'the other side'

By February 1961 Stephen had moved to 17 Wimpole Mews in
Marylebone, London W1 – I still can recall the moment I first went
there. The place is as much a part of *my* London as Big Ben and the
Houses of Parliament are to tourists. It was from there and his consulting rooms that Stephen plotted and talked about Burgess and
Maclean, Kim Philby and George Blake – legendary names in the
spy world. It was where I met Anthony Blunt and other comrades-
in-arms of Stephen's for the first time. Stephen introduced me to
them, calling me his 'little baby'. I would be polite but it scared me.
These men were intimidating.

They would come to the flat to see Stephen while I was there;
Stephen was never concerned about my being present. He would
talk to them about East–West 'confrontations' and about 'military
capabilities' and although I tried to stay away from these conversations I couldn't help overhearing and I somehow became one of
them, one of the players. At the time, I did not realize that this
casual acceptance was totally calculated. I was on Stephen's chess-
board to be moved about or wiped out as it suited him and his
circumstances. One day we were driving along Kensington High
Street when he pointed out a post-like object on the pavement:
'What do you think that is, little baby?'

'I've no idea. Why, what is it?'

'Cameras watching people,' he laughed. 'Spooky aren't they?

And they're appearing all over London.'

But British security was not very effective and he knew it and, with other English traitors, Stephen benefited from that. His consulting rooms were a front where they liaised unsuspected as his patients. One moment he could be treating Averell Harriman, the former US Ambassador to Britain, or John Paul Getty, one of the world's richest and – Stephen showed me – meanest men; the next it would be a Moscow contact. He was a Jekyll and Hyde in every aspect of his life: he would be at Buckingham Palace sketching Princess Margaret during the day and that night at some high-society orgy complaining that he could not get a hard-on

Stephen could carry it all off, including having me around. Some operators, however, were not as comfortable with me present and Stephen would often ask me to make some tea as he 'sorted out a bridge matter'. As time went on I realized what was going on but I was young and tried to ignore it. There seemed to be no other option. And I thought Stephen was right. I believed him. Through Stephen's daily indoctrination, I agreed with him: the Communists were good, the Americans were bad. And, of course, it was much, much more complex than that.

Colin Coote, either a fool or a pawn in spy games being played by Moscow or Britain, had been a patient of Stephen's, as so many of his contacts or dupes were. He had been sent to Stephen for back treatment by the MP Sir Godfrey Nicholson. Coote was also a university friend of the Prime Minister, Harold Macmillan, and a regular golfing partner of Roger Hollis, the Director-General of MI5. It was Coote who supposedly arranged for Stephen and Eugene Ivanov to meet. Before he died he wrote that he simply wanted to help Stephen to get a visa to visit Moscow to draw Khrushchev. Whatever Coote thought or really was, this was just a cover for Stephen and Eugene to be seen together, to be able to operate together. For Eugene was a Moscow spy who arrived in London on 27 March 1960 to work for Stephen.

That long-ago day in the smoke-filled Kenco coffee shop when I first witnessed them together, all I wanted was some company. But it was my first encounter, albeit casual, with the Man from Moscow, a crucial day in my personal history book. And it was two months before 21 January 1961, the day, according to the Denning Report, that Colin Coote invited Stephen to have lunch with Eugene Ivanov. Which was also the day after President Kennedy was inaugurated in Washington. Memory makes me play the game, what if? And what if I had taken offence and never bothered to contact Stephen again? He had been pleasant enough but off-hand that day at the Kenco. What if? But it's a stupid game. I cannot change what happened although others moulded events for their advantage. Stephen's group were after information on nuclear warhead stockpiles in Britain, Germany's armed forces, new missiles, aircraft and submarines and the strategic policy of the British government, especially in UK–US military co-operation. The big question throughout my years with Stephen was: when were nuclear warheads going to be positioned in West Germany? This is what Moscow feared, and most wanted to know.

The Berlin Wall, the Cuban Missile Crisis, it was all about Moscow and Washington having nuclear missiles in strategic places. The soaring commodity in the Cold War was information about the geography and timing of nuclear arms. Where? When? They were the questions Stephen and his spies urgently wanted the answers to. It was a nail-biting time for everyone, for the world.

For people like me who lived through it all, it did feel as though the end of the world might be around the corner. We weren't nuts going around with sandwich boards announcing 'The End of the World is Nigh', just ordinary people terrified of a nuclear holocaust. It all seemed so possible. From about the age of twelve I had lived with advice on what to do in a sudden nuclear attack. I can still remember it because it was so silly: 'Duck into the nearest doorway, close your eyes very tightly and try to cover any exposed parts of the body.'

Can you imagine how unnerving it was for me, listening to all the talk about Moscow and Washington and nuclear bombs? Being at the centre of it? Every day. All the time hearing when? Or where? The network operated, often literally, through Stephen's hands. His spy colleagues recommended friends to Stephen for treatment. Or they would recommend that he sketch them or teach them bridge. It was such a civilized spying game, taking place over drinks or cards. When he was lucky and got to treat or sketch people in their homes he would take a chance and memorize their papers or steal them if necessary.

Stephen liked reading science-fiction books before going to sleep at night. He said that in the future world power would be dominated from space, from the sky. I thought he was talking about supersonic aircraft, not spy satellite systems. His sci-fi books were stacked by his chair and by his bed. Always alongside them was a copy of his favourite book, *Who's Who*, which he studied like an evangelist with the Bible. It was his textbook, his guide up the social ladder. But although I sensed what was going on, Stephen's place was a haven to me.

It was a mews house with two bedrooms and a large basement area which we never really used other than for storage. There was a garage but Stephen usually kept his Jaguar outside the front door; he liked the idea of it being seen. The house was within walking distance of his consulting rooms. Inside, the walls were green and there was a fireplace facing you as you walked in the front door. There wasn't a lot of furniture: a large sofa to the right of the room and a sofa chair over on the other side with a fourteen-inch black-and-white television. You could squeeze six people around the dining table. Stephen had the master bedroom at the back and I had the single bedroom alongside the main room. The bathroom was between the bedrooms. And there was quite a big kitchen.

It was where I first made coffee for Sir Roger Hollis, the Director-General of MI5, and Stephen's fellow spy. For decades, academics and espionage buffs have tried to prove that Hollis was Moscow's man, though all the official investigations have failed – or were intended to fail – to establish that. I witnessed it myself. I saw Hollis and Stephen Ward talking together at Wimpole Mews five times. I saw Hollis and Anthony Blunt there three times.

Was Hollis investigating Stephen? Of course not. When you spy on the spies you send James Bond. Not M, the chief Spymaster. Stephen relied on Hollis to cover his tracks and at that time they were after important secrets. Espionage was on the front pages: George Blake had been charged under the Official Secrets Act but no details were given then. It was a spooky time in all meanings of the word. As far as Stephen and Hollis and Blunt and the others were concerned, they were working on tilting the world's balance of power in Russia's favour.

In the West the great fear was the 'missile gap', that Russia had more nuclear firepower. As a bridge player, I always thought of it as who had the better hand, the most trumps. Astonishingly to me, I was sitting at this card table: I was to be a spy too. It all seems so fantastic now, propositions that out-Bond Bond. I still do not know what Stephen told Roger Hollis or Anthony Blunt about me. These were careful men but they did not seem in the least perturbed about me witnessing their meetings. Or making the coffee, endless cups of Nescafé for Stephen as he paced around the room. Or for the trio as they planned and plotted.

Hod Chapman-Dibben was another visitor but his wife Mariella who, for a time was Stephen's very special secret weapon, never came to Wimpole Mews. In addition to selling antiques Hod also dealt, with Stephen, in secrets. Once, when I walked in on Stephen handing money over to him, I thought Hod was going to faint. He went chalk white, which was a surprise. I didn't think anything could have shocked him. He ran nightclubs in Shepherd Market, Mayfair, with movie-star customers and people like the Duke of Kent and the then Anthony Armstrong-Jones, later Lord Snowdon. But Hod also had to deal with Ronnie and Reggie Kray. It still frightens me to think now that he saw me as more of a threat to him than the Kray twins.

Seeing me while he was passing on documents to Stephen, Hod had gone into shock. Another visitor to be upset by my presence was Sir Godfrey Nicholson who looked distinctly uncomfortable when I was about. Denning called Nicholson 'a loyal Englishman' and maybe he was but I have never understood his role as a go-between for Stephen and the security services. It was a time when it was never clear who was working for whom and what I did not know at the time I have put together since after all these years of research – I know now what had made Stephen and the rest so nervous in the spring of 1961: they were terrified they were going to be betrayed. What saved the spies was the rivalry between the British security services and their US 'cousins'. The focus of their fears was Colonel Oleg Vladimirovich Penkovsky who was the West's most important source of secrets during the most troubling time of the Cold War. And a problem for Stephen Ward.

In Russia, Penkovsky would be denounced as a traitor. In the West, where he was given the code name 'Hero', he was 'the spy who saved the world'. It was MI6, officially the Secret Intelligence Service (SIS), who controlled the debriefing of the colonel in Soviet military intelligence, the GRU. He had failed three times to contact the CIA but scored with the SIS through British businessman Greville Wynne.

From April 1961 to August 1962, the British had a 'mole' in the Kremlin who fed them and their American counterparts vast amounts of material about war plans, nuclear missiles and military manuals and rich information about operatives including GRU men at the Soviet Embassy in London. Through Penkovsky's access and photographs of the files of GRU officers, it was clear that Eugene Ivanov was a spy not simply a Naval Attaché. It was a tiny piece of information in the acres being supplied but vital to my life. Of course, it was all incredibly important, so much part of our modern history. Gary Powers, the American U-2 spy plane pilot, had been shot down over the heart of Soviet Russia in May 1960 and Penkovsky had information that his plane had not been hit by one missile as claimed by Khrushchev but by fourteen; there had not been a direct hit. More importantly, the information showed that, for all the Russian leader's boasts, his nation's nuclear arsenal was smaller than America's, as well as being in appalling condition. When Kennedy went head-to-head with Khrushchev he knew he had the better hand.

This coup for the SIS was timely. Blake, an SIS agent, had been convicted of spying. Fidel Castro had humiliated the CIA at the Bay of Pigs and even out of this world the Russians seemed to be winning – Yuri Gagarin was the first man to orbit Earth. Penkovsky's information was, according to all the material I have studied on the period, a major factor in America's decision *not* to make a preemptive nuclear attack against Russia.

So he was the spy who saved the world. And Stephen Ward's spy ring. Penkovsky's material (more than five thousand documents over fourteen months) was so important that he was never quizzed by the British or American agents about mundane matters like espionage operatives. What mattered was the bigger picture – which left Stephen and the others in the background, although I don't think they knew this. Even after all these years it's hard to nail down the real facts. All I can go by is what I saw, what I heard, and what I remember. And what I remember is that they were always nervous about discovery and I think back now to the moments of great stress when even the smallest things, a broken tea cup, a missed phone call, would set Stephen off on a rant. He and the others were always aware that they might have to run for it but, because of the Russian defector, their position seemed to be even more perilous.

These events played a major part in my life but while I was living through that period I was dealing, first hand, with my own, phenomenal turmoil. I was learning who these people really were and the lessons were frightening. I knew enough by then to be very, very aware that I was at the centre of a dangerous conspiracy. You didn't have to be Sherlock Holmes from the evidence that was paraded before my eyes. Little matters like why was a man like Hollis always coming around for coffee?

Like Stephen the son of a clergyman, Hollis was born in 1905 and went to Clifton College and Worcester College, Oxford, where he was remembered by his contemporary, the brilliant, mischief-making author Evelyn Waugh, as 'a good bottle man'. He worked in China for British American Tobacco for nine years and joined the spies in 1936. He became head of MI5 in 1956 and held his chair for nine years. In 1996, Luise Klas, who worked for Soviet military intelligence, said she and Hollis had a three-year affair in Shanghai before the Second World War.

After I had seen Denning, Hollis had to face three official inquiries into his running of MI5. He retired in 1965 but had to

Nearly tears for the camera,
at two years old.

Me, aged ten, with pigtails
and Rex, my dog.

This is me with my
mother and stepdad
– I can't recall my
friend's name. I was
six years old.

An eleven-year-old schoolgirl.

That's me at the back of the picture with my two aunts, Pam, standing and Betty, paddling her feet.

A family wedding party with (from the right) my mother, me, gran, the bride, Aunt Betty, in the middle. Aunt Pam is peering over the groom's shoulder and Uncle Ron is on the far left.

Posing – I really, really wanted to be a model at sixteen.

Where it all began – my grand showgirl outfit, at Murray's, 1959

Part of my model portfolio by
photographer Edgar Brind, 1960.

Another Edgar Brind shot but in
1964, after the Profumo affair.
'I knew you'd be famous but not
the way it turned out,' he said.

At a Turkish restaurant in London's East End in 1960
with Michael Lambton. He was a good-looking man.

Merid Bayeme, the grandson
of Haille Selaisse, took this
picture of me. He took lots
of pictures of me . . .

Lucky Gordon on the look-out for
me at the Old Bailey in December
1963. I was never his girlfriend and
the thought of him still haunts me.

This is Stephen Ward, the year he died, at a reception for a viewing of his work which included a drawing of me.

The day after the night before: me with Stephen and two of his girlfriends at the pool at Cliveden the day after I met Jack Profumo, who took this photograph.

This is Jack Profumo with his actress wife Valerie Hobson
and their children.

The cottage (above) and main house at Cliveden (below)
as they are today.

Horace Dibben (Hod) kissing his bride Stella Marie Capes,
aka Mariella Novotny and Miss Henrietta Chapman.

This is a 1960 picture of
Roger Hollis, the head of MI5
and a KGB agent. When Denning
showed me a photograph I
recognized him as the man who
visited Stephen's flat, as did
Anthony Blunt and Eugene.

Eugene Ivanov.

come back from retirement to face a fourth inquiry. He was cleared every time by other spies or those willing to protect the Establishment. Hollis, who died in 1972, should be in the same category as Burgess, Maclean, Philby and Blunt. And Stephen Ward.

He was a cool man, Hollis. I never saw him flustered; I suppose he had that trained temperament to survive as a double agent. Stephen, on the other hand, did creak under the pressure and would lose it and start shouting at me for no reason, or screaming at some news item on the television or radio.

Hollis and Anthony Blunt, who were also 'patients', would come round to Wimpole Mews straight from the consulting rooms. It was on those occasions that I made coffee for them. They were concerned about being connected to the Russian Embassy by Penkovsky but could only sit the situation out. Because of the lack of information being passed between London and Washington, no one really knew who was working for whom.

When Eugene Ivanov called he'd just wait for Stephen in the hall before they went to the Connaught Club to play bridge.

People think Colin Coote first introduced Stephen to Eugene at the Garrick Club but that was not true, it was a cover. Because MI5 kept track of Russian personnel, Stephen and Eugene needed an innocent account of how they first met to protect Stephen.

I came to understand through witnessing the meetings that Eugene was tough and could be trusted not to go over to the West. His role was to receive all reports and documents from Stephen personally; he then sent them directly to Moscow Centre, avoiding the Russian Embassy at Kensington Palace Gardens. Eugene never came round when Stephen was chatting with Hollis or Blunt. He was never allowed just to turn up; Stephen thought him 'too Red' and too quick to take offence. He also did not understand that quiet British humour. In other words, he couldn't take a joke. For Eugene everything was for the good of Mother Russia. I began to see how they worked and now, with my first-hand knowledge, I know that Stephen had been in place for a long time when I met him. He talked to me constantly about the Cold

War and who he wanted to win it – and I became part of the plan.

Stephen was not only a spy who was getting money for it; he was a perfectionist and he was definitely anti-American – he thought they were stupid – and he believed in Communism too. He told me that he sympathized with Communists but laughed that he wouldn't like to share his cottage. He had all the old-school-tie formalities off to a tee. His manners were, as he would say, marvellous and part of his cover. But he always had watchful eyes. Where I would see two men in a car, he would detect a plot or a pick-up. He manipulated me and, for a time, I was his monster. Stephen Ward was my Dr Frankenstein – he was never any sort of Professor Higgins to me. It's been written that Stephen taught me how to talk, taught me table manners and how to interact with the rich and famous. I could talk properly long before I met Stephen. Interact? A flutter of the eyelashes was all it took. I learned that before I ever got near London, never mind Stephen. But I also slowly learned, taught by experience, that over time it is the lies of silence that corrupt the truth in minor as well as major ways. It can be deadly. Stephen didn't survive. I did. Every day I wonder why.

It was never a question of *if* he would be set up. It was only a question of *when*. He was the man who knew too much. And not just spying secrets. Through his web of vice he knew the sexual perversions of many of the people who ran the world including unelected 'kitchen cabinet' confidants. He had photographs, porno pictures, but mostly drawings of people indulging in all sorts of sex games. It didn't turn him on – it was just part of the manipulation game. Many were destroyed but I believe some are still locked away in Whitehall. Open government? Don't make me laugh.

Stephen knew the risks. I saw him frightened but he believed in what he was doing. He absolutely believed in it but he also loved his cottage, he loved his life and he was on top. For all his show of Englishness he had several Russian identities ready for escape. As it turned out, he was too strong a man to run. He had a Russian card in the name of Beliakov, Evgenij in his pocket when he was found dead but that was a contact, the First Secretary at the Russian Embassy in London. And he'd been back in Moscow for months.

Passports, paperwork and cards in other names were hidden else-where. They were never found or if they were they were destroyed.

Stephen was running his spy ring when I met him and the machinations were well established: Blunt would come round on his own. So would Hollis, who looked a bit like Sir Godfrey Nicholson though not as tall. When Sir Godfrey saw me with Eugene and Stephen he was very upset that I was there. Stephen kept Eugene away as much as possible because the Russian couldn't be quiet, he couldn't help but show what he was. Stephen took him on a visit to see John Kennedy, an American showbusiness agent with film stars among his clients, who had, by chance, a bungalow near my mother. A friend of Stephen's, Paul Carpenter, was there with different actors and actresses. Paul was talking casually to Eugene when the Russian suddenly punched the wall next to Paul's face – just punched the wall next to him because he didn't agree with something he was saying about America.

Stephen didn't trust Eugene's behaviour anywhere and he never allowed him to mix with Anthony Blunt. Those two were chalk and cheese, peasant and patrician, so Stephen made sure they were never there at the same time. The traitors would come during the day, hiding in plain sight. Eugene would come in the evening and on 'clear' days. On the rare occasions when Eugene came to the flat, he normally had a cup of coffee while waiting for Stephen to get ready – Stephen was usually late. To Eugene I was invisible, I simply didn't exist. He didn't disapprove of me openly or snub me but he kept his distance. He liked to watch what others were doing – someone who took pleasure out of other peoples' activities, rather than participating himself. A slight frown showed his disapproval of people or events. A small, sometimes silly, smile appeared on his face when he was amused by the conversation.

I knew what they were doing and when they talked about nuclear warheads in front of me for the first time I was one of them. Now, I was totally accepted. Stephen knew I did not go around talking about where I had been or who I had seen or been with. I was not a blabbermouth; it wasn't in my character. I know he was very fond of me and it was probably because I'm not a talker about things. He wouldn't tell me not to say anything but he watched and knew my character and was confident that I wouldn't. The only gossip was about fashions, the new French and Italian underwear, ladders in stockings. There were no tights or La Perla and naughty knicker shops then. Well, not on the High Street. Clearly, I was not a candidate for spilling Stephen's secrets and he didn't see me as a threat. Not then, anyway. That would be later.

He used to say that I was a manic depressive because I'd be up for a couple of weeks and all of a sudden down for a couple of days, really down. That's what I'm like, so he had the measure of me. Apart from when he got nervous or under pressure Stephen was mostly up. But we did not have much of a social life at Wimpole Mews; everything seemed to revolve around the visits of Hollis and Blunt. We never had anyone around for dinner, but if he had a girlfriend around, she might be presented with a cheese omelette and a dollop of tomato sauce. There were no bridge parties and I missed my game of cards. We usually watched current-affairs programmes on television. Stephen voted Liberal and couldn't understand why nobody else did. His little joke was: 'You wait and see, little baby, the Liberals will get in next time.'

One morning he suggested I go with him to Jodrell Bank but I was waiting for a call from my agent about the final interview for a modelling job. 'Pity, you'll miss the chance to see the biggest radio system in the world,' he said picking up his pad as he was off to sketch the head man. When he returned he was excited: 'Do you know that a rat gnawed through the mechanism of a missile and nearly sent it off to Russia? You should have come, little baby. There were hundreds of ladders that I had to climb as I actually got out on to the very dome itself.'

Then, without warning, he got angry: 'Damn people will blow us all up and do you know, little baby, another time the radar went wrong, which made it look like the Russians had launched their missiles and apparently missiles were nearly sent off to Russia. What do you make of that?'

'That's terrible,' I said weakly. I was concerned.

Then he laughed: 'Better not let Eugene know. I don't think he would laugh at such a thing.' He carried on laughing and then changed the subject, changed gear: 'Let's have lunch tomorrow, I've no patients after midday.'

'I can't. I've got my final interview tomorrow.'

'Oh forget it, little baby. Let's go to the Kenco for lunch.' Then putting his arms around me he said, 'I don't want you to go – you might leave me if you become a success. I'll always look after you – you know that don't you?' He cuddled me in his arms. I cancelled my appointment and had lunch with him. Stephen just had a way of always making me do what he wanted.

He was not happy when I told him I had made arrangements for Manu to come round, although I explained, 'I'm not interested in him anymore and I'm not going back to him – but he wants to talk to me about something.' It made no sense to Stephen but, of course, I was still interested in Manu. His rejection was a turn-on.

Stephen paced the hall for a while in thought then we heard Manu's car pull up outside. Then the door bell. As I went to answer the door, he said, 'Don't let him into the house – I don't want him in here. You meet him downstairs.' I took no notice of him and went to collect my handbag. As I was leaving he came out of his room. He wasn't relaxed. With a strange, furtive look he handed me a large envelope. 'Would you pass by the Russian Embassy and drop this off for me. Eugene had been expecting me for bridge and he needs these.'

I had driven past the embassy with Stephen and said it was not a problem. I knew I was passing on information but over all the years I have always told myself it was just papers to do with bridge. It was just like posting a letter, delivering something Stephen and his crowd already had. If Stephen had been robbing banks I would have known it was wrong. But this? Of course I knew it was nothing to do with bridge. He could have phoned Eugene about that and this packet was thick with paper. Still, you can make your mind do wonders if you try long and hard enough. I convinced myself for years that it didn't matter, that it was not important, that I was innocent of any wrong-doing. What rubbish, of course, but it kept my conscience in check. I was a stupid young girl. If I had *fully* understood then I would never have done anything, however remotely, that would harm my country. But I didn't think it unusual. I had been with Stephen before when he drove to Avenue Road by Regent's Park in north London to drop off a letter for Eugene, staying in the car then while he went to the door.

This time, Manu waited in the car while I wandered up to the front door of the embassy and handed in Stephen's package for Eugene. I didn't see anyone I recognized, certainly not Eugene. But Manu was watching. And remembering everything.

It was a bizarre time with Stephen even by his standards. He seemed to be more and more nervy. One day Jenny Harvey came round and I cooked her baked beans on toast. Stephen came home from his consulting rooms. He was very angry – and petty. In front of Jenny he shouted at me: 'Where did you get those baked beans?' It sounds so pathetic now. Here was this man trading in the world's secrets and he was worried about someone pinching his can of baked beans.

On reflection, I think it was just a reaction to someone else being at Wimpole Mews. Peter Lewin had visited us but I wasn't interested in having him around at the time. I realized that Stephen didn't want my friends in the house so I didn't invite them anymore: not when he was around. My friend from the Twenty-one Room, Major Jim Eynan, would occasionally come round early in the afternoon when Stephen was at work and he always left me something, pocket money. Stephen never met him.

Stephen's own sexual adventures and erotic experiments were continuing. He would drive around London alone late at night, usually cruising in Paddington. He would look at the girls and talk to them. Sometimes he brought a prostitute back with him. They were usually younger, impressionable girls.

He liked to see them walking round his place in their high heels and black stockings and garter belts. I learned to keep my bedroom door locked after one girl stole the bra and pants I'd bought in Paris and another took my dance costume. Stephen was always looking for girls. Sometimes, he liked me to be in the room with him when he was in bed with girls he was dating. Often I slept between them afterwards. Between them, not with them. I was Stephen's sex antennae.

Opposite the Kenco coffee bar was a dress shop with a very attractive girl serving. I pointed her out to Stephen: 'Have you seen that girl, Stephen? She's very attractive.'

'My, she is nice – but I can hardly go in to buy a dress.'

'I'll go.'

I went into the shop and got chatting with her and then invited her back for coffee. It was up to her after that if she wanted to go out with Stephen or not. As it turned out she liked him. Most girls did. Certainly, Sally Nowells adored Stephen. We were together when we met her in a coffee bar in London. She lived in Beaconsfield and Stephen would drive her all the way home after they started dating.

He wasn't emotionally involved with Sally who he liked to take to parties as she was very pretty. She was impressed by him.

Eugene started staying for coffee in the evening and I would sit with them. One day after he had taken Sally to Paul Getty's for dinner, Stephen told Eugene and me how mean Paul Getty was. 'He lives in that house with his girlfriends all together and they are not allowed out at night. His guests must use a public telephone box he's had installed if they want to make a phone call. Can you believe it? The richest man in the world and his guests have to pay to make a call.'

The Getty phone box got Stephen going on about those he thought were too privileged, complaining about Prince Philip whom he'd sketched: 'Philip's a snob, not like the man he used to be – I used to know him before he was married to Elizabeth.' But then he turned again and was pleasant about Sophia Loren whom he'd also sketched. He peered closely into my face and said, 'She's an extremely beautiful woman – beauty you see is when the face has a defect, like your bower nose.'

He could talk for ever but it was all part of the style, the cover. Stephen found out about NATO policy in Europe, 'The Forward Defence Base' where West Germany was assigned the buffer zone for nuclear weapons as a deterrent against Russian aggression. When

Eugene came round one evening, Stephen looked over at me and all but winked. He was going to wind up Eugene. He started: 'How dare the Americans call the Russians the aggressors when it is they who are the aggressors – moving into Germany. And the Germans are not to be trusted.' I sat there quietly as it had sounded logical to me. But Eugene, of course, got upset: 'How dare America threaten the great Russia.'

Stephen enjoyed getting Eugene going but he was himself angry, always angry, at the Americans. He was happy though when Eugene arranged for him to sketch Madame Furtseva who was visiting Britain. She was the Russian Minister of Culture and closely connected through her daughter's husband to Khrushchev. Stephen not only got the portrait published in Colin Coote's *Daily Telegraph* but he wrote a short account of his conversation with her, which was also published. Under the circumstances the Soviets could hardly complain about the interview even though they didn't like it but Eugene was quite upset about it.

He never went to the cottage at Cliveden but he suddenly turned up there one day soon after the Madame Furtseva sketch was published. Stephen was furious with him: he looked so out of place. With his dark suit, he looked like a caricature of a Russian spook, a Soviet spy. He could have stepped straight out of *From Russia With Love* with Sean Connery. In fact, Stephen had some actor friends visiting that weekend, including Janet Munro who was there quite often. She'd just made Disney's *The Swiss Family Robinson* in Holly-wood with John Mills and everyone wanted to talk to her. Everyone except Eugene. He wanted to buttonhole Stephen but Stephen wasn't having any of it. I saw then so clearly who was the boss. Stephen *ordered* Eugene to go – and he went. Quickly.

Another visitor at Cliveden was Noel Howard-Jones, the most handsome man I had ever seen. He worked in advertising and was very fond of Stephen. He would be one of the few who stood by him to the end. Noel was a gorgeous creature and I fell for him immediately. He came to stay at Wimpole Mews while Stephen was away at the cottage. I didn't tell Stephen as I hadn't wanted to upset him but he found out. He arrived back a day early and caught Noel and me having a party, using the basement area for dancing. He was very upset with both of us. First he nodded towards his friend: 'Noel, I expected more than this of you.' And then he looked daggers at me: 'How could you do this behind my back?'

From then on the atmosphere between us was not good. It got even worse after a visit from a man in a bowler hat. This was 'Mr Woods' who would turn out to be Keith Wagstaffe of MI5.

On 6 June 1961, Stephen brought Wagstaffe round after they had been out to dinner and I made them coffee. There was no mention of me making coffee for Hollis, his boss. Stephen was on the couch and Wagstaffe sat in the sofa chair. He wanted to know about Stephen's friendship with Eugene. We knew that MI5 were monitoring embassy personnel so this was quite a normal interview in the circumstances and Stephen later tried to make light of it but it worried him.

The 'cloak-and-dagger man', as Stephen called him, asked Stephen a lot of questions about his relationship with Eugene. He didn't object to my being there at all. Apparently the Security Service suspected Eugene was not the simple Naval Attaché he made himself out to be. Stephen casually answered all the questions: 'We play a lot of bridge at my club, the Connaught. Occasionally we have a meal together, and we meet for coffee up the road.'

'He's never asked you to put him in touch with anyone you know? Or for information of any kind?'

'No, he hasn't. But if he did, naturally I would get in touch with you straight away. If there's anything I can do I'd be only too pleased to.'

'Carry on the relationship as you have been, as though nothing has happened.'

'Well, I'll let you know as soon as Eugene gets suspicious,' Stephen promised, as Wagstaffe left. 'You wouldn't believe, little baby, that he was a cloak-and-dagger man, would you?' Stephen laughed.

'How about the bowler?' I giggled.

'And the little briefcase, and rolled umbrella?'

'Not to mention the glasses, National Health, I bet. And he

couldn't have been more than four foot eleven.'

'But isn't it exciting, little baby? You know he really had a dagger under his mackintosh?' Stephen joked.

I made more coffee and Stephen seemed to get more serious. He was smoking more than usual, which surprised me for he had been complaining about cigarettes going up in price to one shilling and ninepence for ten.

Stephen and Eugene used to talk openly about East–West relations in front of me. The USSR had become very powerful, building up control over more and more of Eastern Europe. The USA, Britain and France were planning within NATO to position nuclear warheads within West Germany which were going to be the responsibility of NATO troops. For months Berlin had been the focus of attention. Khrushchev wanted to force the Allies to leave West Berlin and bring in Soviet troops. The USSR desperately needed to know when the warheads would arrive.

I knew some of what was going on – there was so much about it in the newspapers and on the radio. Today, modern history tells the big picture: Russia was trying to seduce Britain and France away from America. The French Government was packed with Communists. In Britain, Harry Houghton, Ethel Gee and the Krogers were busy selling nuclear secrets to Russia. Admiralty clerk William Vassall, a homosexual who had been set up and blackmailed, had been sentenced to eighteen years at the Old Bailey for spying for Moscow Centre. It was no wonder the Americans, particularly the CIA, had the mentality: 'You can't trust the Brits.' It coloured all their dealings and was another reason why Lord Denning was allowed, if not encouraged, to conceal all the security aspects of what was to happen to me.

They didn't want the Americans to know another spy ring had been operating under their noses. And what if they had discovered that the Spymaster-in-Chief, Roger Hollis, was a Moscow man? There was much currency in letting sleeping dogs lie – and lie they did again and again and again.

The timing of Keith Wagstaffe's visit was, at the very least, interesting. When he'd gone Stephen was thoughtful and paced around the hall chain-smoking. Then, out of nowhere, he asked me to marry him. Completely taken by surprise I told him I didn't want to have sex with him and thought we were happy the way we were. He told me he didn't want sex with me either but it was still a good idea that we got married. We could have the perfect marriage by doing as we liked, but still having each other. Of course, a wife can't testify against her husband . . .

He could see the suggestion made me nervous so he changed the subject and joked about spies and the cloak-and-dagger man. What concerned Stephen was that Wagstaffe might come back and talk to me and that I could have destroyed him. At that point I was still rather naïve about the information being dealt with but I had heard and seen a great deal. And I could have talked about Blunt and Hollis. When Stephen looked at me that night he was seeing a ticking bomb. What if? Maybe things would have worked out differently had Keith Wagstaffe interviewed me that day.

As it was, Stephen tried to murder me in an 'accident' the next day when we drove over to Maidenhead and Cliveden. It was the beginning of a very warm summer. The beer gardens behind the country pubs were crowded. A friend of Stephen's – I don't want to name him for I do not believe he had any idea of what happened – dropped by in his speedboat and we all went for a ride. I jumped over the side and Stephen threw me a rope so I was pulled along behind the boat. The rope caught around my arm.

It was a motorboat with a cabin and Stephen was perched at the back. When I called to him to stop the boat, he had a strange look on his face and shouted for the boat to go faster. I was dragged under the water. I was nearly finished but I was a strong swimmer from my days swimming with the lads in the Wraysbury quarry pits and got above the surface for some air before being dragged down again. I was on my last gasp, being pulled down under the water again, when the man at the wheel realized there was a problem and the boat stopped and I was able to breathe. It took ages for me to recover. I was coughing up water for some time. I had bruising, purple and black marks, on my arm where the rope had snarled and pulled off the skin.

Stephen appeared concerned and kept asking what had gone wrong. If I had died nothing would be wrong. My drowning would have stopped him worrying. Now that had failed he made plans for someone else to do his dirty work.

8

BAD LUCK

IF I MET UP WITH CHRISTINE KEELER IN THE ROAD,
I WOULD POSSIBLY STRANGLE HER.

Aloysius 'Lucky' Gordon, who claims he is not
a violent man, in a 1989 interview

Stephen always knew exactly what he was doing. After the river incident he was all over me, comforting me and being nice. For some reason that I still cannot make myself understand, I thought that our relationship was back to what it had been. I suppose I wanted it that way – the truth was too terrifying to face.

But Stephen's habits began to change and he involved me. He started driving through the rough areas of Notting Hill late at night taking me with him. He appeared in a frenzy, looking for something but not quite knowing what. He stopped for a coffee in a rough café full of black men, even though I protested; I was now murder material and it was the start of a set-up.

Stephen also took me for late-night drives round Paddington, searching the streets for prostitutes. We used to watch the girls at the all-night launderettes in Westbourne Park Road. A black girl came out of her front door and walked towards the launderette. She went up to a big black guy, pulled out a wad of notes from her purse and handed them to him. He grinned and shrugged. Looking round the launderette, he whispered something before letting her leave.

We watched her walking along the pavement of Westbourne Park Road, then Stephen started the engine and followed her in the car. I knew she would see us and I was concerned. I didn't really know what he was up to, what he wanted to do or was going to do. Stephen had that mad look in his eye. He was looking at the girl but his eyes seemed somewhere else. The girl we were following found a pick-up but didn't seem to like the look of him much. Then she spotted a big man walking along the other side of the road. You could tell she was after him, although he didn't seem to take any notice of her.

'I'll bet you ten bob she doesn't make him,' said Stephen.

The fellow halted as they passed on opposite sides of the street. It was just beginning to rain. He crossed, and they went off together.

'Why don't you have a go?' Stephen laughed.

'You're crazy!'

'I don't mean seriously, silly. Why don't you just walk up the road and see how many men try to pick you up?'

'What for?'

'It'll be a kick. We'll take bets on it.'

'I'm not walking along this road alone.'

'No, not this one. I know, we'll do it on Notting Hill. You can walk up to the milk machine. I'll give you sixpence. I'll park the car a little way off and you can waggle your bottom and trip along to get some milk.'

'What if I'm stopped by the police?'

'Oh, just say you're going to get some milk and meeting me here.'

'OK,' I agreed. So we drove to within a hundred yards of the machine and parked. I got out and walked off, a bit frightened. Two or three cars stopped, but I just kept my head high and walked on. A man tried to pick me up on the way back, but I ignored him. As I got near the car, I could see Stephen was laughing. Suddenly a voice close behind said, 'Darling.'

I rushed to the safety of the car when a hand touched my shoulder. As I turned to get in the car the man backed off angrily and we roared off. Stephen loved the game. He thought it was a hoot.

Notting Hill was a tough area in 1961. There was always trouble on the streets and the police did not seem to patrol although their sirens were as constant and irritating as piped music. It wasn't just fights but the threat of riots. Peter Rachman ran the place and his clients – the white ones – were usually on the fringes of the under-world or prostitutes. It was a melting pot of people, a vagabond assortment of nationalities, a rainbow of colours. For Stephen it was all exciting, a new and – hopefully for him – wicked world.

He made friends with prominent people in the black community and would take coffee with them at a Harrow Road restaurant. It was one of those streets where the garbage was only collected now and again and the kids ran around barefoot. Stephen's passport, as it was to high society, was his sketchbook. He sat among all those black faces which was quite a new and exciting thing to do then. It made a great impression on me, and Stephen seemed as happy there as anywhere. I realized that the common sixties view of black people was a stereotype – every person was different, as in any race. These people were getting on in the world. They had ideas, and they weren't going to let anything get in their way.

Stephen got quite flushed over the black girls he was sketching and went on and on about how great it would be to take one to bed. He really nagged on to me about it. I was appointed his recruitment officer. I pointed out a vast black woman waddling along the pavement with a bundle of washing. 'What about her? Shall I run out and invite her in?' He didn't like that idea and gave me a look and then he made a joke of it, trying to keep me happy: 'I'd never be able to find it to put it in.'

You would have thought Stephen had invented the West Indian scene in Notting Hill. He told everyone about it, including Lord de Laszlo who was a writer friend of his.

De Laszlo was a tall, distinguished man and very upper class. Stephen wanted to show off to him; he told him that as he was always writing about race relations he should see the scene for himself. I was hesitant but went along so as not to upset the older man. On the way there we talked about all the race riots and trouble but when we arrived it seemed quiet. Stephen was crestfallen: his reputation as a lethal man-about-town was on the line. Then the restaurant we picked had no ambience and, worst of all, no customers.

Stephen brightened up when he noticed another place, the El

Rio Café. It was a dive, an extraordinary example of just how squalid a place could be. It was, of course, perfect. We couldn't disappoint Lord de Laszlo. The El Rio staff didn't know us and everyone in there was black. We could have been Martians; everyone stared at us giving us glazed looks. We ordered some coffee and Stephen looked around: 'I think they must be smoking pot. There's that scent in the air.'

I asked Stephen how powerful it was, was it like a double whisky? He said he didn't think it would affect us much but it would depend on the individual – if they wanted to get high. The people in the café looked happy – and high. Of course, we were all desperate to smoke it. Laszlo warned us that any dealer would think we were undercover police or something. Stephen looked miserable – he was not impressing his old friend with the social connections. I summoned up a great display of bravado: 'I'll get some.'

It was that moment, that silly, little moment, when the foundations of the tragedy that was to follow were laid. Stephen, in his search for kicks and information, his determination to impress his friends, was the architect of his own downfall. Stephen and de Laszlo said they would wait in the car. Stephen told me to ask for 'grass' or 'weed'. I marched to the back of the place, around where I thought the toilets would be. They were there, but also a balding West Indian guy in a loud shirt. He had a trimmed, goatee beard and talked to me in drug patois mixed in with a lot of 'Hi, baby' type remarks.

I said I had friends waiting and flirted with him a little and then asked if he would sell me some weed. He wanted to know how much. I had no idea of the price or the quantities. He said I could have a pound's worth or half that amount. I gave him a ten-shilling note. He disappeared down the stairs and returned quickly with a dog-eared piece of paper. Inside was a tiny amount of what, indeed, looked like old grass. I made a face, wondering if I'd been had.

The man was short but strutted to a place against the wall which blocked my way. He invited me to stay but I said my brother was waiting. He wanted to make a date for the next night. I was up, pleased with my 'buy' and I suddenly had an idea: maybe this guy could get me a black girl for Stephen. I said we might be able to meet and added: 'But have you got a sister for my brother?'

'Sure thing, baby,' he smiled, 'plenty of them. Tomorrow, then?'

I told him to ring me when he found a girl and, crazily, I gave him the telephone number at Wimpole Mews. He just lifted his arm and let me go and smiled. He had all he wanted. For the moment.

I was pleased with myself and giggling when I got to the car, offering Stephen my prize with just a little hesitation and saying: 'You don't get much for ten shillings do you?' But he was delighted with the dope and we took off quickly in order for him to get home and smoke it. But he was also grinning at the prospect of the 'little sister' turning up. I had to keep telling him that it would happen the next day. A little later the 'sister' had been forgotten. We had smoked the marijuana. Stephen had a silly look on his face and insisted it was having no effect. I was feeling totally relaxed – and laughing like a hyena. The dope made me feel good.

It also brought lots of trouble. It was forty-eight hours before the 'Hi, baby' telephone call came from that balding man with the goatee beard, Aloysius 'Lucky' Gordon, then thirty-one years old and calling himself a blues singer. He was just a thug who had been thrown out of the British army for having a go at an officer. He'd left Jamaica in 1948 and been in trouble everywhere he went. He had no control. He could go berserk in a moment; for any little reason. He liked to dress in black: leather jacket, a roll-neck jumper and a beret. It was a menacing uniform which matched his background: a long list of arrests and convictions for assault and battery. Lucky was a bad man.

I didn't know how bad when I answered the phone to him at Wimpole Mews. He said he had a sister for my brother; we were to meet at the El Rio Café and he would take us to a party. It was in a basement and it was claustrophobic. The place was heaving with bodies, there was lots to drink and people were dancing and passing around joints. Lucky – his parents called him that because they won a lottery prize the day he was born – told me to hide my cash. He made me push it down the front of my dress and had a good feel as he helped me. This was not going to be easy and the dope and drinks were beginning to have their effect on me. It was not relaxing as it had been in the flat – my legs felt really wobbly and the smell of the place, the sweet dope with the sweat, was horrid. The drums were going at full volume; it was like sitting on a giant speaker at a rap concert.

Lucky brought Stephen his sister and then took command of me. He was grinning with me on his arm telling all his friends, 'This is my girl.' But I was faltering. I soon felt my head spinning from the mixture of cannabis and alcohol. I had to lean against a wall to steady myself. I tried to catch what Stephen was saying to me but there didn't seem to be enough air to breathe. I felt as though I was floating into nothingness and then I was sinking to the ground. Stephen was beside me in a moment. He said he would take me home and asked Lucky to get me upstairs. Stephen went for the car and Lucky carried me over his shoulders. I felt his hand slipping down my bra, searching for my money. I kicked at him to put me down, just as Stephen brought the car round. Stephen tried to lead me away, but Lucky was still holding on to me: 'I'm going with you.'

There was no room in Stephen's two-seater but Lucky started ranting on about a taxi. He had marked me out as his property, put his brand on me, and he wasn't going to let me go easily. Stephen got quite stern and drew himself up shouting: 'She's not well, can't you see that? Let me get her home.'

He told Lucky we would see him again and then he did some drug business. He said his friends might want some 'weed' as it was the latest thing, the 'cool' thing to hand around with the peanuts at parties. He could do business with Lucky and his dope dealer whom he had met at the party.

So we got away that night but Lucky was persistent. He was on the phone all the time and I ran out of excuses for not being able to see him. I got Stephen to answer the phone and make up stories.

One day I answered and Lucky was persuasive. He played what today we would call the race card, saying I didn't want to see him because he was black. I denied that but he repeated that I was too proud to be seen with a black guy. I said it was because I had a boyfriend – I was thinking of Noel as I said it – that I didn't want to see him. I felt guilty, angry with myself. I was tearful and Lucky took his moment.

He soothed me, told me to calm down, take things easy. He just wanted to see me for a moment, to talk about something, to have just one cup of coffee. He poured it on like honey, his voice lower, soft and silky. He didn't want to upset me. I agreed to meet him – to prove to him I wasn't avoiding him because he was black. Double standards. At the same time I didn't want to be seen with him. I suggested meeting in the café in Westbourne Park Road. My mother would have died if she had discovered I'd been talking to a black man. But my prejudice got me into terrible trouble.

I arrived at the café but Lucky wanted to take me off to look at jewellery he had stolen. Stephen and I knew a few crooks and I thought maybe they would be interested. There seemed no harm in it and I agreed to have a look at the stuff at his flat. We walked up hundreds of stairs.

'Keep going, baby,' he said gently. At last he opened the door to his flat and closed it behind us. 'Keep on going, through there.'

I did as he asked and found myself in his bedroom. I was just about to ask where the jewellery was when I realized he had closed the door and was standing back against it, a small knife in his hand. My mind went blank. I was quite numb. I just stared at him. He was peering at me, his eyes hard and cold, the look of a madman. He came towards me, slowly.

'Don't be silly, Lucky. Where are the jewels you were talking about? Look, Lucky. I think I had better go home.'

He flicked open the knife as I moved towards the door.

'Now, look here, Lucky. You can't do . . .'

'Take off your dress,' he ordered, holding the opened knife forward and undoing the button on his shirt with his free hand.

I took the dress off.

He held the knife to my throat. He forced me back on to the bed and pulled off my knickers. He was naked too, and when I tried to argue he got more excited. With the knife in one hand, he had me. Afterwards, I jumped up and grabbed my dress, thinking that was that.

'Stay there!' he shouted.

'What for?'

'You're staying where you are!'

'What d'you mean? You've had what you wanted. You lied about the jewellery. What more d'you want? Are you going to kill me with that silly little knife?'

'You're staying here.'

'Not if you don't get rid of that knife.'

There was something quite pathetic seeing him standing there naked with the knife in his hand. He went out of the room and locked the door. I'd no idea how long he'd be gone or what was going to happen. I looked round the room, but there was no way out, and if he had a telephone it was in another room. Before I had time to do anything else, Lucky came back. He threw the knife on the floor as I pulled a dirty grey blanket over me. There were no sheets and I noticed then an awful, stale smell about the place. Lucky had that mad look again and picked up the knife. He told me to take off the blanket but I pulled it closer. He was standing there naked passing the knife from one hand to another and I could seen him getting erect again. Surely, he wasn't going to do it again. He'd only just done it.

He clearly wanted to do it again and again. I suddenly realized how bad it was. He had been waiting for this: he moved deliberately towards me and then with a quick flick of the knife the blanket fell to the floor.

His eyes and knife hypnotized me. I preferred to watch the knife rather than his piercing eyes. He ran the blade lightly across my calf. I still couldn't look at him. I felt the hatred would have shown. If I tried to defy him, maybe even fight him, I felt he would kill me; the passionate loathing he had was so strong. He wanted power over me, to see me in his control, and I had to go along with that in order to save myself.

Again he tossed the knife aside, and like a maniac threw himself on to me, pumping himself into me. I knew resistance would only anger and excite him, so I lay there passively, waiting for his monstrous energy to subside.

He rolled beside me and lay there, panting.

'Are you going to let me go, now?'

'There's no need to talk that way. Didn't you enjoy it?'

'No.'

'But, look,' he pleaded softly. 'We could be happy together.'

'Yes, maybe,' I said, thinking this might be the only way to get round him. If I told him the truth he would have slashed me, cut my stomach, my throat . . . I said I had to telephone Stephen or he would come looking for me or warn the police. Lucky still ignored me, turning away and pretending to sleep but still keeping a grip on my arm. It was pitch black outside. I'd lost all track of time.

After a while I heard him breathing steadily. Despite his bald head and narrow eyes he didn't look frightening anymore. I was trying to think of a way of getting out. I stirred, and instantly his muscles tensed. I looked towards the tiny window, maybe I could squeeze through. There might be a balcony or a ladder below. I could try that. Perhaps the door wasn't locked and I'd be able to get out that way. I would creep down all those stairs very, very quietly, because Lucky had told me that all the people in this house were cousins or close friends of his.

I lay there and planned my escape. I edged my left leg gently towards the side of the bed and felt the cold air on my toes. Still his breathing continued. I waiting again in that position, staring at my dress on the floor, wondering whether I'd have time to put it on. Slowly I moved my toes to the floor, but as they touched the cold, dirty linoleum, Lucky sat bolt upright and with one swift movement clamped me down. I was too upset to cry. I wanted to, but I couldn't. I must have slept from nervous exhaustion.

The next day was no different. As soon as he woke he was in me again and again. I started to cry, but he liked that. It got him going. I asked for the toilet and he got out of bed. He wouldn't let me get dressed but dragged me with him to the lavatory and stood outside the door. I flushed the toilet and came out, only to be taken straight back to the bedroom. It was like being a dog.

I smiled at him and put my arms out towards him, trying to look as pathetic as I felt. I tried being humble so that he'd think he'd won, that I was his. But he decided not to give in straight away and continued his bizarre love-making for a few more hours. I pretended I was enjoying myself in order to get him on my side. Finally he went next door into his friend's room and brought the telephone back with him on a long extension. I dialled Stephen's number and luckily he was in the office. 'Where have you been, naughty baby? I've been worried about you.'

'Oh, I'm all right. I'm at Lucky's.'

I hoped by the tone of my voice he'd realize I was in trouble. He did and said very loudly, 'Well, you'd better be home in half an hour.'

'All right, Stephen. I'll be right back.' I replaced the receiver and told Lucky Stephen had ordered me home. 'If I don't go, he'll be over here to get me.'

'He doesn't know where I live.'

'He could find out from the café. I know how possessive he is. He'll send the police round,' I said, not realizing how much that was going to frighten Lucky. It was the only thing that he was scared of, really scared. But still he wouldn't let me go. 'I'll come back,' I lied, but he just shrugged.

'I promise. I must go now. Don't you see? Stephen will hit the roof. He might do anything, and we don't want any trouble. You must understand. Stephen wouldn't like it. He's very snobbish and doesn't understand that coloured people are the same as everyone else.'

Lucky looked at me with hate.

'And nor did I, until I got to know you,' I told him quickly, catching myself. 'Naturally, I was frightened of you. Don't you understand? Lots of English girls are brought up to think of coloured people as something evil. It's not my fault that I was frightened of you at first.'

'But you're not frightened of me now, are you?'

'No, no, of course not, and I'd very much like to see you again.'

'You promise you'll come back?'

'Yes, of course I promise.' I was exhausted and it was difficult to say anything at all. I could see that he was beginning to believe that I cared about him and I slowly started to get dressed. At last he said he'd let me go, but added: 'I'll telephone you in an hour.' He said it like a threat. I wasn't free yet.

I didn't rush, just to make sure I got down those stairs and out of the front door without any more trouble. I was trying to be as cool as I could as I said: 'Well, I'd better go now. Stephen'll be frantic.' To help, to show that I wasn't mad with him I gave him a warm kiss. He responded like a child and grinned. Before he knew it, I was saying, 'Goodbye, see you soon,' and walking slowly down the stairs, out of the front door and on to the dirty street. I walked slowly as though nothing had happened but when I got round the corner I took off, running as fast as I could until I saw a taxi.

Lucky had kept me at knife-point and held me for nearly twenty hours. I felt amazed to be alive. Stephen was coldly matter-of-fact and shrugged it off. 'Well, at least you're home and safe now. The trouble is I don't think there's going to be much we can do about it. We'll have to forget this one. There's no point in taking up proceedings, we'd have the entire population of Paddington against us. Besides, you were lucky. I've heard they go for gang bangs quite a bit. There was a case in the papers not long ago.'

And there was nothing I could or wanted to do except forget all about Lucky. But that wasn't going to be possible for in his half-mad brain he believed that I adored him, wanted him. I had only been back in the flat for about forty minutes when the phone rang. Stephen answered. it was Lucky. The lies began again. I knew then that Lucky was crazy and might do anything but Stephen didn't want to talk about it. Stephen had his own ideas about Lucky.

He had a meeting that afternoon with Sir Oswald Mosley, the leader of sinister political movements and one-time darling of the Astor family. Throughout Sir Oswald's appointment the telephone rang. It was Lucky. How strange, a fascist leader on the sofa and a black maniac on the phone.

Stephen kept telling him I did not want to speak to him but Lucky would not give up. Understandably, Sir Oswald was getting fed up and wanted to know what was going on. Finally, he left. Ten minutes later, Lucky was at the front door. Stephen had given Lucky's dope-dealer our address.

Stephen feigned delight that Oswald Mosley had gone and shouted to me: 'Lucky probably would have shot him. The blacks can't stand what he's up to. They've been out for his blood for some time.'

I didn't want to let Lucky into the flat but Stephen insisted: 'I've had enough of this pestering. Let him in, Christine. We'll soon see what's what. Much better have it out with him face to face. Tell him, in front of me, that you don't want to have anything further to do with him. Any reasonable person will see that he can't go on like this.'

Of course, Lucky had no reason. That was the problem. But I took Stephen's fatherly advice and went downstairs and let him in. With Lucky was the dope-dealer Stephen had met at the party. Stephen thought Lucky would pounce on me there, hopefully do away with me there and then.

Instead, Lucky marched in and told Stephen he just wanted a quiet word with me. Privately. Stephen said OK but Lucky followed me to the bedroom, locked the door and dragged me on the bed. I shouted for help and Stephen and the dope-dealer rushed to the door and started banging on it but Lucky, wild-eyed, took no notice.

'For Christ's sake! Let me go, Lucky!' I yelled, 'You're just being stupid. Don't you realize that Stephen will call the police?'

Very slowly and deliberately he released my arm and sat cowering like a cornered animal. I leapt to the lock and turned the key and Stephen fell into the room. 'How dare you behave this like in my house!' he raged. 'We are going to talk this out properly. Make us some coffee, Christine.'

As usual, I did as I was told. On my return, Stephen said, 'Now tell him in front of me.' I knew what he meant.

'I don't want to see you again, Lucky,' I said calmly, standing beside Stephen. 'I've got another boyfriend.'

My mind wandered off and I was thinking of Noel Howard-Jones when Lucky leapt up, grabbing me by the throat and shaking me. Stephen and the other guy pulled him off and dragged him down the stairs struggling and screaming, his eyes wild.

After they had left Stephen was thoughtful and, breathing heavily, he rang the police. Two officers came around. He skimmed over the facts in front of them and sent me into my bedroom. I know now it was then that he made a false complaint about me smoking drugs in the flat.

Stephen created an extravagant story about me and drugs. He said he had taken me to doctors for treatment and received psychiatric advice. It was a device to try and discredit anything I might say. I will be frank. I enjoyed smoking marijuana and believe today that it should be legalized, but I was not and am not addicted to anything. If I was offered marijuana socially I would probably take it but what Stephen tried to do then in a society which was much more naïve about drugs was brand me as some sort of deviant. It was just another cover for him.

He played his game so well. He told me the police said that as there were no marks on me, they couldn't prosecute. Stephen said their advice to me was to go to the doctor's to make sure I hadn't caught anything. The next day Stephen said he phoned Scotland Yard, as agreed, to let them know Lucky was still pestering me. I don't think he ever did. It was just another ploy. He also talked about changing the phone number but he never did.

Within weeks of Keith Wagstaffe's appearance, the visit from the cloak-and-dagger man in the black bowler hat, Stephen got me terrorized, beaten and put on police files. But someone was about to come into my life and save it, save me from Stephen – for a time anyway. He was a man being talked about as a future prime minister of Britain and he knew the secrets that Stephen wanted.

9

A LONG, HOT SUMMER

It was not John Profumo, Britain's Secretary of State for War, who was the victim of a set-up at Cliveden on the weekend of Saturday, 8 July 1961. It was me.

Stephen and his spies wanted to know all about America's intentions, especially in regard to nuclear weapons. This balance of nuclear firepower, as we know, was of utmost importance. The Secretary of State for War could, they very reasonably anticipated, be of great help.

Jack Profumo (family motto: Virtue and Work) was under pressure because British military resources were over-stretched. That ugly George Wigg, who I always thought looked like a pervert, was Harold Wilson's man on the army and he was after Jack. Moscow and Washington were at the brink, playing chess with nuclear missiles. Harold 'Supermac' Macmillan had his own pressures as his consumerist conservatism wasn't making times as good as he had promised. That filtered down as he shared the burden with his ministers.

But the Jack I knew was an easy-going man. He had a way with him and he clearly liked women. He saw himself as a ladies' man and that may have been from his Italian background. When he met me he had been married for seven years but I don't think he was scratching any seven-year itch.

He was comfortable about having another woman. There had

clearly been illicit affairs, dalliances before he ever met me. He knew the technique, what to say and when to brush his hand on your arm or accidentally touch your breast. Later, when he was in purgatory, a friend of mine, the Australian entertainer Shirley Abicair who was famous on television for her zither-playing, told me how Jack had propositioned her, come on to her. The public thought he had learned all the lessons of the events which brought about his downfall but clearly not. John Profumo, the one-time Tory MP for Kettering, was a man with wandering eyes – and hands to match.

But he entered my life at the right time. Over the years much has been said or written about our first and subsequent meetings. Some have tried to make more of it, produced theories and witnesses where there were none. I am the only one now who knows exactly what happened. I was there. People ask me if I've read such and such book about the events and I have but I never needed to. I lived it. Living through it is the miracle. I do not need spy buffs' fantasies or the polluted memories of those on the make to tell me what happened.

I was a mixed-up, lovesick young girl in that long, hot summer when the temperatures soared. It was perfect weather for the cottage at Cliveden and for Stephen to do his gardening. He loved it. I lay about in the sunshine dreaming of Noel Howard-Jones, my pin-up. I was in love with love as far as he was concerned. It was humid during those weeks in London and I looked forward to taking off with Stephen for the weekends at Cliveden. Stephen seemed to live for them. It was where he could get to work. Lady Astor, Bronwen Pugh, had her attention focused on her future child. Stephen had his spy games to play. It was a busy place, a furtive time.

The weekend that all the world *thinks* they know about began for me with a casual drink with a Persian friend, Leo Norell. Stephen had been nagging me about getting a girl for him for the weekend, saying that he could use more relaxation than ever because of the heat. But the right girl never materialized in London and we took off for the cottage, just the two of us: Leo and me.

Just after passing Heathrow Airport on the now so familiar road out to Maidenhead we saw a girl waiting at a bus stop and stopped the car. I thought it might be fun to have another girl along, someone to make it a crowd, a party. I knew Stephen wouldn't mind. I chatted to her and she got in the car with us and we were on our way to Cliveden. We joined Stephen that evening. There were four of us at the cottage that night.

At the big house Lord and Lady Astor were entertaining nearly forty people including Ayub Khan, the President of Pakistan, Lord and Lady Dalkeith, a group of Conservative MPs and John Profumo, Secretary of State for War and his wife, the former leading actress Valerie Hobson. Before the war, Jack, who had a reputation as a man-about-town before his marriage, had run Bill Astor's Conservative association in Fulham so they were long-time, good friends. And they both liked girls.

The marvellously appointed house and its guests were glittering in their finery. I was happy at the cottage with a drink and the cool evening air. It was a perfect summer's night. Bill Astor allowed Stephen and his guests to use the swimming pool, a grand, walled pool. Stupidly, I had forgotten my swimsuit but it didn't matter as there were always spare clean suits in the pool-house. I put on a black one-piece but it was a bit old fashioned and was tight around my bottom. I liked to swim with lots of energy and I just couldn't get going in that suit. I must have complained about it for Stephen told me to take it off as it was only us.

Nude, I felt a lot better. It was cool and free in the pool and I happily swam about thinking about Noel Howard-Jones and our plans to meet the next day. I had left the bathing suit by the deep end of the pool.

Stephen was lighting a cigarette when Bill Astor strolled in with Jack Profumo. I had water in my eyes and couldn't make them out at first but then I recognized Bill. I had no idea who John Profumo was. The two men were smiling and laughing. Stephen got up to greet them and at the same time threw my swimsuit into the hedges. I was stuck naked in the pool. There was a small towel at the deep end and I quickly splashed over there and grabbed it. The men were all watching my mermaid act.

It was impossible to be dignified. I could either cover my breasts or my backside but not both. I tried for somewhere in the middle and attempted to walk out at the shallow end without giving them the fully monty.

They had obviously had a few drinks and with Stephen's encouragement started trying to whip the tiny towel away from me. I ran around the pool with Lord Astor, head of a legendary family, and John Profumo, one of Supermac's most important government ministers, chasing me.

I had been drinking too and accepted this as great fun. I was giggling and enjoying the game. The towel would slip or I would let it slip a bit and there were schoolboy shrieks from the two of them. Bill Astor turned on the pool's floodlights and I didn't feel so brave in the spotlight.

Just then more of Bill's guests arrived including Jack's wife. The women were in stark contrast to me in their evening gowns and jewellery. All I had on was this sad square of towelling. With dripping wet hair down my back and not much of me covered up I smiled and smiled and hoped the ground would swallow me up but everybody was nice and then I said I was frightened of getting a chill and must change.

Before I went, Bill Astor glanced at his wife and then invited us to join the party up at the house for a drink. Jack nodded his approval of that idea. I was rather taken with him, impressed with him. I didn't mind having a bit of fun with Jack even though I was dreaming of Noel.

I had never been to the main house before and I was impressed; there were rooms galore, one after the other after the other. I wondered how much it would cost to heat – especially with shillings in a gas meter. I felt like Cinderella, finally getting to the ball. Jack Profumo had pointed out some of the paintings and photographs and invited me to look around with him. He said he would be my 'tourist guide'. As room led on to room, I rushed on to the next door.

It became a little game for the two of us: what was behind the next door. Jack suggested: 'A kiss?' It got a little naughtier with him stroking my back as we walked and then he was chasing me around the furniture. I said I needed protection from him. There was a suit of armour in one room and I put it on. It was a struggle but Jack obviously enjoyed watching me pull it over my head. The others heard the noise as I clanked about and, thankfully, Bill thought it was all great fun, a super party.

I hadn't noticed Stephen earlier but he was suddenly there and he was watching Jack and Jack's eyes on me. He knew what had happened and what could happen – it was part of his tradecraft. Stephen started to make plans.

Leo and the girl we'd picked up at the bus stop – Joy was the name she gave us – had clearly become friendly. I don't think she ever realized what she had seen or how important it would be to the world for she never surfaced again. She vanished into the night after returning to London with Leo in the early hours of 8 July, 1961. We stayed at the cottage that Friday night. But only after Stephen had gone to the village to use the phone as the cottage, his beloved sanctuary, did not have one. I now see that Stephen had the last piece of the jigsaw with which to compromise me. He had Lucky Gordon as a weapon, possibly a fatal one. And he had Eugene who he could order around. He also had me to use against myself. He knew I was crazy about Noel. After all the swimming and excitement I slept well at the cottage but a couple of times in the night I thought I heard Stephen pacing around. I was too tired to get up and see him. I slept on quite happily.

Stephen made coffee early the next morning and on the way back to London we stopped at the main house; Stephen had arranged to give Bill a massage. I talked to Bronwen about the hot weather and how cooling the pool was. She didn't say anything about me running around half-naked.

Stephen wanted to try and find out information from Bill about the delivery of nuclear weapons to Germany. It had been hinted at in previous conversations and there was some paperwork at the house. While Bill was changing, Stephen stole some letters which he later handed over to Eugene. The letters were useful information about the Skybolt missiles which were to be Britain's nuclear weaponry with the help of the Americans. Jack Profumo was involved in the negotiations with the Kennedy administration, talks that would eventually see Polaris weapons in the UK and the CND on the march. Later, that plan would all go wrong and cause a great fuss between Washington and 10 Downing Street, but then, in the summer of 1961, it was a tremendous triumph for Stephen to get any information about the missile programme. It was also even more important that he was not found out, not betrayed.

Poor Bill never suspected Stephen, in all the years he had known him, of being a traitor and over the years had confided many things to Stephen. They say spying is the second oldest profession but it seems to me that it is the least honourable because it can only work through treachery, deceit and hurt.

But Stephen was a happy and busy man when we got back to Wimpole Mews. He phoned Roger Hollis while I started to make some lunch, but he asked me to go into the bedroom while he was on a 'private' call. It was then, I believe, that he and Hollis decided that I was again expendable and should be the dupe if their activities were discovered. I was to be compromised with Eugene whom they could get out of the country while I faced the music dead or alive. They had lots of circumstantial evidence against me if things went wrong. Their plan was simple. I was to find out, through pillow talk, from Jack Profumo when nuclear warheads were being moved to Germany.

They did not know if Jack would go along with my questions and refrain from taking any action because he had compromised himself. Stephen, I know, felt Jack would blow with the wind. What about me? Should I betray him or if Jack should betray me, Stephen wanted to be able to blame me and Eugene – and cover himself. It was so important to the Russians to have that date that Eugene would have flown home with the information. Stephen could cover himself by telephoning his 'cloak-and-dagger man' Wagstaffe and informing him that Eugene had asked him when the Germans were to receive nuclear weapons. The very thing he intended getting me to ask Jack.

But first he had to totally link me with Eugene and he used me and my lovesickness over Noel to do it. Stephen had always been against my association with Noel and had tried to break us up. It wasn't just that we'd had the party at Wimpole Mews while he was away. It was more than that. I think Stephen wanted Noel and me in separate compartments. He wanted to control both of us, but very much separately. He knew I had planned to see Noel that Sunday, 9 July 1961. When he got off the phone on the Saturday afternoon I presented him with lunch, just a couple of ham and cheese sandwiches – I was still no gourmet cook – and coffee. Stephen was happy and told me that he'd invited Noel and Eugene to come along to Cliveden the next day and that they had both accepted.

I was hurt that Noel had let me down; I wanted him to myself in London. I was also surprised that Stephen had invited Eugene who would be so out of place with that weekend crowd at Bill Astor's. The image of that big bear of a Russian with all those elegant ladies and very cultured British men didn't seem to work for me. Anyway, I didn't want to see Noel and tried to get out of going back to the cottage but Stephen insisted, saying he needed me as he'd invited both his current girlfriends by mistake. I would have to help him control that situation as his girls always knew of our platonic relationship. 'And anyway,' he said, 'Eugene has to get back early. You can drive back early with him.'

His girlfriends and Eugene arrived in the morning and we all set off. I went with the two girls in Stephen's car and Eugene followed. I'd taken each of the girls aside and told both of them the same story: Stephen was going to dump the other one for them. It was another hot, sunny day and the roads were busy – people out for a Sunday run in the country. It took us longer to get to Cliveden than usual and I was desperate to get there and dive into that cool, welcoming water, for Bill Astor had invited us back again for a swim.

We all arrived at the pool together. Bills' guests were lounged on one side of the pool so we took up our positions on the opposite side. I was feeling quite glum about Noel but the water cheered me up and we all splashed around in the pool. A few of Stephen's friends had turned up as a surprise and he didn't look too glad to see them but he quickly changed his mood. We were all messing around in the pool when some of the men decided to have a race. Jack, Eugene, Ayub Khan and Bill Astor got in the deep end and were to get to the shallow end without walking – none of them were good swimmers. It was obvious Jack was walking, using his legs, at the shallow end and Stephen and I were in fits of laughter. Jack won without any trouble. He'd cheated, mercilessly.

But it all seemed good fun and he laughed as he shouted to Eugene whom he only knew as a Soviet Naval Attaché: 'That'll teach you to trust the British . . .' I said we should have a girls' race but Jack wanted it to be a mixed doubles. The same men were in the race and we girls climbed on to their shoulders. I was on Jack's and he hoisted me on to his neck; I had my legs wrapped around him as we started to race but then we decided the winners would be the couple who could stay afloat the longest but we were all flapping about, falling over and sinking.

Everyone was having fun when Noel arrived with the most attractive girl I'd ever seen and my heart sank. I wanted to run away there and then. Of course, Stephen knew I'd want to leave and he had already told me that Eugene had to get back early to the Embassy. I was in a foul mood, very depressed. So when Jack asked me for my contact number I snapped that I lived with Stephen and maybe it would be better if he asked him. I was rude because I was upset about Noel and, anyway, I did not think it mattered. What could Jack Profumo be in my life?

I left Cliveden with Eugene that fateful day as I'd been hurt by Noel. Eugene was also in a bad mood. With no sense of humour, he had not appreciated Jack's tactics in the race. At the pool he'd been very quiet, hardly mixing with Bill and his guests – he'd kept his distance from them, under Stephen's strict orders I expect, as he was so tactless. He was nervous and in a bad mood, and as we drove back we both complained about the other drivers. We were like a double act performing a routine.

Eugene started: 'Look at that car. How dare he drive in such a dangerous way.'

'We call them roadhogs here,' I told him.

'In Russia, houses like Astor's are for all the people not just for the few.'

'Yes, I know. Stephen told me. But even though he is a Communist sympathizer, he would never give up his cottage.' I laughed.

'The Russian people are honest. We don't need ticket men on our buses like you people have to. Our people are trusted to pay their own bus fares themselves into a till when they get on the bus.'

It became childish, Eugene boasting that his country was better than mine.

'We don't have queers in Russia like you have here. People odd like that are sent to the country,' he went on. I hit back.

'When you send queers to the country do they have to do hard labour?'

'Of course,' he shouted.

Eugene certainly didn't have a sense of humour. He was always so serious about everything. When we arrived back in London, I was surprised when he asked to come in, but I didn't refuse: he was Stephen's friend. He then produced a bottle of booze from the boot of his car. 'In Russia, we drink vodka.'

We drank and talked more about his country. He bragged about the size of Russia, how much had been achieved by the Party, how loyal its people were. We drank glasses of vodka and he got annoyed because I kept putting tonic in mine. Then he started kissing me. He wasn't very enthusiastic at first but it was clear what he wanted to do and he got carried away. I could feel him get more excited. He thrust me to the floor. He took his time. He wanted good, old-fashioned sex without any fuss or trimmings. He was a Soviet warrior. He did what Stephen had ordered him to do. And he was pretty good at it.

I had just had sex with a Soviet spy, a man from Moscow. If anything went wrong from now on I was the wanton woman who had betrayed her country by bedding a spy and selling secrets. I was not that willing a partner and he didn't like it much either but he'd carried out his orders, even if it made him feel a little ashamed of himself. In all of it, Eugene thought he was doing the right thing, acting for Mother Russia in the most honourable of ways. When he'd gone I had strange dreams that night. I can't remember them other than they made me feel uncomfortable, hot and overwrought.

Stephen arrived back in a fabulous mood on Monday morning to announce that he had given Jack my phone number. He was jubilant. And he laughed about me and Eugene. I saw the mischief in him and he said: 'With the two of them you could start a war.' Stephen, as he always could, got the full story from me. He knew Eugene and I had made love. He wanted the details. How had Eugene got me in his evil, Russian clutches is how he put it, making a joke of it. But he wanted to know just what went on between the two of us. Had he got my knickers or my bra off first? What was he like, gentle or rough? He asked about everything in his soft, convincing, sincere voice while all the time making light of it. And, of course, I told him. Later that day a woman friend of Stephen's – I think she was called Jan – turned up. She was older than his usual girls, well built and attractive with long dark hair. She paraded around half-naked in blue stockings and a garter belt and Stephen gossiped about me and Eugene. He let her know that I'd had sex with Eugene to cover himself with a witness. He had his triangle, his plot, in place.

And so he waited for the right moment. At first, he had trouble with me as I was not interested in Jack. I liked him, but I thought I loved Noel. And I was irritated with Stephen. 'Why did you give him my number when you know that I'm not interested in him?'

Stephen became his cool, headmaster type – how he always behaved when I was annoyed with him. He wouldn't let the matter rest: 'How could you not want to go out with such an important man? If only to find out what he is like, how he treats his men, why he was the youngest ever MP. And he is tipped to be prime minister one day. You don't have to do anything silly but surely you're interested in what he works at?' He made me feel quite stupid in not wanting to find out about Jack. He was at his best, silky self. He had only to wait for Jack to ring me then he'd telephone Keith Wagstaffe at MI5 and not only tell him that Eugene had asked him for information but he'd warn him about me: 'Christine Keeler drank a bottle of vodka with Eugene and had him. She is in demand with cabinet ministers. John Profumo wants her telephone number – this could turn out to be a very awkward situation.'

And all the time this espionage information, had to go through Wagstaffe's boss Roger Hollis. Hollis would then make sure that Jack was not warned off me until I had got the information for Stephen. Jack did as expected for he really wanted me. I've had men hot for me but Jack was panting, absolutely rampant. You could smell the need on him. Nothing mattered to him but getting his way with me. Stephen had spent a lifetime reading such men.

Jack telephoned me on 12 July 1961; on the same day Stephen telephoned Keith Wagstaffe. MI5 knew all about Eugene and me and Jack's pursuing interest in me at least eighteen months before anyone else, including Macmillan and his government. But it was kept quiet by Hollis and, later, ignored by Lord Denning. I sit here in north London thinking about it now and just shake my head: how did they get away with it? If I had known then what I know now. What a silly girl I was.

It was hot and Jack suggested a drive to anywhere I wanted to go. You have to remember I was only nineteen years old and this was a government minister. I wanted to show some respect although I knew what he was after. I had no idea what to say and I blurted out: 'We could drive by where you work.'

I have no idea why I said that. I didn't care. I was just trying to be polite. It was like asking: 'Do you think it will rain today?' But the Secretary of State for War was not concerned. He just wanted to impress me. 'I'll show you the army barracks too, where I inspect the men.'

On 12 July we went for a drive around London. Jack had collected me from Wimpole Mews and casually greeted Stephen who, incredibly, was leaving for a meeting with Eugene, a Russian espionage agent. Jack asked about Stephen and I assured him that Stephen and I were just good friends. He was most polite. My nineteen-year-old self was impressed, flattered by the attention. We drove to the War Office and down Downing Street which you could still do in those days. Jack was forty-six then, more than twice

my age, but he had a natural style about him, something you get
with pedigree: confidence and an aura of being totally in control. I
had climbed into Jack's polished, glistening black car without much
thought other than keeping everybody happy.

And so I began the Profumo Affair.

10

LOVE LETTERS

DARLING, IN GREAT HASTE AND BECAUSE I CAN GET NO REPLY FROM YOUR PHONE.
ALAS SOMETHING'S BLOWN UP TOMORROW NIGHT AND I CAN'T THEREFORE MAKE
IT. I'M TERRIBLY SORRY ESPECIALLY AS I HAVE TO LEAVE THE NEXT DAY FOR
VARIOUS TRIPS AND THEN ON HOLIDAY SO WON'T BE ABLE TO SEE YOU AGAIN
UNTIL SOMETIME IN SEPTEMBER. BLAST IT. PLEASE TAKE GREAT CARE OF YOURSELF,
AND DON'T RUN AWAY.
  LOVE J.

P.S. I AM WRITING THIS 'COS I KNOW YOU'RE OFF FOR THE DAY TOMORROW AND
I WANT TO KNOW BEFORE YOU GO IF I STILL CAN'T REACH YOU BY PHONE.

One of John Profumo's letters to Christine Keeler, 8 August 1961,
quoted in the Denning Report, September 1963

I don't remember the sex with Jack that much other than it was furtive
at first and increasingly pleasant. It seems incredible looking back over
the years that our liaison could have resulted in so much tragedy and
damage. It was no grand romance. I've felt sad for Jack over the years
but never sorry for him. He was a grown-up, much older man and I
was clearly not the first girl he chased. Or the last.

To me, it was Jack's wife, who died in 1999, who was the strong
one. She stayed with him for nearly forty years and never said a bad
word. About anyone. The Profumos had a lot of family money and
Jack had a taste for luxury. He used to pick me up in a big black
chauffeur-driven car with a flag on the front. The government car
he took me around London in had soft leather seats you sank into
and that smell of polish on the walnut finishings and the leather. It
was like being in a Bond Street store.

When the car pulled up back at Wimpole Mews the only thing bothering Jack was running into Stephen. He was desperate to see me again, the next day if possible. But he wanted to know about Stephen and we arranged for him to call me, make sure the coast was clear as it were, and then arrive. It was 'our plot', as he put it with a big smile. He didn't seem to think he was doing anything wrong, taking any risks. He was just looking for a good time.

Of course, Stephen wanted to know exactly what had happened with Jack and I told him about driving along Downing Street and past the War Office which Jack had been running since 1960; how Jack had delighted in showing me around Regent's Park. Stephen wanted to know if we'd had sex so I told him we hadn't and accused him of having a 'dirty mind' which, in the circumstances, was a bad joke. Stephen didn't care: he relished all of it. He called it dramatic and I thought he just wanted to know all about the habits – sexual or otherwise – of a future prime minister.

Stephen subsequently spent more time than usual at his consulting rooms and Jack and I became lovers. The first time was in the front room of Wimpole Mews. We had been talking and he was being charming and flirting and the next thing we were kissing and then he was leaping on top of me.

Jack never gave me a chance to think about rejecting him. He was anxious to move on and we were on the sofa. I enjoyed it for he was kind and loving afterwards. I never thought about the implications; it was all very agreeable and I began to look forward to his visits.

Stephen bumped into Jack a few nights after I had met the minister at Cliveden. Russia's first man in space, Major Yuri Gagarin, was in Britain. He had lunch with the Queen and the Duke of Edinburgh and then attended a mobbed press conference in Earl's Court. It was like a Hollywood welcome for him.

The Russian Embassy went to town. They held a lavish reception for Gagarin and Stephen was invited. He took Sally Nowells, not me, with him to the function. Jack was there with Valerie and naturally enough Eugene was there. Stephen told me had met them all and he and Sally had had drinks – vodka – with Jack and Valerie and also with Gagarin. Nothing was said about me but Jack must have been thinking about me because I received word from him.

It was insane of him to write me notes, but he did. There would be a couple of lines like 'Looking forward to getting to know you better . . .' a little innuendo about our love-making. And there were a couple of notes changing arrangements always signed 'Love J.' and with a message for me to take care of myself for him. I did not keep the letters as I never wanted to hurt Jack and I never considered blackmailing him over them. The only letter that was ever published in full was the 'Darling' letter and that got most circulation through the Denning Report.

At first, I just put the letters in my top drawer. I don't know what happened to them all. I know that I gave one to the *Sunday Pictorial* which apparently was returned to Jack and that I left two at Michael Lambton's who I assume passed them back to Jack, being the type of man Michael was. He was old school tie. I never wanted to cash in on Jack's disgrace. I went on seeing him after our affair had supposedly ended but I covered for him after it became public by saying it was all over in August 1961. And until now I have never said anything about that or becoming pregnant by him.

That summer I was happy having our illicit love affair. It was exciting. I had the upper hand for I could always get rid of Jack by saying that Stephen was scheduled to be home. That got him away for he was very wary of Stephen, but he never seemed concerned about others finding out about us. I told Denning he was concerned about his wife finding out but if he was he never showed it to me. He even borrowed his friend John Hare's Bentley to take me for a drive. And Viscount Hare was the Minister of Labour whose car had a unique bonnet mascot, a silver hare. I don't know if Jack was being reckless or was just too arrogant and thought he could do what he wanted with impunity.

Also, it was not the sign of a worried man to take me to his marital bed and make love to me. He had turned up in his red Mini and was cheerful. We took a drive through Regent's Park but this time we stopped at his home, an impressive Nash house. We rushed up the steps and into an oblong-shaped hall. At the bottom of a huge staircase there were two big ornamental dogs which Jack said Valerie had bought. He didn't sound too fond of them. Stephen had known Valerie before she married Jack and he contacted her a couple of times during that summer of 1961. I believe he went to see her at their house in Regent's Park but he never told me what occurred between them. That surprises me for he knew Jack had taken me to the house and we would, in our 'normal' circumstances, have gossiped about the size of the rooms and the interior decoration. It was fine and rich and tasteful, and Stephen would have adored it.

Jack, as he had done at Cliveden, offered me a tour of the house. He showed me the dining room. 'We often have the Queen for dinner here.' I stared at the table. He rolled his eyes: 'She's my favourite girlfriend.'

'The Queen?'

He laughed as he led me up the great staircase to where his office was situated and the master bedroom. We entered his office: 'And this is where I work.' He tried to kiss me. His desk looked like a telephone exchange and one phone looked unusual. 'Oh, that's a scrambler. I use that if I want to phone the Prime Minister. It scrambles our voices. No one except us can understand what we're saying.'

Then he took me into the next room which was a grand en suite bedroom. Jack went into the bathroom as I looked around. When he came out he seemed to me a most powerful figure. Soon we were making love in his own bedroom. It was a great turn-on for both of us. I enjoyed being with him. Jack would try to buy me presents or give me money, but I always refused. I didn't want his money. I felt that what was happening between us was above that. Once, he gave me twenty pounds for my mother and I got perfume and a cigarette lighter from him. He said he wanted to be generous to me as I was generous with my gifts to him. I didn't like taking the twenty pounds from him but I did. Jack seemed oblivious to people finding out about us. The next time we went out he went to a club in St James's to collect a package and I waited in the car for him. But then we went to Chelsea to visit Georgie Ward who was the former Air Minister. Jack told him about meeting me at Bill Astor's pool and they laughed about it. Georgie was a jolly sort of man and thought nothing of us being together. The following day Stephen took me for a drive and I pointed out Georgie Ward's house to him.

A couple of afternoons later, Jack turned up uninvited. He was more confident with me now. We'd made love at the flat about half a dozen times but this was inconvenient – he'd arrived about five minutes after my long-time friend Major Jim Eynan had come to see me. I heard a car and looked out of the window. I was frightened that it was Stephen as he knew nothing about Major Jim's visits. But it was Jack and I can laugh now because I sounded like someone from a Whitehall farce.

'Goodness, it's the Secretary of State for War. He's come to see me,' I said in a matronly, Hattie Jacques voice; it was a bit of a squeal. Major Jim looked astonished and seemed to stand to attention. He became an old soldier, part of the act. 'Don't worry about me, I was in the army. Let him in, I'll go.'

I let Jack in and introduced him to Jim who mentioned something about being an army man and made his excuses: 'I just popped by to see Christine and I was about to leave . . .'

Jack and I made love that afternoon and later Stephen returned from a trip to the cottage. Late that night he came into my bedroom. I was half asleep and he paced the room puffing on a cigarette. It was his usual routine when he couldn't sleep, when he wanted to talk. But this time the talk was of world importance – and would affect the rest of our lives. It's extraordinary how a small moment in time, a half-awake moment for me, can transform your world. For you can never change what happened, take back the words, reverse the deeds. It's done, it's said. No matter how much you want it, things can never be undone, unsaid. That night in the bedroom, between drags on his cigarette, Stephen just asked me straight out to ask Jack what date the Germans were going to get nuclear weapons. I knew Stephen was a spy but had not allowed myself to think how great his scope was or what his actions could mean. This seemed so bold. I had dropped off letters to the Russian

Embassy but, as I said, that was just like posting a letter. This was different. This was gathering information. Spying. Properly. Or, rather, improperly.

I leant over and put on the night light and could see that Stephen looked worried. He lit another cigarette and went on: 'We know they are going to have them but we don't know when – you could find out as Jack would have been invited to the ceremony.'

Months later 'Supermac' Macmillan would suggest that Jack could not have known such details, but Jack was in negotiations with the Americans all the time over weapons and their placement. The Russians – and Stephen – knew Jack would have some inside information, if not every detail. And so, of course, did I – having heard them talking about it and Eugene and Stephen's heated discussions on the East–West battle of power.

I became afraid and begged him not to ask me to do such a thing, that I couldn't betray my country. He then told me not to worry and abruptly left my room. I lay awake wondering what to do. I loved and I feared Stephen for I knew what he was capable of. I also knew that if I did not do what he asked my life would be in danger again. The reprieve would be over. I would be back on Death Row. I decided to ignore the incident and put it out of my mind for ever. But that was not to be. Stephen followed his plan. He rang Hollis and Wagstaffe's report on me or at least part of it was given to Jack – exactly one month after Stephen had warned Wagstaffe about me.

The next day I received the 'Darling' letter with Jack changing our plans, but not cancelling out future meetings. The next meeting we did have was complicated, we sat outside Wimpole Mews in his distinctive red Mini and we argued. He said he could no longer see me if I stayed with Stephen. I had no option: I had to either leave Stephen or never see Jack again. I got confused and angry and he said, 'Why don't you get a flat on your own somewhere, Christine? I could find one for you.'

I thought of the movie *The Apartment* where the girl, Shirley Maclaine, is used by some big-time business executive. It's Jack Lemmon's apartment and is always available for the executive and his friends to come round. I thought my Jack wanted me to be available for all the Tory government and I was livid. I shouted at him that he didn't own me. I said I didn't love him and I enjoyed living with Stephen, with our arrangement. I said he was being jealous and possessive, and it wasn't as if I loved him, although I did enjoy being with him and I liked going to bed with him.

Jack again said he couldn't see me any more if I stayed at Wimpole Mews. I jumped out of the Mini saying, 'Don't then,' and slammed the car door. Without looking back, I also slammed the front door. I thought all was over with Jack Profumo. He wrote to me once after that, saying that if I would like to see him again, I could get in touch. I didn't bother reading the letter twice but I did get in touch. When I was frightened for my life again.

11

CORNERED

WHEN CHRISTINE KEELER WALKED INTO A ROOM,
THE WHOLE PLACE LIT UP.

Lucky Gordon, April 1989

By August 1961 the Berlin Wall sealing off the western sectors of the city was getting taller and stronger by the day. It was snaking across Berlin and as it grew and grew like Topsy, so did the crisis.

The happenings in Berlin had Eugene in an anxious mood when he came round one evening. I sat there quietly while he and Stephen discussed events and Eugene lost his temper, smashing his fist down on the coffee table, shouting: 'Those bloody Americans. Who do they think they are, threatening the great Russia. If I were there I would blow their bloody tanks off the face of the earth. When will the order come, Stephen?' 'Don't worry, Eugene, it will come,' Stephen assured him.

Eugene was not aware of Stephen's deep fears about me; he didn't know then that Stephen had plotted my death. Stephen hadn't told him that he feared MI5 might come back and talk to me. I might have been one of them as far as Stephen was concerned but he was upset at Eugene's questions in front of me. I made a show of leaving the room. I could feel Stephen's eyes on me. I swear I could hear his mind ticking over: my stay of execution was over. Stephen began again his nomadic, nocturnal drives down to Notting Hill and his behaviour made me think he had turned into a crank. A murderous one.

He would take me sometimes and for some reason I went but I thought he was being crazy and selfish because Lucky Gordon knew his car – had been about to jump in it after I became sick at the pot party – and had taken a note of the registration number. Lucky would spot the car in a moment – this wasn't the congested London of the twenty-first century. But Stephen always got his own way.

One afternoon we went to Notting Hill and I didn't mind the daylight visit so much but I was still wary. We went to see Ronna Riccardo who had dark hair and almond-shaped, gullible eyes. She was a quiet-spoken, shy girl and I did not know then that she was a busy prostitute. One of her clients was a police detective called Samuel Herbert. Herbert committed suicide after playing a crucial role in all our lives. She had been to Cliveden, to the cottage, with Stephen. I don't know how she had figured in his plans but, later, she would turn on him. Then, we just had tea and she and Stephen talked quietly in the her small kitchen. I presumed she was just one of his girls, one he would call round to parade for him. I had no idea she would find her way into FBI files and be of interest to the American president. As I was to be.

The man in my nightmares was far closer to home. Lucky Gordon was still roaming the streets and haunting the clubs where Stephen was taking his late-night drives. The more I thought of Lucky, the more frightened I became. I felt I saw him standing on street corners when I went out and I was always looking over my shoulder. It got worse for me as the weeks went on and the nights began to draw in. Summer was disappearing and the colder it got the more I worried, the more I shivered. But it wasn't just the weather. I thought Stephen was putting me in danger and so I contacted the man who, by happenstance, had saved me before: Jack Profumo.

In his last note Jack had said to call. He seemed pleased to hear from me. It was late October 1961, and the weather had turned very cold. We were more discreet for he did not want Stephen to know and neither, of course, did I. I thought Jack's offer of a flat might be a chance of escape. Later that night Jack and I went to Murray's. We were not worried about being seen there as long as Stephen never found out. Jack was not a member of Murray's so I whispered to Peter on the front door who Jack was and Peter made an exception (after making a meal of it) and allowed us in. We sat at a corner table. The girls were impressed as was Toni, the head waiter. It was a lovely evening. I felt warm and good to be back with Jack.

We talked about lots of things including where I might go to live away from Stephen. After we left the club we drove around and stopped somewhere. I don't remember where, I wasn't paying attention to anything but Jack. We made love in his car and that is where and when I became pregnant.

I didn't tell Jack about the baby but I never heard from him again. About the flat. About anything. Maybe it had been one last fling with me, one last great risk that excited him. I don't know and I don't suppose I care that much now. At the time I was lost and didn't know where to turn. Stephen, who had always been my escape was now the man I wanted to escape from. I knew he was risking my life trying to set me up with Lucky Gordon but for the time being I was stuck at Wimpole Mews. Or visiting the cottage.

One November weekend at the cottage I met a well-known show business personality, a marvellous character. She had a great fan club of young men – not surprising because she was very attractive with a fabulous figure. She still looks wonderful today. But she was in trouble: she was pregnant.

Now she was going to have an abortion and would I be with her? I went to her flat where the baby was aborted. It was difficult and painful for her and she kept thanking me for being with her. She also told me that the Duke of Edinburgh was the father.

I was getting a lot of headaches at the time because there was so much going on. I felt like some fun, some escape. I hadn't seen Mandy since we returned from the South of France when she had gone to stay with her friend Nina Gadd but I managed to track her down through one of Peter Rachman's boys, a friend of Serge.

She had been living in Bryanston Mews like I did, courtesy of Peter Rachman. She often 'left' Peter but furs and jewellery kept being bought and she was getting more than sixty pounds a week from him. She tried her best to keep Peter happy but she was still a kid and wanted more excitement. A young lad in Bournemouth was providing that.

I moved down to the coast and we got a flat together. It was a pretty miserable place but there was a view of the sea if you stretched far enough out of the window. Mandy later said this was when I mentioned Jack Profumo or Eugene Ivanov to her but I have no memory of doing so. And the story she told to the newspapers about Stephen leading me around by a dog collar – well it never happened, but at that time the press were desperate for any juicy gossip. I was just pleased to be getting on with my own life.

I found Mandy through Peter's boys. So did he. He was furious I was there – he had still not forgotten how I had humiliated him with Serge in front of his boys – and he slapped me in the face. I took it – there was not much choice. Mandy went back to London with Peter and, as I had nowhere else to go, I returned to Stephen. He was as skilled at manipulation as ever and he got me back into that El Rio Café again. This time with the help of the actor and comedian Alfred Marks and his wife. They were very friendly with Stephen and they turned up at Wimpole Mews for a drink. Stephen didn't have any gin – not even the tonic to go with it – or so he said. It was part of his plan to get us out of Wimpole Mews and once again to confront me with Lucky Gordon. He told the Marks about Lucky, the 'dreadful maniac who forced his way in and attacked both of us'.

He made it sound exciting, not terrifying, and suggested that we went off to the El Rio. 'It'll be a real laugh. We'll see if Lucky Gordon's there – that's the wild man who attacked us. Honestly, you must see him for yourself.'

Alfred was all for it, ready to go. He was almost jumping out of his seat. When we arrived at El Rio, Lucky was there. I was frightened, but Stephen played the whole thing as a huge joke. 'That's him over there, do you see? What d'you reckon our chances are?'

Alfred's wife looked cautiously over, but nothing happened. Lucky didn't move all evening, and when we got up to leave, he didn't acknowledge us. But I could feel his eyes. He had seen us all right, and everything we had done. It was such a stupid mistake. I should have refused to go. If I had known then that I was pregnant

I would never have gone anywhere near the El Rio or Lucky Gordon.

Peter Lewin was still in my life and he saved it. I had always been fond of him and when I found I was pregnant with Jack Profumo's baby I dreamt that maybe Peter and I could marry and we could have a life, a family life, and escape from the horrid mess I found myself in. Peter was also fond of me but, looking back, what I was asking a young man to do was unfair. Peter and I decided to remain friends and we still are. Ironically, later, he did want to marry me but by then it was not an option for me. Life plays dirty tricks.

Stephen appeared to be sympathetic to my pregnancy. I never told him who the father was for that would have been too much of a trump card for him. He would have gloried in that information as would MI5, the CIA and, eventually, the world. It is only now as I grow older that it needs to be told, to take its place in the history of some of the most misrepresented events of the last century. As part of his apparent concern, Stephen made arrangements for me to see Teddy Sugden who was the 'in' abortionist of the fifties and early sixties. All the showgirls and actresses went to him. He also created his own business by throwing elaborate sex parties. He was a watcher, a voyeur who got off on watching others at it. His friends, like Stephen and lots of prominent actor types, would attend these parties, the girls would get pregnant and Teddy would charge them two hundred pounds for an abortion. It was all a game of Monopoly for Teddy Sugden, but he was more into Snakes and Ladders.

Stephen was very close to Teddy who would do abortions for nothing for his pals. All the men liked Teddy but he was an amazing character who kept collections of live reptiles in glass cases in his surgery. He liked girls to fondle snakes and pretend to be having sex with them. I thought he was a horrid man but he was a friend of Stephen's so I went to him. He had a frozen face which made him look odd, like Jack Nicholson as the Joker in the Batman film. When I saw that movie, I thought of Teddy Sugden: that fixed smile.

I watched it across his big, mahogany desk in his consulting rooms as he said he could not help me. I appealed to him saying that Stephen had said it would be fine, that payment, extra payment if necessary, would be made. It was late – I needed to be taken care of quickly. But this man who was doing a dozen or more illegal abortions a day refused to help me. Stephen got Teddy to turn me down to humiliate me. I knew it was another way that Stephen was harming me and it was the last straw. I was so angry with Stephen and determined to leave Wimpole Mews. I had not been in touch with Mandy but, by chance, she contacted me.

She had broken up with Peter Rachman again and had moved into a flat in Dolphin Square in Pimlico. Through Peter she had the money for the flat and invited me to move in with her. We would start our modelling careers again. But, as I've said, Mandy didn't like working and although I got in touch with my agent Pat Glover yet again, Mandy soon went back to Peter. In fact, he kept her until he died.

I stayed on in Dolphin Square; it was good to have my own place. Especially, with the pregnancy. I had found a woman who would carry out the abortion for twenty-five pounds but I don't remember that much about it. It was, again, a horrific experience. I was thankful to live through it. I was half asleep, almost in a coma, when Peter Lewin came round to see how I was. The abortionist woman had gone, just left. Peter was shocked but took control. He knew I was in a terrible state – dying. Peter saved my life by getting me to the Chelsea Hospital for Women in Dovehouse Street – just in time. I don't even remember seeing him. He took me in his arms and carried me to a car and got me to the hospital. I was haemorrhaging and the doctors saved me. It was on 20 January 1962, and I still have a copy of the note I wrote to Peter that night thanking him. I said I was sorry for not 'seeing' him. A copy of the letter, headed from the Annie Zung Ward at the Chelsea, was given to me by Peter. He wanted me always to know what I had felt at that time. Forgive the shaky grammar which I have left as it was that day. It reads:

DEAR PETER,

DARLING I WAS SO PLEASE TO YOU FRIDAY, ALTHOUGH I WASN'T QUITE AWAKE, I CRIED WHEN YOU LEFT, MIND YOU I FELT BETTER, THAN WHAT I DO NOW.

Cornered

PETER I AM GOING TO ASK THE DOCTOR TODAY IF I CAN LEAVE SUNDAY SO
I CAN GO WITH YOU, BECAUSE I CAN'T SEE ANY DIFFERENCE SUNDAY OR
MONDAY, ANYWAY IF NOT WE CAN STILL BE ALONE FOR AN HOUR AND A HALF
SUNDAY PROVIDING YOU COME ON TIME.

YOU MUST HAVE RECEIVED MY OTHER LETTER BY NOW SO I WONT SAY
MUCH NOW, AS YOU ALREADY KNOW THE WAY I FEEL.

DARLING CANT WAIT TO SEE YOU SUNDAY REMEMBER I LOVE YOU,
BE GOOD.

LOVE CHRISTINE

XX

Peter saved my life. I blamed Stephen then and I still do for
risking it. Teddy Sugden may have been a weird guy but he was a
terrific doctor. With him, there would not have been any complications. Instead, the woman I'd arranged nearly killed me. I
discovered then that I was resilient, that I would and could stand up
against a stacked deck. I refused to be arbitrarily dismissed by
Stephen or anyone else, to vanish like the other girls. I vowed to
myself that I would live as much as I possibly could.

I was young and I recovered quickly. Pat Glover had managed to
get me some work, some modelling assignments. I did a Camay
soap commercial for West Germany, some work for the glossy
magazine *Tatler* and some jobs for artists. Stephen was still keeping
closely in touch with me and asking me to go back to him, but I was
happy with the way that things were. He'd introduced me to Paul
Mann, a bridge-playing friend of his from the Connaught Club.
Paul liked racing cars. He was a bit of a mother's boy but sharp and
fun to be with. We entertained a lot, held gambling parties, playing
for fifty-pound stakes, and generally had a lot of fun, though we
never had an affair. I felt that I had grown up and was in charge of
my life. Stephen came round with John Kennedy the American
agent. He was quite handsome and a bit wild and came to parties
that Paul and I gave without inviting Stephen. Once we all landed
up in the bath with our clothes on drinking champagne. Although
I was happy in Dolphin Square I kept on seeing Stephen. One day
we went to lunch with Fred Mullally the writer and novelist at the

White Elephant. Fred was looking for a girl for the cover of his new book but nothing came of it.

Stephen was trying to impress me with the people he knew, the celebrities, and one of these was Sidney James. Sid was very popular because of his appearances with Tony Hancock and the start of the Carry On films and we had dinner with him at the Room at the Top. He liked a laugh and the girls and had enjoyed a long affair with an actress friend of Stephen's. Stephen liked the reflected glory and so did I. We also went to a cocktail party where I met Lord Kimberley, who later took me with him gambling but the woman who owned the gambling house threw him out. He told me it was because he had made too much money there.

I was still looking for an escape from it all and I tried marijuana again with Paul Mann. I hadn't smoked since that time I was out with Stephen, the black girl and Lucky Gordon. It meant a return to the black clubs and one night, sitting round the flat smoking pot, now the Chelsea set smart thing to be doing, we decided to go to the All Nighters Club in Wardour Street in Soho. It was the only late-night, loud music spot and a crowd of us went.

A soon as we walked in, I saw Lucky. He came up to me and hung around our crowd. We tried to avoid him; everyone had guessed who he was, but he wouldn't go away. He just wanted Paul and me to know that bygones were bygones and that he wouldn't cause any more trouble. He was so persuasive that we believed him, and to show goodwill we invited him back to the flat. Looking back, I can hardly believe we did that. It was one of the most thoughtless things I have ever done. We had decided to make a party of it, and when we got back everyone was there. Paul put on a Johnny Mathis record and I was sitting on the sofa. I saw Lucky go out of the door and return moments later – with an axe. He came towards me and sat down on the sofa, putting the axe beside him.

Johnny Mathis sang on as everyone, except one of my girlfriends, disappeared. They just got out of that flat as fast as they could. No one bothered to wait and see what was going to happen. Not one man stayed to protect us. Paul was thrown out – Lucky threatened to kill him and me, if he stayed or called the police. I couldn't blame

Paul. What could he have done? As the room cleared, Lucky jumped up and locked the front door. Then he pulled me off the sofa and dragged me to the bedroom, brandishing the axe, his eyes blazing.

'I'll kill you this time! Kill, kill, kill!' he screamed, waving the axe round his head. 'Get your clothes off.'

I tore my clothes off. I had been this route before. I thought that after he had his way with me there was a chance of controlling him. A chance. There was no sound from my girlfriend. He hurled the axe at me. It sliced through the air, just missing my head. He hit me, knocking me almost senseless on to the bed. He wanted me subjected and terrified into being gentle with him. He wanted sweetness, but I wasn't ready yet. I was getting used to this treatment.

Lucky kept us in the flat for two days, wielding the axe to get his way. He never let up punching and slapping me until I was bruised and covered in fiery red sores. I cooked the meals while Lucky watched over us. He never let either of us out of his sight. When he took me into the bedroom, he left the door open, so he could keep an eye on my friend.

Smarting with pain, I realized that I was going to have to make up to him, pretend that I liked him, if we were to get out alive. There was no way of communicating what I was doing to my friend, and she clearly thought I was off my head when I started, gradually, to soften towards him. I got the strength to go through with it from knowing that only this way might we get a chance to escape.

As I became more pliable, Lucky relaxed. He still slept with the axe in his hand, but he had become a bit more pleasant to be with. Towards the end of the second day we ran out of food.

'Someone will have to go and get some, or we'll starve. There's a shop round the corner,' I told him.

'She can go,' he said, pointing to my friend.

'She'll call the police.' I explained simply, as you might to a child. 'You'll have to go, Lucky. I'll give you the keys.'

It was extraordinary, but he believed me. We'd run out of cigarettes, so he was keen to be off. As soon as he had gone, I rang the police. They rushed round and were ready for Lucky when he got back. There was no messing about. This time the evidence was there in black and blue, and Lucky was charged with grievous bodily harm and taken into custody. I wondered how long he would get, and what state he would be in when he got out. Shortly after the police left, Lucky's brother telephoned. He pleaded with me: 'We've all been trying to get Lucky to go straight. Look, don't charge him this time. I promise we'll keep him away from you.'

I told him it was too late for that, the police had taken Lucky but he insisted: 'You've got to drop those charges. He's my brother, see. And he's coloured. The police will have him in for a long time. They'll have no mercy. You drop the charges and I promise you won't see him again.'

I said I had to think about it and got his telephone number promising to call back. I wasn't sure what to do. I was dreading the thought of confronting Lucky in court. I would rather never see him again than have to go to court. The press would get hold of it, who knew what might come out? I decided it was better to let the whole business die out quietly. I rang the police and said I was going to drop the charges. They weren't at all happy about that, and demanded to come round to talk about it.

The officer was as insistent as Lucky's brother: 'Don't you understand he's a very dangerous character? He has a string of convictions behind him. Assault, larceny, even attempted murder. You were lucky this time, Miss Keeler, next time you might not get off so lightly.'

But I had made up my mind. I was fed up with other people controlling me, telling me what to do and when to do it. I was dropping the charges.

It was another stupid mistake. The next day Lucky Gordon was lurking round Dolphin Square, leaning up against the wall, watching and waiting. In those days, I believed people when they told me they were going to do something. There was plenty more for me to go through before that attitude, that belief in honour, was knocked out of me.

With Lucky in Dolphin Square, it was time for me to leave. I packed my bags and returned to the only person who I thought could help me, Stephen. But Lucky caught up with me. I put on a strange voice when I answered the phone, but Lucky knew it was me. I just couldn't relax, knowing that wherever I went, I was being followed. Every time I left the flat, Lucky would be there, lurking. Then there would be a couple of weeks when I wouldn't see him. I began to breathe freely, thinking maybe he'd given up. Then there he was again, for no particular reason.

The fear became unbearable. The worst of it was not knowing when he might strike. It was slowly driving me mad. Gradually, his obsession became mine. I found myself thinking about him day and night, trying to understand him. Thoughts rushed through my head, mad ideas. It was almost perversely flattering to arouse so much attention, to be in someone's mind every hour of the day. Yet I was scared. Scared to answer the phone, or walk out of the front door. I was scared to go out in the street, not knowing if he'd jump on me, and if Stephen and I got back late at night Stephen would drive straight into the garage and we'd jump out and quickly close the garage doors. It was a nightmare.

I think it was the feeling of total imprisonment that made me do what I did next. I had to confront my fears, meet them head on. The only way left was to seek out Lucky and I knew how to do that. I went to the All Nighters. Alone. I was quite unafraid that afternoon. Who was this, anyway, who had the right to make my life a misery? I hadn't even worked that out. I only knew that if I enraged him, he would try to kill me. But that afternoon I couldn't have cared less.

As soon as I entered the club and saw him standing there, my fears rushed over me. I would have run straight out again, if he hadn't already seen me. He walked over, took my arm and ordered me a cup of coffee. I started talking. Quietly, I told him I couldn't carry on living in the same town as him if he was going to continue pursuing me. He told me he loved me and that I was not responding because he was black: 'You must understand that I love you. That's all. I don't mean any bad for you. I just love you. I can't go away. It's better I see you at a distance than nothing. But you won't give yourself a chance to love me. That's it, isn't it?'

Somewhere in me, amazing as it sounds, I felt sorry for him. He might be wild, but he obviously did love me. I did mind what people would think, my mum in particular, about me seeing a black man. I would have lost my friends. Stephen would have drifted off, and everywhere I went people would have whispered. It was different in 1962. Today in London no one would give you a second glance. Then, a white girl walking with a coloured man was something to stare at. No one had ever told me that it didn't matter what people thought of you, only what you thought about them.

I said I could see him now and then but he had to promise no violence. Lucky was so delighted, he was almost crying. He took me to his brother's house and everything was different. Lucky laughed and chatted as we drove to Leytonstone in a minicab. He kept pointing out where we were going and told me all about his brother's family. He told me how long he had lived with them, how long he had been staying there, how well his sister-in-law cooked and how pleased they would all be to see me. When we arrived we went straight up to Lucky's room. There wasn't much stuff: a single bed, a chair and a chest of drawers with a television on top, plus Lucky's sister-in-law's washing, which hung off a clothes-horse in the middle of the room.

Lucky was a different person. He smiled instead of snarling, and his eyes were brown and gentle. Those hands which had scratched at my throat now tenderly washed me with a flannel dipped in a basin of hot soapy water. I wasn't allowed to do a thing for myself. He brushed my hair and brought meals up from the kitchen.

We stayed together in that room for three days and all that time Lucky waited on me as though I were a princess. I was so mixed up inside that I thought this was the escape I wanted. I was just a stupid girl but his love was so persuasive and the marijuana made it all dream-like. He was totally content making love to me and talking about plans for our future.

I soon got wary of the controlling situation. I was no druggie although I enjoyed smoking the joints. I wanted all of myself back, my life, and to be able to do the simple things like buying my own cigarettes again, chatting to people. I didn't have the heart to tell him that things could never work out for the two of us, so I left, telling him that I'd see him again. He was so relaxed that he let me go without a fuss.

I went straight round to Stephen's, but I didn't want to stay long because I knew Lucky would be on the phone. Back at Stephen's in my own familiar world, I realized too late that I had lit a fuse with Lucky – he would go berserk when I did not return. Why it didn't dawn on me before, I don't know. I can only put it down to the nervous state I had been driven to. I was too scared to think straight, and now I knew I had got myself in a dreadful situation. If there had been trouble before, there was certainly going to be more when I didn't go back to Lucky. All afternoon the telephone rang but I left it ringing. When Stephen got back, he picked it up and of course it was Lucky.

I told him to say I was not there and then I told Stephen of my three days with Lucky.

'You're mad – the man's a maniac. He could have killed you.'

Stephen was bemused as I told him, 'He was very gentle. He wouldn't even let me wash myself. He waited on me. Did everything for me. Even washed me all over.'

Stephen liked the idea of that but he had a frown on his face and it only went when I told him I was going to stay with Michael Lambton for a little time. We both knew Lucky would soon be on the doorstep. That there was more trouble ahead. Neither of us could have known just how much. But we didn't tell each other everything. I decided to buy a gun. I was going to kill Lucky if I had to.

12

THE SMOKIN' GUN

A MAN LIKE JOHN KENNEDY WILL NOT BE ALLOWED TO STAY IN SUCH
AN IMPORTANT POSITION OF POWER IN THE WORLD, I ASSURE YOU OF THAT.

Stephen Ward, October 1962

It is only over the years that I have learned and understood just what
was going on and how I was at the centre of world political intrigue.
And just what an international mess I was involved in. The USA, the
Soviet Union, Kennedy and Krushchev, were pointing nuclear
missiles at each other. Britain's interests were in the middle of it all
and I had slept with the Secretary of State for War. And a Soviet spy.
At the same time, I had lived with and worked for Stephen Ward,
another Russian agent. It was little wonder that the FBI were
watching me but even now, with the whole story clear to me, it is
staggering when I contemplate just what role I played. I have to shake
my head to believe it. Or flip through the documents on my desk.

I now have hundreds of pages of FBI documents which began
being created when President Kennedy took a personal interest in
my affair with Jack Profumo and liaison with Eugene Ivanov. Many
of the papers are entitled 'Bowtie' which was the American security
services' code name for their investigation of Jack and I and Eugene.
Many of the documents, which only became available years after the
events they refer to, have blacked out paragraphs and lines; there are
still names and events the Americans want to protect but nevertheless they are still more forthcoming than the British authorities. One
of them caught my interest immediately. It brought back the
memories and story of a daft summer with Mandy in America.
The memorandum is headed:

The Smokin' Gun

Christine Keeler;
John Profumo
Internal Security – Russia – Great Britain

It is from J. Edgar Hoover, the Director of the FBI, to the US Attorney General, Robert Kennedy. Copies had also gone to five highly placed FBI agents. It astonishes me that so much attention from such powerful people went into my jaunt to America with Mandy. I smile to think of Bobby Kennedy knowing me as 'Christine' and J. Edgar Hoover having to supply my surname. And the FBI knew nothing about me sleeping with the captain of the *Niew Amsterdam*. He was a wonderful-looking man especially in his whites. But they were more interested about whether I had slept with a Kennedy. The White House was clearly scared – we know now just how much of a serial philanderer JFK was – that events would link the President with the Profumo scandal and all his sexual shenanigans might be revealed.

My trip to America was for far less world-shattering reasons. I was still trying to escape Lucky Gordon. And Stephen was spying. Events which would lead to my five jolly summer days crossing the Atlantic began in the spring.

America was still threatening Russia with NATO's 'Forward Defence' so Stephen used Sir Godfrey Nicholson, who always supported him, to make an appointment for him to have lunch with Sir Harold Cassia of the Foreign Office on 5 April 1962. Stephen's plan was to get information from Sir Harold about British intentions over disarming and over Berlin but he got nowhere with Sir Harold. In May, Stephen twice went to British security to be recruited by them to allow him better access to people with information. It was also a cover for him – he could tell them that he was with MI5. It was a desperate attempt but, again, Stephen achieved nothing. The security investigators decided he could not be trusted as he talked too much. What a laugh.

We went to a party at Robert Pilkington's and Robert gave me a doll which looked a little like me and said: 'Look after her – her name is Cookie'.

Stephen laughed as he told everyone present about a black man who was after me. I tried to protest but he took no notice. He was creating another alibi.

From then on, Stephen more or less abandoned me and I was a little like a gypsy between Wimpole Mews and Michael Lambton's. Michael still adored me and yet again I was going to use his love to get my own way.

I felt like a sitting duck for Lucky. I didn't know what to do. I was lost. Stephen was ignoring me and he knew I would get nervous. He knew me so well – I swear he could read my mind as he had setting me up with Eugene at Cliveden.

It was Mandy who presented a possible escape to America. She wanted to leave Peter Rachman and get out of Britain for good. The strange Nina Gadd was around. She was going to the States with Mandy and they both got on my case arguing that America was the place to be. My protests about having no money didn't stop them. Mandy never thought that a problem – there was always someone with some money to help.

We set a date to leave in late June or July and I was to stay with Michael Lambton and get him to pay. I reckoned I needed at least five hundred pounds, which was a great deal of money then. Compare that amount to Stephen's delight that Nina Gadd would pay him five pounds a week in rent. At first, Michael refused me the money point blank. I worked on his jealousy saying I'd get it from someone else. I liked the thought of Michael sitting there feeling jealous at the prospect. He didn't know much about me, or about Lucky Gordon, nor did he see much of Stephen's or my friends, but I felt safe with him and I was very fond of him. He had asked me to marry him, and I was seriously considering the idea. I changed into a wonderfully sexy dress, and swayed back into the room: 'I'm off. See you later.'

One thing Michael did know was that I never made idle threats although I would never have made the threat if I hadn't known that Michael would give way. It wasn't as though he couldn't afford the money. He had lots of it. He agreed on condition I returned to him. I agreed and meant it: I just wanted to be away from London and the horror of Lucky for a time. But then, over the next few days I had such a lovely time with Michael I decided to stay in England. I really didn't want to leave him. He was one of the few men that I really respected. He never stood for any nonsense from women, and at the same time he didn't throw his weight around trying to be macho.

I called Mandy to say I wasn't going to the States. She was terribly upset. Soon after I put the phone down, Nina rang to apologize: she had just given my number to Lucky Gordon, not realizing who he was. That ruined everything. I had to escape to the States: anything was better than that Michael should get caught up in this Lucky business. Then there was a silver lining. Michael's company needed someone to go to America and Michael fixed it for himself. He would join me in America.

Mandy and I were like nuns let loose on the high seas. We cajoled and urged each other on. I fell for the captain, the first officer and a couple of others: the ocean breeze was an astonishing aphrodisiac. It felt as though you could do anything you liked; there were no barriers, no taboos. I had sex with the captain and the officers because I could, because I had the power to make them want me.

We were ready for the New York clubs as soon as we arrived. Were they as good as everyone said, better than London? Immediately, it seemed to be the place to be. I loved it, it was a brand new world. I wanted to see all of it. We set off to explore: it was blistering hot in New York, uncomfortable and tiring and we made for the seaside. We knew no better and went to Fire Island – then the homosexual summer capital of America. Not exactly my scene but it was all so new, it was fun. Our knowledge of the ways of America, of sophistication, was such that Mandy had brought the mink coat bought for her by Peter Rachman. I hate to think of how silly we must have looked trying to fit into the beach crowd.

We arrived on the ferry with no hotel reservations and no car. We got friendly with a couple of guys and shared their room for a night but I was terrified all night that Mandy's mink might be stolen. I had seen too many Hollywood gangster pictures. The next day we found a hotel in Cherry Grove. We lay on the beach and sunbathed, stupidly sniggering at the gay guys strutting their stuff.

They were having a lovely time displaying themselves. The only two men who weren't gay were the policemen. We made a date with them, but when they arrived we were so sunburned that all they could do was rub our backs with lotion. It was sunshine all the way after that but Mandy spent all her money in no time. Her first reaction was to make plans to return to London and Peter Rachman, the apparently bottomless bank account. Nina Gadd had never shown up and Michael was not scheduled to arrive for another two or three weeks.

I like to be where I know – I still get nervous in strange supermarkets when I don't know where the bread is – so I had no intention of staying in America on my own. I telegraphed Michael, reversing the charges, and asked him to wire me some more money, so that I could get home. Later, when I spoke to Michael, I was nearly in tears, which is unusual for me. I never let people know when I'm upset, I bottle it up and I suppose I do brood about things. But that way I have learned to get everything sharp and clear in my mind before I act or make a decision. Things are rarely what they seem the first time you examine them.

But to get home I had to face the transatlantic flight and I hate flying. I had a few drinks before take-off. I had a Manhattan iced tea thinking it was what it sounded like and not realizing it was full of different spirits. For the first time I was relaxed on a plane and fell asleep almost immediately. I was terrified when I woke up to find the pilot standing talking to the passengers and thought: Who's flying the plane? Touching down at Heathrow was one of the happiest moments of my life – I could hardly believe we had arrived in one piece.

I have obtained copies of the FBI investigation of our trip. The memo from J. Edgar Hoover begins:

> Reference is made to my letter of June 24, 1963, which you returned to the Assistant Director C. A. Evans on July 2, 1963. At the time you inquired if we had learned what Christine (Keeler) and her friend did in the U.S. when they were here.

It has been learned that Christine Keeler and Marilyn Rice-Davies arrived in the U.S. aboard the *SS Niew Amsterdam* on July 11, 1962. They registered at the Hotel Bedford, 118 East 42nd Street, New York City, July 11, 1962, and re-registered on July 16, 1962. Hotel records do not show a date of departure; however, they did leave the U.S. on July 18, 1962, by British Overseas Airways Corporation plane.

The last paragraph has been blacked out, censored.

All that concerned Michael was that I'd spoiled our plans but he got over it and we went back to being a couple and the plan was for me to return to America with him when he had to go on business. It was all fixed – but there were problems.

We were only happy when we were on our own. If we went out with friends, Michael was terribly possessive and jealous if I talked to anyone else, man or woman. It was not for me – I was not able to deal with Michael so I let him go to New York alone. Where did I go? Back, like a fly to a spider, to Stephen. For me and the way I thought then, there was nowhere else to go.

Stephen introduced me to Paula Hamilton-Marshall who lived near his consulting rooms in Devonshire Street. She used to come around to Wimpole Street and have sex with Stephen. Now, she was pregnant by a black US Air Force officer who had gone off to America and left her. She had to look after her brother John who was a bisexual and a druggie. To help out with money, Kim Proctor, a photographer, was staying with her and paying rent.

The day Stephen and I went round, a West Indian called Johnnie Edgecombe – he liked to be known as 'The Edge' – was visiting her. We told them about my problems with Lucky and Johnnie told me that he knew Lucky and that he could have a word with him. He sounded so positive that he could deal with Lucky. Stephen and I thought that perhaps this was the answer for one black man to have a word with another and that Lucky would accept that. To me it seemed a solution. But I was still living with Stephen and Lucky knew all about getting in there. I got on with Kim Proctor and we decided to take a flat not far away in Sheffield Terrace. Johnnie Edgecombe said he would be there to protect me from Lucky. Stephen just smiled about all of this especially when I told Paula I wanted a gun for protection in case I should be confronted by Lucky in the street. I was so boiled up about him I would have shot him knowing that I would go to prison for three years at least. All our thoughts were how to get Lucky off my back. The chain-smoking man came round to Paula's and sold me a Luger and ammunition for it, two magazines. I put all of it in a new, big handbag. I felt I was ready for Lucky – ready to kill him.

I felt more relaxed about things and that was helped by the marijuana. With Johnnie Edgecombe, I smoked pot again – something I hadn't done for months. I was being a little too carefree and found myself leaving the gun under the bed and not always taking it in my handbag. It was early in October 1962 when Lucky turned up again. I had been to the hairdresser's with an American girlfriend I had met through Paula, Jackie Brown. It was near my old flat in Comeragh Road – and Lucky appeared from nowhere.

He punched me to the ground without any warning. Jackie screamed and several people ran to ring the police. I told Jackie I was going to prosecute Lucky and shouted at her: 'I'm sorry I didn't have my gun, or he wouldn't be alive.' But Jackie did not want to get involved with the police. She had run over her time in the UK and had not applied for an extension. She'd be kicked out of the country so I told her to lose herself. Now I had another excuse for not getting involved with the police. I got in a cab and took off for the flat I had with Kim Proctor. 'The Edge' was there, and he lost it when I told him about Lucky's aimless attack. He vowed that he would deal with Lucky.

Johnnie called Lucky and they had a long argument. He told Lucky where we were, and Lucky came round to have it out. Johnnie went downstairs to face him. I stood six feet from the door of our flat pointing the gun. Kim was hysterical so I told her to go and sit down. There would be no problem as far as I was concerned: if Lucky got past Johnnie, I was going to blast him, kill him. I waited, arms stretched out. Then Johnnie came back upstairs. Lucky had run off. But he knew where we were. Kim went to stay with Paula, and Johnnie and I moved into a Kensington hotel, a sort of hotel-bedsit place in Lancaster Gate.

I wanted to get away from Johnnie as I knew Lucky was looking for us and we were just sitting around waiting for him. I was more afraid of Lucky than ever now. On 25 October 1962, I went round to see Stephen to ask him for my old room back. Stephen had been responsible for Lucky in my life and I felt he owed me some protection. I sat on the chest in the hall as he paced around waiting for Eugene. President Kennedy had announced a naval blockade of Cuba and told the Russians that any move on their part would be immediately answered in kind. It really did seem as if the world was on the brink of war. Selfishly, my concerns were all about me:

'It's terrible, Stephen. I can't go on like this. I'm safer with you, could I have my old room back?' I asked.

Stephen then said something which meant little to me then but was to mean so much to Stephen, to all of us: 'No you can't, I'm renting it to an Indian doctor for twenty-five pounds a week as he wants a room available for an afternoon screw once a week which suits me as he won't get in my way.'

'But I've got to do something – I'm so worried about everything.' I was so very miserable that Stephen relented a little: 'Maybe you could take on the Indian doctor as he hasn't found anyone yet.'

'No, I wouldn't want that.' I could not see myself living with Stephen like that. But, what if?

The doorbell rang and Stephen bundled me into his bedroom as he wouldn't allow me into my bedroom. I kept the door open to see Sir Godfrey Nicholson arrive with Eugene. Sir Godfrey looked worried when he saw me. The Cuban Crisis was at its height and Stephen – and Eugene – were most agitated. They talked about weapons and defences and missiles. I heard Sir Godfrey say he had made an appointment for them to have lunch with Lord Arran on 27 October, two days later. After they left together, Stephen came into his bedroom and put his arms around me. He looked very worried.

'What is it Stephen, what's wrong?' I asked him.

'Some televisions have just gone down in the Channel.'

'What do you mean? A boat has sunk?'

'No, silly. *Under*water televisions so you can see *under* the water.'

Stephen explained that the West had positioned surveillance cameras deep in the water and it was a problem, it was 'spooky'. All this meant nothing to me. I really couldn't care about it or understand all the implications. I was interested in only one question at that moment: 'What am I going to do about Lucky?'

I wanted Stephen to reconsider renting my room to the Indian doctor but all he said was: 'Let me have a think, little baby. Come back in a day or two and I'll have sorted something out.'

I spent forty-eight hours worrying before going back to Wimpole Mews on what was to be a turbulent, landmark day. Eugene was there. He and Stephen were just off to lunch with Lord Arran, the Permanent Under-Secretary. I sat and waited for Stephen as I blamed him for my predicament and was determined to make him take notice and to get me out of the mess. They returned later and Stephen was in a temper as they had been turned away from Lord Arran's door. Immediately he sat down, still in his raincoat, and telephoned Sir Godfrey. Eugene was at his side.

'That bloody man said that we were not expected. How dare he!' Stephen screamed and raged down the telephone. He didn't care about me as I stood waiting for him to get off the telephone. Then he put the telephone down, took his coat off and turned on me:

'We have to go out. You had better leave.'

'Stephen, I thought that I might be able to come back?' I asked.

'You can't come back here, Mandy's moving in. I arranged it with her yesterday that when she comes back from France she's coming straight here.' I was astounded, unbelieving. I must have looked it.

'Go look for yourself if you don't believe me,' he said firmly.

I went into my old bedroom and looked in the wardrobe; there was one suit hanging there which I knew belonged to Mandy.

Eugene stood in the hall still in his coat. He and Stephen were going to see Lord Arran again if they could. Eugene had a sympathetic look on his face. I was very hurt and confused as I returned home to Johnnie.

That same evening Stephen, taking Eugene with him, turned up at Lord Arran's house and told him that he was a Russian intermediary and he demanded Lord Arran call a summit conference in London. Arran suspected right away it had been a plot. Later, it was implied that Stephen was Eugene's man rather than the other way around but Eugene acted like a butler to Stephen. I saw it all the time, and there was never any doubt who was the boss, the chief operator. Stephen's clever use of cover – of putting other people in places with him to protect Eugene and his other conspirators – certainly worked as far as Denning was concerned. And with the British intelligence services – unless of course they never told their political masters what they knew. If they had, it would have been a first. The motives and machinations of them all are fascinating.

But late that same night, I didn't much care about anything. Yet again, I felt lost, abandoned. Johnnie and I went to the All Nighters Club – I was angry with life and I didn't care about Lucky Gordon or the consequences of meeting him.

What a stupid woman.

Lucky was there as usual, smoking and drinking with his cronies. And mad-eyed. As soon as Johnnie and I appeared, Lucky rushed over and grabbed a chair as a weapon. Lucky chased me through the club. I got lost in the crowded dance floor and Johnnie caught up with Lucky. Girls were screaming while the men stood back enjoying the macho show. Lucky made a rush for the exit. Johnnie was up behind him and the bouncers were blocking Lucky's getaway.

Johnnie seemed to stroll towards Lucky and then whipped out a knife. It was over in a second. The knife flashed and then Lucky's face was pouring with blood. Lucky had his hands to his face. He screamed with rage and pain. The cut ran from his forehead to his chin down the side of his face, and the blood poured into this eyes, blinding him. 'You'll go inside for this!' he screamed. 'I'll get the law, you'll go inside.'

'Come on! You're coming with me,' Johnnie ordered, pulling

me towards the door. He grabbed me by the arm and we took off from the All Nighters as fast as we could. 'He'll get the police on to me – and his brothers,' said Johnnie, back at his hotel room. In a panic he telephoned a friend and arranged to go into hiding at a place in Brentford, out on the old A4 – now the M4 – just beyond Hammersmith and Chiswick. He started packing his clothes and shouting at me to help him find his socks. He had decided to take me with him and I didn't argue, even though I had been shocked by the knife. I didn't realize that Johnnie had taken it with him. What had I got myself into? Johnnie was as deadly as Lucky. And probably as crazy.

I had gone from one maniac to another.

I used the telephone in the hall to call Stephen as I was now desperate to get away from Johnnie: 'Stephen, Johnnie's slashed Lucky and the police are looking for him and Johnnie wants me to go with him.'

The last thing Stephen wanted was me talking to the police – about anything. He drove straight over in the middle of the night. I was relieved that he was going to help me get away from Johnnie whom he hadn't seen since he first introduced me to Paula. He tried to reason with Johnnie to let me go but Johnnie insisted that I went with him. Stephen was not used to dealing with someone like Johnnie so I stepped in and promised Stephen that I'd be back the following day to talk to him. Stephen put my case in the boot of his car and I jumped in a car Johnnie had ordered with only the clothes I stood up in. And my gun.

I went to Stephen's the following day, 28 October 1962, desperate to find somewhere away from Johnnie. At first Stephen suggested that I come back to live with him but I refused because of Lucky. Stephen said that he knew someone who was looking for a girlfriend and that I might like him. Michael Eddowes was a lawyer who had become a rich businessman and Stephen said he could be useful with his money and legal expertise – he might put me up in a flat. Eddowes owned Bistro Vino, a chain of restaurants, and Stephen arranged for me to have dinner with him at El Bistro.

Later that evening Eugene arrived and Stephen cooked up a

spaghetti dinner for us using a tin of tomato soup. On the television news it said that Russian ships had turned back from Cuba and Eugene was furious. He started shouting about President Kennedy and how the English were a bunch of sheep and how Russia had nearly been blown up twice by accident before. I left them talking loudly to return to Johnnie as I too was in hiding from Lucky until I found a safe place to live.

I kept my date with Michael Eddowes but he was far too old for me. He was nearly sixty but he certainly was interested and wanted to set me up in a flat – in Regent's Park of all places. He tried to keep in with me and drove me to see my mother where I showed off my gun to her and Dad and shot it into the earth. After Lucky's daylight attack in the street I didn't go anywhere without it. Stephen called, saying a flat had come up and I went straight over. I couldn't find my gun and I didn't want to make a fuss about it and alert Johnnie that I was off. Permanently. I left the gun at Johnnie's and he knew where to find it. I left unarmed and I felt naked without it.

At the mews Stephen introduced me to Rosemary Wells. Her cases were unpacked in the hall. She worked for Wallace's dress shop, was the daughter of a friend and looking for a flat-mate. Stephen gave me some money for my share of the rent on a third floor place around the corner at 63 Great Cumberland Place. Rosemary was a nice girl and I liked the flat being high up for security. We were due to move in the following day so I decided to chance staying at Stephen's. Rosemary was to sleep in my old bedroom and I would bunk in with Stephen just like old, platonic times. Rosemary didn't seem to think it strange.

That night William Shepherd arrived. He was a Tory MP and – something I didn't know that night – a friend of Jack Profumo. Eugene was there too. Rosemary and I were too busy getting to know each other and didn't take much notice of them although we were in the same room. Stephen had told Shepherd that Rosemary and I were moving into a flat the next day. We were talking about decorating our flat but I still overheard Eugene saying to Shepherd that President Kennedy was a madman. Later, I wandered into the sitting room to offer to make coffee. Shepherd had gone. Stephen was standing by the fire and Eugene was over by the window with his coat on ready to leave.

'Don't worry, Eugene,' said Stephen, 'a man like Kennedy will not be allowed to stay in such an important position of power in the world, I assure you of that.'

Stephen turned around and saw me and shouted: 'Kennedy nearly blew up the world.'

'What do you mean?' I asked him.

'Well he had his key in the lock – you see, there are keys. One the president has and the other is held by a general.'

'What sort of general?' Eugene asked.

Stephen didn't miss a beat: 'An air force general.'

But for all their talking it seemed that the world was not going to end. Just yet, anyway. I was keen to get on with my life and now had a good opportunity with Rosemary, who had gone to bed earlier. She was so different from Mandy and keen to work in the fashion business. Well, keen to work, full stop.

At Great Cumberland Place life appeared to return to some sort of normality. I felt safe and secure . . . but not for long. Stephen telephoned to tell me that Lucky had been around earlier that day. He had given Stephen seventeen little pieces of thread. They were the stitches from the wound, from his forehead to his chin, that Johnnie had inflicted on him at the All Nighters. I was horrified. I started breathing heavily, gasping for air. Stephen said that Lucky had warned me through him saying, 'Give them to her – she'll need them soon.'

Mandy meanwhile had been trying her luck in Paris. Peter Rachman had tried to get her to stay with him: he told her he was dying but Mandy did not believe him. Later, that would really upset her. She handed him back the keys to Bryanston Mews and took off. Peter was distraught and it was near the end of November that he died, wiped out by a giant heart attack, and the scavengers were soon all over his empire. Mandy had called Peter from France wanting money but had not been able to reach him. She got back to Bryanston Mews with a stuffed doll toy for Peter but it was all quiet. She went round to Stephen's but knew that Peter was dead before he finished telling her his 'bad news'. Her first question about Peter's death was: 'Did he leave a will?'

As planned, Mandy now moved in with Stephen who, after the débâcle over Lord Arran, was trying to keep a low profile. Certainly, Hollis and Blunt were not around for a long time. But 'the Indian doctor', Emil Savundra, was.

Emil Savundra was born in what was then Ceylon and was a friend of a gentleman called Bobbie Mckew who Stephen said had introduced him to the 'Indian doctor'. Savundra wanted women, women, women and the idea was for Stephen to help him in his horizontal endeavours which were by all account prodigious. Savundra was head of Fire, Auto and Marine Insurance which was soon to crash and remains a landmark for spectacular fraud. Savundra had girls on tap: he ordered them like pizza. But it was his sex with Mandy at Wimpole Mews, costing about twenty pounds a time, which was to do most damage to all of us.

Mandy and Stephen were not getting on that well – he never had liked Mandy. They rowed and he gossiped about her. Then, to my surprise, she tried to do away with herself, not very successfully. I went to visit her one day and she was still in bed though it was mid-morning. She wasn't getting out of bed at all. I made some coffee to try and get her going but she had swallowed a bottle of aspirin. She looked awful and I rang 999. The ambulance was quick and they pumped her out at hospital. She recovered quickly but had no energy, no interest in life. I tried to get her to spend money – she liked doing that so I thought getting her out to the shops would help. Finally, it worked and we arranged to go Christmas shopping on 14 December 1962. I was in the flat waiting for her to get ready and at that damn moment the phone rang. No one answered. Mandy was in the bathroom. It rang again. I hadn't answered a phone since I'd been back in London, fearing it might be Lucky. Now, of all things, I did. It was Johnnie Edgecombe.

I told him I was not living at Stephen's, simply visiting Mandy. I was rude, angry with him because I really hoped I had got all this business behind me. He insisted on seeing me but I slammed down the phone.

Then Mandy wanted me to call Peter Rachman's widow Audrey to see if she had been left anything by him. I had already called her to tell her Mandy was distraught at Peter's death and had tried to kill herself. Mandy wanted people to know she was upset. After Johnnie's call I wasn't going near the telephone. I sat and smoked and Mandy did her hair. It took at least ten minutes before she was happy with it. The front door bell jingled. I was going to answer when Mandy looked out of the window and announced: 'It's Johnnie.'

He had come straight round in a minicab. I was terrified. I looked at Mandy's hair and said: 'Tell him I'm at the hairdresser's.'

Mandy leaned out of the window: 'She's gone to the hairdresser's. She left a few minutes ago.'

Johnnie said he was coming in. Mandy looked at me. She tried to reason with him but he would not believe her. I went to the window. We argued and I warned him I would call the police. I was frightened he had the gun but he said he hadn't. I think he thought I might let him in then but I wouldn't. He started raving and I dialled 999. As I spun the numbers he started shooting at the front door of the house. I dropped the phone and rushed to the window.

'Johnnie! What are you doing?'

He heard me and aimed the Luger I had left at his place straight at me. I dived down and waited. Then slowly I raised my head to see if he was still down below. He was ready for me and took another shot and, before he took the next one, I rushed downstairs to make sure that the garage door was closed.

Johnnie started shooting at the lock on the front door. As I ran back upstairs Mandy had finished the 999 call. 'The police are coming,' she whispered from the floor where she was trying to hide under the bed.

'What if Johnnie breaks open the door? He's shooting at the lock. We'll go near the window. We'll have a better chance . . .'

We stood on either side of the room, waiting for something to happen. There was silence. I peered out of the window. Johnnie's minicab driver was still waiting outside, but there was no sign of Johnnie. He had emptied the one magazine of ammunition he had brought. The next time I looked the cab had gone. The police arrived soon afterwards and searched the house and garden. They examined the bullet-holes and found the gun hidden in the drawer of an old table in the garden. I rang Stephen.

'Get Mandy out at once. I'm not coming back to the house until she's gone,' he said.

I told him we had to go with the police but he said, 'Then make sure you take her back to your place. I don't want to be involved in any of this.'

'It's bloody mean of him,' Mandy said. 'He's just a mean, vicious old man. I'm fed up with him. I'll be glad if I never see him again.'

The police got to Johnnie at Brentford. He was for it. They charged him with the shooting but also with cutting up Lucky. The game was also over that day for Stephen. I knew when I telephoned him after the shooting, by the way he told me to get Mandy out of his house, as she was my friend and not his, that he was going to blame me for everything.

Wimpole Mews was a sea of police and press. Everyone wanted to know what had happened. Some of the newspaper people had heard rumours or been tipped off about the action. They had got to us faster than the police. They were hungry. I was not feeling good about being asked *any* questions but the feeding frenzy had begun.

When we left the police after making statements – they told us we would not be questioned until the New Year – I took Mandy with me as she had nowhere else to go. Poor Rosemary had to move out as there was only one bedroom with two beds in it. I think she was glad to go – it all seemed out of control, like a brushfire. Stephen got Paul Mann to move in with him.

I had been having a good run with my modelling but the next day's publicity stopped all that. A photographic shoot for Knight's Castile soap was cancelled and so was a whisky promotion in Scotland. I was twenty years old and it seemed my life was over, finished. And Stephen was to blame. I was determined to bring him down with me and I only knew one way to do that. In time, I told what I knew to the police and others: of Hollis and Blunt, of the intrigue, the sexual blackmail, the insidious movement in and around so-called high society, of the underbelly of corruption and the greed and disdain for ordinary people. In time, all the press wanted me to talk about was a British government minister and a Moscow spy. And they were anxious, I can tell you, to know all about that. However, that was not the information the people in charge wanted to be circulated. They wanted it to be all about sex.

They wanted to brand Stephen as a perverted character who had lived off immoral earnings, a pimp. They needed Stephen as a scapegoat for their ineptitude and their guilt, a fall guy to divert attention from the government which was being hounded by Harold Wilson's revived Labour Party. Wilson, the dynamic new Labour leader, could scent a political kill. The atmosphere was of bloodlust. As a principal in the hunt, the hypocritical hounds were after me too.

From the moment the press pack started baying in Wimpole Mews there was no escape from being Christine Keeler.

13

RABBIT IN THE HEADLINES

THERE IS NO TRAP SO DEADLY AS THE TRAP YOU SET FOR YOURSELF.

Raymond Chandler, *The Long Goodbye*

I was a victim of lies from the beginning and they have just become more colossal over the years; the cumulative effect is that everyone has a blurred view of what really happened. It is why I have always wanted to tell all the truth about Stephen and his spying and all the other horrors. It's just that I have not had the strength before, I was too frightened; but now my sons are grown, I want the world to know my real story. The plight of Monica Lewinsky brought it home to me again when in 1998 she became a dirty joke with all those smarmy remarks about cigars and President Clinton and racy sexual happenings in the Oval Office. It wasn't the first time there had been sex in the Oval Office, or so Mariella Novotny told it. Mariella had been part of an elaborate string of girls who were 'available' internationally to prominent men. She had talked of sleeping with important men like John and Robert Kennedy. Her encounter with JFK was supposedly before he became president but she always alluded to having actually had him in the White House. I'm surprised J. Edgar Hoover didn't have kittens.

Knowing all of this and what I personally survived, I am one of only a few people in the world who could hope to understand something of the architecture of the shaky, nightmarish life that Monica Lewinsky endured at the height of that scandal. And will suffer for ever. I only had to watch her being manipulated and turned into a scapegoat to think of Denning.

And Clinton's confidants and sharp-suited aides appearing on television with one story and then another and then a new version – it made me shudder. Sincerity? The truth? Sorry, I'd heard and seen it all before. I could empathize with what really happens to a young 'scarlet' woman when the world is watching every moment: the constant whisperings, sniggering, finger pointing, head turning, the simple surface signs that you are disturbingly different. Also, about the insecurities and fears, the paranoia of living around the clock with the certain knowledge that someone, somewhere, is always after you. There is no escape from such high-profile political scandal after the threshold between nonentity and notoriety has been crossed.

You can never be you again.

I have lived scandal and all its satellite machinations ever since Johnnie Edgecombe blasted away at Stephen's front door and tried to shoot me dead. Then, I felt like a rabbit in the full glare of car headlights. My mind was frozen. I did not know where to turn. And now, as I sit in relative comfort in my flat in north London, almost four decades later, I realize that most of my life has been like that: wondering where to go, who to trust.

My life has been cursed by sex I didn't particularly want. Jack Profumo was all over me and there wasn't much I could do about it. He was a much older man, not someone I wanted to be with. It just happened. At least Monica thought she was in love with Clinton. Older men do impress young girls. I think she had some fantasy, fairytale idea about it. Clinton is a good-looking man and I can understand the attraction – of him and the power he has. Jack had power too and that was part of it for me. Monica had her power kick with the world's number one man. And obviously there were moments when she had control over him – that's an aphrodisiac too.

But whatever happened in those moments she will always be known as the woman who had oral sex with the President of the United States and she will have to live with that for the rest of her life: with her neighbours, her in-laws, her children. It's not some-thing you can wipe out in any way. You have to live with it, live with the scandal, suffer it and fight to find your identity again and, My God, that is not easy. Everybody wants the scandal – not the person. To many people you are a pariah. To Clinton she was 'That Woman'. That must have hurt. I've gone through so much and I don't know if it would have been easier if I'd loved Jack Profumo, if it had been an affair of the heart. But I know my life would have been better, happier, if it had never happened at all.

If I had just married one man I would probably have been better off. You are deluding yourself if you think you can build a career from scandal. All that follows scandal is more scandal. Every time I thought it had gone away something would knock me back . . . there would be something in the papers, someone on the telephone or the doorstep.

If Monica thinks Clinton betrayed her she's not seen anything yet. The wolves are at her door but as the years go on they will be roaming the house. She will find as I have that hell is around the corner and she will have to fight fiercely to preserve herself, her sanity, her own life. A year, two years, a decade and the rest, it never goes away. There are nutters out there and you always have to be on guard. There is a point where you feel you can't take any more. But, somehow, you do.

What you lose is your identity, not just your individuality but what makes you *you*. Your personality changes. You don't trust and if you do you find yourself used or betrayed. You are an object, a commodity. I used to be invited out and find that another dozen people had been invited too – just to look at me. I was an excuse for them to have a party. Before Profumo I knew that people looked at me because I was attractive. Afterwards I couldn't be sure.

But they *were* still looking. I couldn't know why. They were always looking. I hated it. I was only twenty, what did I know? It's like being the lady with the moustache at the circus, the Fat Lady, the Elephant Man . . . I don't know. It's about being a curiosity. You are a curiosity and you will never stop being one. And to have to live your life like that is no picnic.

People want to look at you and hear your voice not because of anything you have or might do but because you're a curiosity. You have to deal with all the personal horrors in the middle of the night when you know that you have lost who you are and must find yourself again. I still talk of that 'Christine Keeler' in the third person. Because she isn't me. I have found myself and my identity. It has taken decades, but I have never found the me that existed before Jack Profumo. I never can, for you never know what could have been. If it had been different and I had settled down and married what life would I have had, who would I have been?

I was young and naïve. When it all went wild I had to hide my mother to protect her – not the other way around. I had no back-up. I was on my own. I became a pawn, shorthand for scandal, for sleaze.

I became a dirty joke. Men were always staring at me, undressing me with their eyes. You felt they were having you in their imaginations. It's a horrid feeling, being an object. When it all happened for me the world came to an end. You wait for the situation to change but, of course, it didn't. It never does. The soap advertisement and other work dried up. My modelling career ended: people didn't want me. One afternoon I went to play cards at a club in Kensington. It was a ladies bridge club and I played well – I come from a family of card players. But I was never asked back again. The ladies didn't want *me* there. Then there are others who want you – the wrong way.

In the summer of 1964 there was a disco, one of the first in London with loud music, called the Ad Lib, in Leicester Square. Everybody was there, people like Terence Stamp who had just made *Billy Budd* and Michael Caine who was the toffee-voiced officer in *Zulu*, co-starring with my friend James Booth. I didn't fancy Caine – he was spotty, very quiet and nondescript – but he came round to the flat with rest of them, just to look. Just like the autograph hunters do to him all these years on. Yehudi Menuhin came and played bridge; he and I won. London was happening. London was swinging. Beeching might have been closing the railway lines but the Pill became available on prescription and the Beatles were belting out 'Please Please Me'. I met Peter Cohen of the Tesco family and brother to Dame Shirley Porter. The East End was meeting the West End, taking it over in some cases. The talents of people like the tailor Douglas Hayward and photographers like David Bailey and Terence Donovan were blurring the geography of what was acceptable and where. It was fun and exciting and all happily acceptable in the brave new world of the Sixties sexual revolution.

Everybody wanted to know me because of the notoriety. I could have bedded any man I wanted. I was an attraction, a thrill in an E-type-Jaguar world with ever-relaxing sexual codes. I was on all the lists – there wasn't a restaurant I couldn't get a table at. There were movie stars like George Peppard and Maximilian Schell around – they all wanted to know me. The only two people in the world who wouldn't take my phone calls were the Pope and Marlon Brando. I tried.

When Frank Sinatra's 'Rat Pack' came to London in the mid-sixties I ended up in bed with Peter Lawford who was married to President Kennedy's sister Patricia. I met Lawford and Sammy Davis Junior at the Mayfair Hotel in London; there was a crowd of us and it was a fun evening. Peter Lawford drank a lot and talked loudly about his connections and the movies he'd made with Sinatra and dropped names like Judy Garland, Paul Newman and Gina Lollobrigida, trying to impress me. Lawford was persistent but not perverted in his love-making. One published report said he wanted women to bite his nipples, to be so savage that blood was drawn. Some of his lovers had said that, but he wasn't like that with me. I just thought he wasn't quite what you would call a well-built man.

I became a sexual scalp. Powerful men wanted me in their bed and on their arm so they could boast: 'Look what I've got.' It doesn't last. They get you up on this wobbly pedestal and then they start chipping away. I've had it most of my life. You think it's gone away and then something else happens. Someone else is on your doorstep or more likely someone else is making up a story and your picture is in the paper again.

One time I was in a club with a friend and a man recognized me and tried to pull me. He wouldn't take no for an answer. He was so abusive I ended up hitting him and running out to my car to escape.

He just thought that because of who I was he could have me. You become a sex object, as though you were walking around with a neon sign flashing 'available'.

I went through the wringer but people, all sorts of people, squeezed for more and more. You think you will move on, escape. But where do you go from being Christine Keeler?

I was used and manipulated. I was interrogated time after time by the police in what any civil rights lawyer today would call harassment. Looking at the damages people get in lawsuits nearly forty years later, what I went through would probably be worth millions. And there are always people on your doorstep. No matter what you do you will be found. Probably I should have left Britain but I am English, I didn't want to go abroad. What do you do? There would be a lull and I'd be in the newspapers again. One time when things had calmed down there was a giant headline in the *Daily Mail* saying 'Keeler A Liar' with Eugene Ivanov denying he ever had sex with me.

Earlier, when he wanted to sell a book, he wrote that he had sex with me twice. That also was a lie. It was only once. Sex sells but you pay a terrible price yourself. I made money but I never think such money made me prosperous, if you understand my meaning. There was no delight in it. It was about survival.

You tell yourself that you deserve the money and, finally, you convince yourself that you do. It is a conscience cushion. You need some sort of mattress for your mind for, psychologically, it's playing hell with you. You get an inferiority complex, believe you can't achieve anything and it is terrible. I worked with the drug group Release and tried to do some good. You try and help yourself by helping others. Jack Profumo, who was Jack the Lad, got an honour for what he did but all I got was heartache. Heartache or honours? We were all victims to one degree or another of one the greatest carve-ups in history. Who spies on spies?

People wonder why I am careful with my trust. It is because of all that has happened to me and those around me. I don't get on with many men now. It's strange but I don't. I am quite happy with my own company. Relationships are always difficult. There were a couple of men I wanted to marry but they didn't want to marry me. An American guy who was totally caught up with me wouldn't commit to anything because of who I was. At a house party – and it was a big house – I wasn't allowed to stay the night because of who I was. The family thought I might corrupt everyone.

I don't think anyone ever wrote anything nice about me – oh, Rebecca West wrote that I spoke like a university don – because everyone always put me down. It fitted the story, the plot. Another lesson is: Everybody wants something, a piece of you. Nobody just wants to be nice, to pass the time of day. It's not 'Have a cup of tea,' but 'What's in it for me?'

Normality, normal human contact is gone. I've had to work at finding myself. I found out who I am and it was OK but it has taken a long, long time. I have achieved things and I have found contentment within myself but, My God, it has been a struggle. You have to be strong to do it. I pride myself on that and on surviving. You have to go out there and disregard and not be bothered by what other people think. You can only believe in yourself and if people do not like who I am, well they can get lost. The pressures of being Christine Keeler are there every day. That didn't help my marriages but I don't know if they would have worked out anyway. As I said, I'm not good at getting on with men.

Dealing with people is pivotal in life but there is always a shadow. Why do they want you? Business-wise, is it to exploit you? Personally, is it to exploit you? They are always the questions. What happens when you meet a man you like and want to marry and have a family with? If he rejects you is it because you are *that* Christine Keeler or just that he doesn't feel happy with you? I never knew. I had to tell my sons much about what had happened to me and it was the most difficult thing.

Every day I have to prove to someone that I am not a bad or wicked person. It is a pressure that never goes away. It remains a narrow-minded world in the twenty-first century. Attitudes don't change. Just imagine what it was like when the hue and cry went up in Wimpole Mews. I needed *all* my pride and strength then.

14

CRUEL INTENTIONS

I found myself desperate for a shoulder to lean on. I needed advice, guidance. I needed someone to turn to. Stephen did not want to know. The press were pestering Mandy and me all the time but she knew nothing and thought it was all a giggle, a bit of fun. Her ignorance did not help my feelings.

The fears to me were immediate ones and surrounded the trial of Johnnie Edgecombe which was set to be heard a couple of weeks into the New Year. The prospect of the trial at the Central Criminal Court, the Old Bailey, dominated all my thinking. Everyone else seemed to be preparing for Christmas and the lights were on in the West End. I had a stack of invites to parties and to drinks get-togethers but I was thinking about being asked in court if I had had sex with a black man, which in the early 1960s was a great stigma. It was like being an unmarried mother, a dreadful thing. But as the sixties got older and celebrities began having babies out of marriage that became more and more acceptable. Just as inter-racial relationships have become commonplace. Then, you didn't stir the melting pot for fear of the prejudice disguised behind net curtains.

I thought Michael Eddowes might help me. He clearly found me attractive and had been keen to get me into bed. All I wanted was his advice for he had a distinguished legal background. Money was short and forty-eight hours after the shooting on 14 December 1962, I picked up the phone to Eddowes hoping for free advice down the line. Instead, he wanted to visit me in Great Cumberland Place. He was terribly self-important, a florid-faced man who talked loudly and did not expect interruptions. He was used to speaking in court. He did not paint a positive picture. Johnnie would say anything to escape a long sentence. He would say he was protecting me when he knifed Lucky Gordon and the gun he used in the shooting was mine. Why had I got a gun? Was it all *my* fault? Eddowes made it very clear that the story could be made to suit whoever was telling it. I told him Stephen was terrified of being mixed up in it. I did not tell him it was because Stephen was a Soviet spy.

One important element of the story that was relentlessly spun in the years that followed was that I blurted out to Eddowes all about my affair with Jack. I didn't. I simply said, 'Stephen asked me to ask Jack Profumo what date the Germans were to get the bomb.'

Eddowes, who was a conspiracy freak and later investigated the shooting of President Kennedy, was bright-eyed when I told him this. He clearly saw all sorts of implications. He had seen a lot of Stephen and must have had an idea about Jack and even Eugene. But not from me. What information he had came from Stephen and was part of the scheme orchestrated by him with Roger Hollis.

Eddowes had the scent: he asked me about Lucky and about the All Nighters and then kept coming back to espionage, matters of state. He had an evangelical look about him; a singled-minded determination. He seemed to lose track of what concerned me most – the Johnnie Edgecombe trial. I was terrified of mentioning anything about Hollis or Blunt. The way Eddowes looked and talked I could see myself spending the rest of my life in the Tower of London. I had visions of Traitors' Gate. Eddowes seemed to take over the small living-room with his bulk and questions.

I was happy to tell him what seemed to keep him happy and that was being asked by Stephen to ask Jack about the bomb. I said nothing about my own activities, of dropping off papers. He kept threatening me with fire and brimstone but I never confessed to any involvement with Jack or Eugene. Eddowes was like so many of the men at the time: he was putting down others for what he talked of as moral misdeeds but wanted to have me himself. He didn't like Stephen because he thought Stephen stood between him and my bed.

I finally got him back on track about the Johnnie Edgecome trial. Or so I thought. He said he would enquire about the charges against Johnnie but his eyes told a different story. It was humbug and he had no more direct contact with me. Almost immediately, Eddowes confronted Stephen with what I had said. Stephen fed him the line he had prepared with Roger Hollis for just such an eventuality: it was Eugene who had asked me to find out about the bomb. Eugene was dispensable – and had a 'safe' escape established. The confusion and chaos of how events were reported and interpreted from then on was always in question. A virus, like a computer virus today, was injected into events by the spies and those like them wanting to hide the truth: most, if not all truths, were distorted.

Stephen was scheming. He disdained the events as squalid, nothing but a guns-and-drugs affair. Lord Astor was petrified, but not altogether inhibited. The pressure seemed to arouse him: he got my telephone number from Stephen, rang to make sure I was in, and then arrived at the flat very red-faced. There was about a week to go until Christmas Day. I gave him what I thought was an early present: I told him I would be saying nothing about having sex with him as I hadn't. Then he very physically propositioned me but I did not want to know. Nevertheless, he said he would help me with lawyers, getting and paying for them. Then, still stimulated, he went to bed with Mandy. The rose-tinted view taken of Bill by so many over the years always makes me smile. He was a man who wanted his pleasure. And no concerns. He had, of course, no conscience about his illicit desires and needs.

Bill Astor's offer to help me never materialized. Nor did the call from Eddowes. Instead it was Lucky Gordon who appeared like an evil genie: but not on my doorstep. My mother called almost weeping with anxiety. I don't know whether she was more terrified about what the neighbours might think with a black man in the vicinity or whether she would be killed by him. The newspapers, reporting the shooting with headlines like 'Model Shot At', had published her address and Lucky turned up demanding to see me. He had sat in the field opposite watching the house before asking about me. I was furious with the papers for printing the address but they did it to me again and again. I was even more perturbed at Lucky being back as I had hoped that he was out of my life. I realized he wasn't and I began treating Great Cumberland Place as a fortress. I changed the locks and put special chains on the windows.

I did go out to a Christmas party given by my long-time friend Jenny Harvey who had been my saviour in the past. It was a sort of Murray's Club reunion with people like me who had worked there and favoured customers. It was a mistake for there I met one of the most evil men of the whole affair, the vindictive John Lewis. Later, I was told, someone chewed off his nose as a reprisal for 'putting your nose in my affairs'; that was before he died in 1969 and I was not surprised. He had been a Labour MP in the 1950s but a rogue in business. Stephen had played a part in his bitter divorce from his wife, Joy, and Lewis was, even years later, after him. He believed revenge *was* best cold.

On the surface, the man I met at Jenny's party on Christmas Eve 1962, could not have been more helpful. I didn't know he was using me as a conduit to get to Stephen. He bragged about getting hundreds of thousands of pounds in legal actions against newspapers. My legal troubles involving Johnnie and Lucky were nothing. I was so grateful when he said he would get his lawyers to help and even more pleased that he actually rang, as promised, the next day. He invited me to his house and bamboozled me with his confidence and connections: Frank Sinatra and Ava Gardner had stayed in his flat. He pointed out the fat dossiers he kept on people. He was the same as Stephen but more deadly: he became more familiar with me and made a pass. Our meetings got fraught as I insisted my relations with Jack and Eugene Ivanov had nothing to do with the case against Johnnie Edgecombe.

He, like Eddowes, threatened me with gaol and he was more intimidating than Eddowes. Nastier. Eddowes had taken an interest, been understanding. I told him about Stephen asking me to get details about the bomb. I told him about Jack. He told George Wigg, the powerful Labour MP with the ear of Harold Wilson. Wigg, who was Jack's opposite number in the Commons, started a Lewis-style dossier; it was the official start of the investigations and questions which would pull away the foundations of the Macmillan government.

I thought John Lewis was helping me but he was trying to destroy Stephen. Strangely, if he had known the truth, that would have been to my advantage – he would have been more willing to protect me. The only people I now allowed in the flat were Kim Proctor, now my closest friend, Mandy, Nina Gadd and Paul Mann.

I was frightened of everyone and concerned about what Stephen was doing. If I had known then what I do now, I would have freaked: he was enlisting the help of the CIA in America to get me out of the way. He told the CIA agents that Eugene had asked me to get the information for Jack; that I was devoted to Eugene, mesmerized with love for the Russian, and a traitor. All along, all the spying I had done, however haplessly, had been for Stephen, who had now moved out of Wimpole Mews. He had also warned Eugene to be ready to flee.

He had spoiled things for Mandy by moving into Bryanston Mews, the flat she believed was hers through Peter Rachman, to try and escape the growing crowds of pressmen. Stephen continued to attempt to destroy my image, my character. Kim Proctor told me he was telling everyone that I had introduced him to the delights of Paddington rather than vice versa and that I was into drugs. He gave out quotes to help his version of events. He told the *News of the World* that he was concerned about me: 'I feel so sorry for Christine. She could have done so well for herself. But she was utterly oblivious to my warnings that she could not trifle with the affections of engaging but primitive people.'

I called Stephen and confronted him with it and stupidly shouted down the phone: 'I'm going to tell the truth!' He hung up with a rattling bang. Later, Mandy had a row with him about the flat. They were not fans of each other but this was poisonous. Like John Lewis.

George Wigg's inquiry into Jack had begun and, over two or

three weeks, Lewis, unknown to me, had been recording our conversations. I had a row with Lewis and locked him out of his office while I searched for his files on me, Jack and Stephen. He made such a fuss, I got nowhere. But neither did he when he offered me five hundred pounds to sleep with him. Did he want to tape that as well as evidence of my easy virtue? I don't think so, not by his reaction. When I turned him down he called me all sorts of horrid names and shouted, 'You're not going until I fuck you.' I walked to the door but he pushed me back and shouted what he wanted again and again. Then he locked me in his office and disappeared. When he came back he had a gun in his hand.

Astonishingly, he handed me the revolver, saying, 'If you won't make love to me, you'll have to shoot me if you want to leave. It's loaded. Go ahead.'

I would happily have shot him and told him so. He wouldn't move so I pointed the gun at him and pulled the trigger. The gun wasn't loaded. I will never forget the look on his face when he heard the click of the hammer. I left. One game appeared to be over. But it wouldn't be long before I had the urge to kill again.

The circus was about to start.

The press had kept a vigil outside the Great Cumberland Place flat since Johnnie Edgecombe had played his version of the Gunfight at the OK Corral at Stephen's front door. About six weeks had gone by and they were getting impatient. Nina Gadd was, like Mandy and Paul Mann, going in and out of the flat but I had turned protectively reclusive and kept out of the way. The reporters and photographers seemed to be working in shifts and it would not have surprised me if they had arrived squeezed into double-decker buses. They turned up in all different sizes and attitudes, some gruff and pushy, others relaxed and amiable; it was good guy, bad guy. What they all had in common was one thing – they were desperate for an exclusive interview with me.

Nina Gadd thought she was going to make a killing. Nina had been feeding the gossip columns and called herself a freelance journalist. I suspect now that she was the source of a glossy magazine snippet in *Queen* in the late summer of 1962 which began the

Profumo affair rumours. It was so vague in linking Jack, Eugene and me that it was only understood by an elite cognoscenti who were working on equally vague, circumstantial evidence. Now that the hunt was on, Nina could be more provocative. She arrived at the flat as usual on 22 January 1963, but with a man she said was her fiancé. Of course, I allowed the guy in – he was engaged to my friend.

Mandy and Paul Mann were present. It was a set-up, the first of many. Nina started talking about Jack and the problems with Lucky. In front of her fiancé who I was meeting for the first time? But I was so wrapped up in my world that I did not see how ridiculous this was. When you are in a corner and the people facing you are, you believe, your close friends, you are blinded sometimes; it is sleight of mind because you can't think for thinking.

They all suggested I sell my story to the newspapers. What had I to lose? There was only profit in it – and my modelling prospects were nil.

Nina's man was very clued up, asking if I had evidence. I had the 'Darling' letter from Jack but I did not want to hurt him. That was not a problem because the newspapers could not print his name. He would be an anonymous government minister. To Miss Naïve, 1963, it all sounded so simple. The money certainly appealed to me for it could bankroll an escape from all the problems. But how much would I get?

Nina's friend took out his business card and identified himself as from the *Sunday Pictorial* which was a heavy-hitting competitor of the *News of the World*, the *People* and the *Sunday Mirror* of the time. He suggested I could make as much as one thousand pounds – maybe more – a tantalizing figure at the time.

I justified it to myself. Kim had seen Lucky near the flat and what harm could it bring to Jack? I went to the *Sunday Pictorial* office the next day. Mandy came with me. We talked through my story and I showed them Jack's letter. The deal was done as long as I left the letter, the hard evidence. We haggled. I left with £200 and the newspaper kept the letter. The agreement was that when I signed the story the rest of the money would be paid. They were going to write everything, I just had to put my name to the proofs.

Then the police arrived and more traps were set.

And one would lead directly to the death of Stephen. I betrayed Stephen to the police – I told them that Stephen had asked me to get the date of the bomb delivery from Jack. Detective Sergeant John Burrows from the Marylebone station came to the flat to interview Mandy and me about the shooting. He told us the magistrates would take evidence in early February 1963. He asked how I had met Jack and I told him that I'd met him at Bill Astor's home and I let him know that I had given Jack's letter to the *Sunday Pictorial*. I also told him that I had met Eugene, a Russian, through Stephen on a few occasions and that was that, I thought. I had done my duty. However, Mandy was still furious with Stephen over the Bryanston Mews flat and blurted out: 'He uses young girls – he's a sexual pervert.'

Burrows went away and wrote a report using both mine and Mandy's words. In a statement which he wrote, and was never seen or signed by me, he said:

> She said that Doctor Ward was a procurer of young women for gentlemen in high places and was sexually perverted: that he had a country cottage at Cliveden to which some of these women were taken to meet important men – the cottage was on the estate of Lord Astor; that he had introduced her to Mr John Profumo and that she had an association with him; that Mr Profumo had written a number of letters to her on War Office notepaper and that she was still in possession of one of these letters which were being considered for publication in the *Sunday Pictorial* to whom she had sold her life story for £1,000. She also said that on one occasion when she was going to meet Mr Profumo, Ward had asked her to discover from him the date on which certain atomic secrets were to be handed over to West Germany by the Americans, and that this was at the time of the Cuban crisis. She also said she had been introduced by Ward to the Naval Attaché of the Soviet Embassy and had met him on a number of occasions.

It was this initial report which became the key to the conspiracy to cover-up. All my information about Stephen passing on documents and information to the Russians was ignored. As was my witnessing his meetings with Anthony Blunt and Roger Hollis. It was all part of the plot to which Denning gave official approval by deflecting questions about Stephen's espionage machinations and manipulations. The attitude that originated with that report was: let's blame Christine Keeler for everything. Stephen Ward a spy? Never. The man was a pimp. That was a much better solution. Ward the ponce was much more acceptable than Ward the spy, another one missed by the Brits. How would the Atlantic 'cousins' like that? They did not want another name to add to Burgess and Maclean, Philby and Blake. Certainly not Stephen Ward and – God forbid – Roger Hollis. Anthony Blunt's treason was discovered but remained secret for years. Stephen Ward as the pimp was best. The charges said so later in the year at the Central Criminal Court, the Old Bailey. Stephen pleaded not guilty to five charges:

> That between 1 June 1961 and 31 August 1962, he knowingly lived wholly or in part on the earnings of prostitution.
>
> That between 1 September 1962 and 31 December 1962, he knowingly lived wholly or in part on the earnings of prostitution.
>
> That between 1 January 1963 and 8 June 1963, he knowingly lived wholly or in part on the earnings of prostitution.
>
> That between 1 May 1961 and 30 June 1961, he incited Christine Keeler to procure a girl then under twenty-one years to have unlawful sexual intercourse with a third person.
>
> That on 3 January 1963, he attempted to procure a girl then under twenty-one years to have sexual intercourse with a third person.

That such charges were even brought was one of the great miscarriages of British justice, something that many legal experts as well as scholars of the time now recognize. Stephen never lived off women like a pimp. He never did that. The charges were just a weapon.

Detective Sergeant John Burrows visited me about the Johnnie Edgecombe case. I had felt safe with him and told him as much as I dared.

Stephen I now regarded as the enemy. He was no longer the witty, warm man I had known before. I knew he would be happy with me dead. How could he? The man whom I had always respected, who had taught me to feel again, how to live, had denied and betrayed me. I felt crucified. It hurt too deeply. I had accepted him, his orders, his life; I'd laughed with him and never at him, had known when to be silent, when to be talkative. We were a team. No more.

The policeman was intrigued by Stephen's girlfriends, the cottage and Cliveden. As he asked his questions Mandy was more obdurate than me about Stephen. 'I should think he's had about every girl in London. It's all right for a time, but then he just drops you. It's the same with all of them. He threw me out and then took my flat. Now I have to live here. I had the flat Peter Rachman left me, and Stephen's taken everything in it.'

Mandy pointed at me. 'All that's happened is his fault. He got her into trouble and now wants her to take the blame. He won't have anything to do with either of us now. Christine's had to sell her story to pay for legal help.'

The story came out, most significantly for the authorities, that Stephen had introduced me to Jack and Eugene and Bill Astor. He was the one getting girls for the boys. Many of Stephen's girlfriends, including Bill Astor's wife, had met their husbands through Stephen, but that didn't concern Burrows.

Stephen was playing for time but the strain was beginning to show. People told me he was looking worn and unkempt. I was avoiding him, afraid of what he might do. I was running around like a rabbit and stayed in a hotel while Stephen was trying to put together a parcel of excuses. When he found out about the *Pictorial* story he tried to trump me with his own. He told Bill Astor and Jack about me agreeing to do a story for the press. He also used a friend of his, the barrister William Rees-Davies, to try and stop my story being printed.

Rees-Davies, maybe sensing something, kept his distance and other barristers got involved. They were a conniving bunch. I didn't feel anyone was telling me the whole story. One deal was that I would be paid £5,000 – via Jack Profumo's lawyers – not to publish my story. It turned out that they were acting for Stephen as well. Paul Mann had got involved and through him I dealt with a solicitor called Gerald Black. It was all a trick. He had been chosen by Stephen. Black tried to buy me off for £500.

He was a smoothie: 'Your story could do a great deal of damage.' He treated me with much courtesy and then got threatening. I gave him the number of Jack's solicitor and finally left. The following day I rang him and was told that Mr Profumo had no intention of buying me off. Stephen's barrister, Rees-Davies, with whom Black, a former pupil of his, had agreed on Stephen's behalf to pay the £5,000. I was happy with that. Black gave me £50 that afternoon so that I could pay my hotel bill. He asked me to collect the balance the next day. Paul seemed quite happy with the arrangement, so we stalled the *Sunday Pictorial*.

Black offered me £450 the next day. He had, he said with a small smile, already given me £50 in advance. I was livid. What a bunch. But as I built up steam in my anger Black was telling me that there were conditions too: my family had to go into hiding, I must never see Mandy again and, after the Johnnie Edgecombe case, I must leave the country. I left his office instead. I almost squealed I was so mad. Before I stormed out of his office I hit him with my handbag.

The *Pictorial* was nervous about my story and some time had gone on. I was fed up with all of them and thought I'd rather have the balance of the £1,000 the paper would pay so I signed the proofs. Jack's name was not mentioned.

They had written what I had told them and added what Mandy had told them she 'overheard' me tell Eddowes. It was the beginning of a pattern in my life, my version of events being obscured and distorted. At that particular moment I didn't care. I saw the money as an escape from it all. From *all* of them.

While the *Pictorial* dithered, as Stephen was also negotiating his own story about me to them, the *News of the World* published one of my portfolio photographs taken by Edgar Brind with the caption story: 'Model in shots case. Attractive Christine Keeler features in a case at the Old Bailey this week in which a man is accused of shooting at her with intent to murder. He is a 30-year-old West Indian, John Edgecombe of Brentford, Middlesex.'

The chase was even more intense after that Sunday, 3 February 1963. I had the press hard on my heels. And the CIA. The CIA's man was Earl Fenton who seemed amiable and walked with a limp. He had been at a party I went to with Kim Proctor to celebrate the arrival of 1963. After that New Year's Eve party, Stephen had driven us home in his two-seater. We were obviously squeezed in and he tried to leave Kim behind, wanting to incriminate me with Fenton. Instead, I jumped out of the car with Kim.

Now, only a few weeks later, I recognized Earl Fenton's voice on the telephone the day after the *News of the World* published the swimsuit photograph of me. Stephen had been telling him lies, feeding him false information and indicating that I was spying for the Russians because of my love for Eugene. The message was to leave the country, say nothing about anything I might have seen or heard. Just six days earlier, 29 January 1963, Eugene Ivanov had vanished from London. Contrary to custom, no successor had arrived for him to hand over to. The Admiralty had him scheduled to leave that May. He was presumed to be in Moscow. I thought he could be anywhere.

The telephone call from Earl Fenton made me jumpy but I was more scared of Lucky Gordon turning up than a voice on the phone. Then I got angry and reported it as a threatening call to the police but they said they could not trace it and could do nothing. Other strange things were happening: the newspaper people and police who had been on my doorstep now seemed to have gone to the moon. It was, I now understand, a ploy to put pressure on me, leave me in a vacuum, to worry, make me more vulnerable than I already was. And it worked. I had nothing but questions. Detective Sergeant John Burrows had also left the scene. What was he doing?

What the *Pictorial* was doing was publishing Stephen's story – not mine. There was another strange call with an American voice saying I could be hurt. I was in a corner again and didn't know which way to turn. Kim and I had already tried to get away by moving to the Park West Apartments, a block of flats near the Edgware Road.

I was down as a witness at Johnnie Edgecombe's trial which had been postponed until 14 March 1963 because the cab-driver who had taken him to and from Wimpole Mews was ill. I was legally bound to attend but with everything that was going on around me, that was not a great concern.

Stephen knew I would run. I had told him how terrified I was of going to court. He knew me so well, predicting how I would react to the 'leave-the-country' message fed to me by Earl Fenton. Mandy went off – to live with Earl Fenton – and Paul Mann, Stephen's friend, suggested we go to Spain. He had rehearsed Kim Proctor with supposedly innocent stuff about the sun being good for me and she was enthusiastic, all for a spot of sand and sangria. I was not keen. What I was worried about was my life – and rightly so.

Lucky Gordon had been given my new whereabouts by Stephen. One evening I was in the hall of our flat at Park West taking out the garbage when Lucky leapt out of the rubbish hatch. I just couldn't believe it. He was shouting at me, telling me he loved me. Kim appeared at the door of the flat, saw what was happening, went back into the flat and reappeared with a dining-room chair, like a lion tamer. She tried to get Lucky up against the wall but he was too much for the two of us and forced us into the flat. Paul Mann then turned up and Lucky seemed to calm down once he was inside talking to us.

We talked him into going to a club called the Roaring Twenties and, while we got ready, Paul packed our stuff and put it in his red 3.4 Jaguar. He was a racing driver, which would turn out to be useful. We planned to get away to Spain without Lucky.

We were all dancing at the Roaring Twenties when first Paul disappeared, then Kim joined him in the car and finally, at the last moment, I raced out of the club with Lucky right behind me. I just got to the car and jumped in. Paul zoomed off. He just *zoomed* from that club. It was unbelievable. Lucky was still holding on to the back of the car as we roared off. But then Paul accelerated again and Lucky was left way behind.

We drove through London and down to Dover. Luckily, my one-year passport was still valid from my American trip the previous July and there was no fuss. After crossing the Channel, Paul aimed the car at Spain. It was Friday, 8 March 1963. We stopped in Paris for a couple of days then just drove and drove. We had about £100 between us and some American dollars, not a lot. Paul had an insurance cheque for £175 from a claim over a car crash. Even in those days, that wasn't going to mean a luxury trip.

We drove through France and into south-east Spain. We stopped at a place in Marbella and met Arthur Corbett. It seems I could not keep away from characters no matter where I was; Arthur was the son of the former Chief Scout, Lord Rowallan. We were looking at a place near a villa which belonged to his fiancée, April Ashley, who started life as George Jamieson and had a sex change in 1960. April, who now lives in California, married Arthur later that year but after twelve days he sued her for not being a woman and they divorced. But the flat near her villa was too much money.

So we drove on to a fishing village called Altea and, for thirty shillings a week, we got ourselves a 'villa' which was freezing. It had cold stone floors, bars on the windows and little furniture. We sat in the sun and played cards. Alicante was the nearest place of any consequence and Paul went there for supplies and to try and cash his insurance cheque. There was a phone at the café but it was difficult to get through to London, to anywhere. I wanted to see the newspapers – what had happened to Johnnie Edgecombe?

On 14 March at the Old Bailey, Johnnie was charged with the slashing of Lucky and shooting at and trying to kill me. I was the no-show witness and became in the next day's headlines 'The Missing Model'. Later that day, Johnnie was cleared of these charges but convicted of possessing a firearm with intent to endanger life. He got seven years from Mr Justice Thesiger and protested that it was all an Establishment fit-up. It certainly looks that way to me.

Especially now, with hindsight, when you see how everyone was being taken, however harshly, out of the picture.

Except me. Despite all the efforts. On the second day of Johnnie's trial the *Daily Express* had a clever front page with a banner headline reading: 'War Minister Shock'. There was a confusing story about Jack resigning but not resigning. They couldn't put directly into print the rumours that were all over Whitehall and along Fleet Street. It was a journalistic device to link me and Jack. Across to the right on that front page was a photograph of me with the headline: 'Vanished Old Bailey Witness'.

So, as I sat winning pennies playing whist in Spain, Jack Profumo was the architect of his own downfall.

George Wigg brought up the rumours about Jack and me in the House of Commons without specifying names. Barbara Castle called me a 'tart' under the protection of parliamentary privilege. There were stories that Jack had paid for me to vanish. The people writing had not met Lucky Gordon or they would have understood my real motivation. Everyone was speculating about who had paid for the 'missing model' to go missing. The inside gossip rattled on about Jack and Bill Astor and Stephen. Who *had* paid the bill? Harold Macmillan's government was under siege from the Labour Party and the press. We were starting to hear about 'thirteen years of Tory misrule' and how familiar is that? But it was all rumour because few knew for certain that Jack and I had had sex. Or that I had also slept with Eugene. And nobody knew about Stephen's spy ring with Roger Hollis and Anthony Blunt. That *would* have been a story. But the whiff of scandal was now strong enough to encourage anyone who felt like it to join in a great banshee cry about morality and security.

Finally, Jack made his now legendary 'personal statement' to the House of Commons just after 11 a.m. on a Friday, 22 March 1963. Here it is, paragraph by paragraph:

> I understand that in the debate on the Consolidated Fund
> Bill last night, under the protection of parliamentary
> privilege, the Hon. Gentlemen the Members for Dudley
> (George Wigg) and for Coventry, East (Richard Cross-

man), and the Hon. Lady the Member for Blackburn (Barbara Castle), opposite, spoke of rumours connecting a Minister with a Miss Keeler and a recent trial at the Central Criminal Court. It was alleged that people in high places might have been responsible for concealing information concerning the disappearance of a witness and the perversion of justice.

I understand that my name has been connected with the rumours about the disappearance of Miss Keeler. I would like to take this opportunity of making a personal statement about these matters. I last saw Miss Keeler in December 1961, and I have not seen her since. I have no idea where she is now. Any suggestion that I was in any way connected with or responsible for her absence from the trial at the Old Bailey is wholly and completely untrue.

My wife and I first met Miss Keeler at a house party in July 1961, at Cliveden. Among a number of people there was Doctor Stephen Ward whom we already knew slightly, and a Mr Ivanov, who was an attaché at the Russian Embassy.

The only other occasion that my wife or I met Mr Ivanov was for a moment at the official reception for Major Gagarin at the Soviet Embassy.

My wife and I had a standing invitation to visit Doctor Ward.

Between July and December, 1961, I met Miss Keeler on about half a dozen occasions at Doctor Ward's flat, when I called to see him and his friends. Miss Keeler and I were on friendly terms. There was no impropriety whatsoever in my acquaintanceship with Miss Keeler.

Mr Speaker, I have made this personal statement because of what was said in the House last evening by the three Hon. Members, and which, of course, was protected by privilege. I shall not hesitate to issue writs for libel and slander if scandalous allegations are made or repeated outside of the House.

Ironically, the pressure on Jack had been stirred up by my story for the *Pictorial* which was never printed. Together with the fact that I had gone missing – initially only to escape from Lucky Gordon. But now I was literally running for my life, forever fearful, paranoid with everything that was going on, that the CIA might quietly get me permanently out of the picture while I was already on the missing list. What stories could Parliament scream about then? Earl Fenton had helped temporarily to manoeuvre me out of the picture; I kept thinking his CIA friends would like to make it permanent, simpler for everyone.

Which is why the two matadors were a most welcome sight. When two bullfighters arrived in Altea on their way to Madrid it was a welcome opportunity to move on. Ignorant of what had gone on in the Commons, Paul and I got a lift from them and arrived in Madrid on 25 March. We had baths in their hotel and changed into the few clothes we had brought from the villa. I wanted to see the town and we went to some nightclubs, ending up doing the twist in some club until about four in the morning. The Spaniards like a late night. It was great fun after the bridge games and knock-out whist of Altea. We met some Americans at a party and the next morning, before making arrangements to get back to Altea, we went to say goodbye to one of them.

By then I was on the international press radar and the British Consulate in Madrid knew I was there. The American looked at me and said, 'You're the missing model, Christine Keeler. I've been reading all about you and Parliament.' He produced the paper. I read the report of Jack's speech and my first question was: 'What's impropriety?'

I was soon told. Paul Mann contacted the consul and the American said he would go out and try and get more English news-papers.

He came back in about twenty minutes with three reporters – I could spot the suede-shoe shuffle a mile away by now – and a black guy. I denied who I was and Kim backed me up but they were not having any of it. They had me cornered: the set-up began again. They suggested I went for a cup of coffee with the black guy while they talked to Kim. I knew the photographers were waiting. Me – linked to a British government minister – wandering through Madrid with a black lover. That's how it would have been made to look. I needed to escape and I pretended to compromise.

'I am Christine Keeler. But I'm not going to say a word until that photographer you've got waiting gets lost.'

They agreed to write a message and order him away. I insisted on delivering it myself, posting the card under the door to the photographer. I took the American aside and suggested that he took Kim for a coffee, somewhere I could meet them later. He gave me the address of a bar and left with Kim. I then turned to the pressmen, asked about the coffee and walked towards the door. I walked right through that door shouting I'd be back in five minutes.

I slammed the door and rushed for the lift. Out on the street, I found a taxi to the Palace Hotel where I had planned to meet Paul Mann. No Paul, so I fled to the police station. I gave them my name and they started looking in the phone book for the Hotel Keeler – they thought I was a lost tourist.

My agitation must have concerned them because they sent for an interpreter. Things finally started to move, Spanish-style: slowly and with a negative result. The consul's telephone was not working. The police invited me to wait until morning; I could rest on a couple of chairs or use a cell. I took the chairs; it felt safer. I had time to think but all I had to work with was half the information, the newspaper reports and what their representatives were telling me. I desperately wanted to talk to someone in London – indeed to get back so I could find out what was really going on.

As I sat there with my mind in turmoil, I felt eyes on me. Word had got round the station that I was the 'missing model' and the Spanish policemen were taking it in turns to look at me. It was the start of a process that has been going on all my life: I was a curiosity. In the morning the latest line of cops turned up but at least this lot invited me to breakfast with them. When the consul's man turned up at the police station he was concerned: the press were everywhere. He took me to the consulate where I met up with Paul Mann. The official advice was to deal with the newspapers in Spain. I could have gone home by train but why not face it now?

The *Daily Express* in 1963 was *the* middle-market newspaper which, because of its circulation, could afford to walk tall along Fleet Street. Paul and I were going to deal with the *Express*. They sent ten men including a younger guy whom I liked called Frank Howitt. He always wanted to take me for a drink. The rest of them acted as though they were extras in *Deadline Midnight*.

They wanted to manipulate my every move, my thoughts, what I wore, what I ate and drank; they even escorted me to the bathroom. This was losing control of my life and I didn't like it. There has always been that rebel element about me. I will only take so much. I did not want to become someone else's property – I never have. *I* run my life.

But at that moment I was stuck and although fighting my corner I allowed Paul Mann to do the negotiating with the *Express* men. It went on through the night before a fee of £2,000 was agreed for *my* story. But the contract Paul and I signed did not make it clear what his fee would be. I thought he should get something, but not the fifty-fifty split which was his intention. There was not much time to discuss it as we were under siege from the rest of Fleet Street. Some newspapers had hired helicopters, the phone was almost melting with the heat of the calls and the roofs around us were covered with bougainvillea and photographers. The fact that the *Express*, the Street's top dog, had got to me first only seemed to make the others more determined.

More *Express* men arrived. About a dozen of us spent the night in a tiny flat and in the morning we took off. Elaborate plans were made to get me back to London without the other papers catching us. The idea was that we would drive to France and fly from there. We zoomed even faster than we had from the Roaring Twenties. Life had got much more complex since then.

The *Express* men kept asking me questions about Jack and I was thankful none of them mentioned anything about my role in espionage. I said I knew Jack and had met his wife, they were friends. But I backed up Jack in saying that I had not seen him since

December 1961. And that was true despite the years of speculation from those looking to make money from 'seeing' us together after that. Stephen was telling a similar story – friendship, not sex. Clearly, it also suited him for the whole business to blow over as quickly as possible.

I had to keep my wits about me, keeping the story straight for the *Express* and not talking myself into a corner where I did not have an explanation for the meetings, for the contact. But the newspapermen did not delve thoroughly into the more important aspects: they were happy with a tale of a pretty young girl and a government minister and I did not enlighten them.

As we made our way to France I told Paul I thought it would be fair if he took a quarter of the *Express* money, £500. He tried to avoid talking about it. Paul wasn't as supportive as he had been and kept avoiding the money issue with me. But I made them stop on the journey; a deadline was closing, they wanted a photograph and I used that to get a new contract which specified that Paul got £500 and I had the rest. The deal was done, the camera clicked, and before I knew it we were on our way again. The *Express* now wanted to lose Paul but he had too much invested in me. He followed us in his car and not far behind him were the cars of rival reporters.

With nine of us in the car it was a madcap drive. We had a puncture and I was wrapped in a blanket while it was repaired. I sat sweating in the sun hidden from the camera lenses of the *Express*'s opposition. I thought we were doing a hundred miles an hour which worried me but then I realized it was a hundred kilometres. Nevertheless, it was a hair-raising trip. Even though I hate flying, getting on the plane in France was a relief: I was going home. I didn't know it then but I had become one of the most famous people in the country and my life would never be the same again.

What the police wanted to know, however, wasn't so much to do with my affair with Jack; they wanted to know if I had stolen top secrets from my country, if I was a traitor.

15

CONFIDENTIAL AGENT

Stephen Ward is still rearranging history from beyond the grave and I still marvel at how brilliant he was. I have studied the now unclassified US files and seen what information Stephen was supplying as a 'confidential informant' to the Americans through Earl Fenton and other contacts.

All the time he was protecting his own role and the Bowtie files reveal how determined he was to discredit my character. From 1 February 1963, I had been known by the code name 'Kolania' in the British government files which are kept much more tightly sealed than the American documents. It was extraordinary for me to sit at home recently sipping tea in north London and read through these pages and pages of US documents released under the American Freedom of Information Act. It seems like another world, another life. I just didn't realize for so many years how concerned some of the most powerful men in the world were over me. It doesn't make me proud. It makes me shudder when I understand the cumulative effect of the years of lies on which history has been created. Truth is the victim of politics.

For nearly forty years the Americans have believed a great deal of nonsense that was supplied to them by Stephen who they did not know was working for Moscow. In accounts of the affair they have had their own agents interpret events and spin other stories on that basis. What they were supplying, a little changed and then recycled, was Stephen's misinformation. No one ever asked me but then I was too fearful to speak out until now. They said the father of the boy I aborted and called Peter was a black member of the US Air Force and not the true father, Jeff Perry. The FBI said it was Jim Calfie – who was white – and insisted that Jim was black in an attempt to discredit me further. My affair with Jim resulted in international cables between J. Edgar Hoover and British Intelligence.

The Americans also said I had relationships with three black American airmen who had access to classified material. The *Daily Telegraph* even printed that in October 1999. Without question! They just simply accepted it as fact – because it was in a declassified FBI file they had just discovered in Washington. Years earlier, it got so high up in the US government that the Secretary of Defense, Robert McNamara, said, according to the documents, that he felt he was 'sitting on a bomb in this matter'. One declassified FBI document reads:

> Colonel Walsh indicated the trio are being flown from England today for interrogation and to insure that the thrill-seeking English Press does not get to their story before the AF does. The three airmen will be housed at Bolling AF Base and the investigation is designed to determine whether Keeler had attempted to pump them for intelligence data which they might have in connection with their AF assignments.

These three were quizzed at the Ruislip, Middlesex, headquarters of the US Third Air Force, before going home because of what were called their 'rumoured connections' with me. I swear I never met them. Why would I deny it now if I had? What benefit is there in lying about something that is accepted? But I'm damned if I'll accept this any more. For decades my self-esteem has been chipped away at, time and again, piece by piece, sometimes little bits, sometimes great chunks. I have been placed at dinner parties and in situations I was never near when actually it was Stephen or Eugene who were present. By placing me across and around his board of play, Stephen was constantly covering himself. I was the stooge, the fall guy.

Stephen's information put me in the same clubs as the three airmen; in the mid-summer of 1963, the Americans were putting intelligence officers from the CIA, FBI and Air Force special agents on my case. J. Edgar Hoover, chief of the FBI who officially reported to Bobby Kennedy but detested the Kennedy clan, was in overall charge. He wanted all the dirt he could get on them. At the time, Arthur Sylvester, the US Assistant Defense Secretary, said: 'Security is our basic concern.' But, interestingly, he refused to identify the airmen because of the 'thinness of the rumours' although their names were leaked. A couple of them told lurid stories of meeting people I knew but not of meeting me – they hadn't. The implication in the files, however, was that I was intimate with them.

It is also clear from the documents that the Americans knew more, if not all, about my relationship with Jack Profumo and Eugene, long before Harold Macmillan or any of his government's security services. The police didn't have a clue what was going on. At vital moments they just withdrew from the scene – or more likely were hauled off. Stephen was the conduit for the information and he could back it up: he had witnessed it or set it up.

For the Americans there were the delicate issues of world security and the difficulty of keeping secret John Kennedy's enormous sex drive. Only a year earlier Marilyn Monroe, his lover through the devices and help of Peter Lawford, had died in circumstances still never fully explained. The last thing they wanted was for JFK to be involved in a British spy-and-sex scandal. They could see the 'thrill-seeking' headlines rolling off the presses.

One memorandum from J. Edgar Hoover to Bobby Kennedy, the US Attorney General, is both fascinating and frustrating for many, but I believe I can shed some light on it. Dated 18 June 1963, the memo reads:

> In view of the President's forthcoming trip to Europe, it is believed you would want to know of the following information which was obtained from a confidential informant who furnished reliable information in the past:

The next two paragraphs are censored. The fourth paragraph reads:

> In view of the extremely delicate and sensitive source providing this information, it is being furnished only to you with the belief you might want to personally advise the President concerning this information.

A note at the end of the memo is partially blacked out and only the words 'grave damage to the US' can be made out.

It is clear from the documents that the FBI was worried. Quietly, in one security area, the FBI were investigating the President because of his alleged affair with a Chinese woman who, when I knew of her in London, was called Suzy Chang. The FBI had linked her to me and thereby, of course, Kennedy to Profumo. It was the connection between JFK and Suzy Chang, who agents said had worked for a Hungarian madam with Iron Curtain contacts, that got Washington going. Bobby Kennedy had alerted the FBI to stories which suggested that his brother could have been exposed to a Communist spy ring – and me. The declassified documents show claims by Mariella Novotny that President Kennedy slept with Suzy Chang. Mariella said in a New York article that Suzy had been procured by Stephen, another link with me and Jack Profumo. The declassified American documents have bizarre details including a claim that Eugene had an affair with Mariella. I saw that previously secret document for the first time in 1999 and it made me consider again how close Stephen had been to using Mariella in a Mata Hari role.

I believe that if I had been killed in the boating incident Stephen would have used Mariella or Ronna Riccardo or another girl, Yvonne Brooks, another victim of the spies, who killed herself in 1964, to try and get the information about the bomb from Jack Profumo. Stephen was certainly recruiting more and more girls. I know Ronna Riccardo was interviewed by the CIA after she ran off to America. Yvonne Brooks got into all sorts of games in Italy but did away with herself at the Hilton in London. Apparently, she had simply had enough. I could understand that, the pressure, and the feeling that life was just too much to endure. On reflection, it is clear to me that Mariella was too notorious, too well known, dressed or naked, to the movers and shakers of the 'Supermac' times to be very useful in an espionage role. But Stephen was cornered at the time and under a great deal of pressure, so there may have been thoughts or plots we will never know about. He took them to the grave.

When the FBI investigated they were able to involve Mariella with a Hungarian madam in New York. What alarmed them further was my association with Eugene. You could see how two and two could add up to a very big number indeed with all this information. I believe the Americans were convinced that a worldwide sex-for-information network, an elaborate blackmail operation, was going on. And that the most powerful man in the world, their president, had sampled the pleasures of these female sex spies. Certainly, Bobby Kennedy did not conceal the concerns of himself and his brother.

The Bowtie files talk of Stephen's American connections such as Averell Harriman, the former US ambassador to London, and the billionaire Paul Getty. There is mention of the 'Man in the Mask' party. Mariella's story was published on 29 June 1963, and she talked only of Chang and 'a US government official who holds a very high elected post'.

At 3.05 p.m. that same afternoon, the President's brother called Courtney Evans, a senior deputy of the FBI chief J. Edgar Hoover, to tell him about the story and order an investigation. According to a memo, 'the Attorney General stated that the President had expressed concern regarding this matter'. The FBI, which had been concentrating, foolishly, on the air force guys, now went all a-flutter. Memos were circulated between Hoover and his deputies about the possibility of 'an espionage-prostitution ring operating in England with American ramifications'.

Bowtie files show that FBI agents were sent out all over America, where Suzy Chang and Mariella had worked. They identified Chang as Esther Sue Yan Chang, the daughter of two Chinese immigrants who lived in New York, but who had herself been refused a visa to live in America.

The FBI men in New York were already familiar with Mariella because two years earlier she had arrived from London and set up in business but was arrested under the White Slave Trafficking Act before she skipped back to the UK.

But the documents show they discovered that Mariella and Suzy had mutual friends and that Mariella organized orgies for well-connected clients. There's still much blacked out in the documents which will refer to the leak over the Skybolt missile, the information stolen by Stephen from Bill Astor and passed to Moscow. It was, for J. Edgar Hoover, another example of Britain 'screwing up' and, from the memo, he clearly thought Kennedy should reconsider his trip to Europe, particularly the UK. Harold Macmillan's cabinet believed at one time that Kennedy would cancel. He didn't.

For Kennedy, the Skybolt programme was over. The missile system had been cancelled a year earlier. Britain was to have Polaris. I suppose the sex stories would have meant more embarrassment for his administration. And that's probably why Hoover dwelt on them.

When some details of the declassified Bowtie documents were published in October 1999, they brought uncomfortable attention on Suzy Chang, who was by then known as Suzy Diamond and living in a Chinese-temple-style home in Long Island, New York and, after three wealthy husbands, living well in the island's exclusive Gold Coast area where mansions sell for fifteen million dollars. Her passion then was for rescuing stray cats. She was sixty-five years old and a great-grandmother; devoting her time, she said, to public works and animal welfare.

This was the woman that Mariella said had a fling with JFK, arranged by Stephen Ward, shortly before he took over the White House. I had heard stories about that in London for there was a lot of gossip about which girls were seeing who and the more important the man, the more important the girl. Suzy the great-grandmother was described as pencil thin but with a face and figure which could be imagined as stunning with the years stripped away.

If only we *could* take away all the years.

The files do make it clear that even before Jack Profumo lied to the Commons about his relationship with me, the FBI was deeply concerned at how far the activities of Stephen and Mariella would go. How far and how high up? They also show the lack of cooperation from Roger Hollis's MI5 which is, of course, understandable. The Americans complain in the Bowtie documents of Hollis stonewalling them.

I was also intrigued by the story Suzy Chang-Diamond told in 1999 for it involved so many people that I had known. She was quoted as saying of JFK: 'I definitely was not his mistress, I was dating a lot of men in that period.'

The 1999 interviewers were good; they got the material they really wanted and it was not a denial. Suzy rather played around, saying:

> 'For a while I had a sugar daddy. But never was I a pros-
> titute, any more than poor Stephen Ward was a pimp.
> And let's face it, do you think Kennedy would need to
> buy a prostitute? I knew Jack a long, long time . . . Well,
> I only ever met him on two occasions and both were
> public. What I remember is he was very nice to me,
> always kind.
>
> 'I don't think our relationship was something you can
> call sleeping with someone. I don't think I had an affair
> with him or went to bed with him. I never have been in
> a bedroom with him, OK? We flirted, I think. I used to
> drink a lot of wine and I'm near-sighted, but I didn't
> think he was attractive. I flirt with a lot of people but I
> don't like old men. I think he was too old for me. You
> must remember at that time there were very few Oriental
> girls in London.'

About Stephen she said, 'He was just a nice, kind guy who wanted to be a big shot. He had no money. I met him at a party given by an American friend.' She was then asked about me:

'Sure, I met Christine . . . And I met Mandy Rice-Davies . . . They were what we called party girls. I bumped into Mandy after the Profumo affair and I said, "I'm going to kill you for the bad things you said about Stephen." Of course, I'd begun to hear the things they said about me, the trash they put out. So what if I knew Kennedy? I knew a lot of people. I knew his sister-in-law, Lee Radziwill. I knew Jackie Kennedy.'

Truth? An elusive beast. But for the newspapers and magazines it is the headlines that count. A denial is often as good as an admission. I found that there is no winning. You say one thing, it is interpreted as another. However, the early sixties were astonishing. These were the days of incredible characters like Suzy Chang. Ian Fleming, you could argue, only had to make up the plots of his Bond books. The characters were wandering around.

The 1,189 pages of declassified documents that make up the Bowtie papers include a note of a visit to the American embassy in Grosvenor Square on 29 January 1963 by Thomas Corbally, an American friend of Stephen's. Corbally told his friend Alfred Wells, the secretary to David Bruce, the ambassador, that everything about Jack, me and Eugene was going to come out. That was because of my dealings with the *Sunday Pictorial*. It was also the day Eugene vanished to Moscow. I thought Corbally seemed a tricky character. He was usually talked of as an American businessman, but I always wondered if he was more than that and having now read the FBI papers I am even more suspicious. According to Bowtie he was frightened that I might escape from Britain, run off. It was more likely that he thought that Stephen was going to make for Moscow. Stephen was certainly packed and ready to go with his 'escape kit' of passports and false identities.

Corbally said in the American memos that Harold Macmillan had been told about Jack and me on 28 January 1963. The British cabinet papers released by the Public Record Office in 1994 indicated he was told three days later, on 1 February. Corbally – according to the documents – hosted sex parties in London. The link here, if we accept the FBI's Bowtie file, is Mariella. I am haunted by her for I believe that I took her place in Stephen's scheming. If I am correct, and I swear I am, it means my life could have been so different. When I appeared in Stephen's life he clearly saw me as the perfect instrument to guard him in his treachery. He used me as protection in the same way the Establishment employed the tales of sex in high places as a blind, to camouflage the truth. But all the stories of sex and perversion were a useful smokescreen while the authorities tried to figure out just how big a security mess Britain was in. Of course, it was mostly one of their own making and I was a convenient fall guy. With the dice loaded against me, on my return from Spain I walked into a set-up.

16

MIDSUMMER MADNESS

I HAVE BEEN GUILTY OF A GRAVE MISDEMEANOUR.

John Profumo in his letter of resignation to
Prime Minister Harold Macmillan, 4 June 1963

The police did everything but shove a spotlight in my face to get
their information. They thought they knew the whole story. I just
had to answer their questions and back up their theories. They
knew nothing but that did not stop them building a case. At first, I
thought they were building it against me but then I began to
understand: they wanted Stephen. Someone wanted him out of the
way.

The *Express* brought my mother to a hotel in London they had
arranged for me and what she told me there was a surprise just when
I thought nothing ever would be again. She said that Stephen's
friend Michael Eddowes had turned up and told her that I had been
spying. He ranted on that I would be gaoled for treason and he
terrified my mother by telling her she could be shot by an assassin.
What did Eddowes know? Was he cleverer than all of them? I was
panicked by this news: I had, after all, passed on that thick packet of
papers to Eugene and I had witnessed Stephen's meetings with
Hollis and Blunt and may have heard what they had said.

Then, my mother surprised me again: she and my stepfather had
actually been interviewed by British security. They had called the
police about the visit from Eddowes which had terrified them but
the police had sent a spy. Why? My parents knew nothing but it
seemed the spooks Stephen had so often talked about were on my
trail, watching me. This was bad. To stir things further, Nina Gadd

had also been to see my mother with a team of reporters looking for more headlines. I thought they would have overdosed on news by then, but no, they were insatiable.

And then came yet another surprise: Stephen called me. I had not talked to or heard from him for many weeks and there was his voice again. 'Come over, little baby. I've got a film producer, John Nash, here with me and he wants to pay us to make a film about everything.'

I went. Even after all that had happened I hoped that he'd take me in his arms and confess everything so that we could be close again and face him being charged as a spy together. I was willing then to stand up for him, to go to gaol for him. I was so afraid that I just needed someone to trust, to lean on. Stephen had been that in the past and had appeared to me so very knowing and sophisticated. Nevertheless, I was not so naïve that I wasn't a little afraid when I arrived.

The film people were already there: David Pelham, Dominic Elwes and John Nash. They were all friendly enough but they allowed Stephen to make the running: 'Look, little baby, you must sign something or you won't get any money. After all, why shouldn't we make some money?'

I was wary but eventually Stephen got me to sign over on the back of an envelope my rights to be played in a film for two thousand pounds.

Then they told me that I'd have to wait for the money as the script had yet to be written; Stephen was going to get a reporter from the *Express* to write it. As I left, Stephen told me that he would be in touch about a book for us to do together. I knew that I had been tricked and that Stephen would blame me in the writing of the script; it was more subterfuge. I was angry with him again and that was fuelled by my uncertainty for I was not sure what sort of game he was playing.

I had to appear at the Old Bailey for being the missing witness in Johnnie Edgecombe's trial. The *Daily Express* at this time was selling more than four million copies a day and was a rich, powerful newspaper. I was still under contract to them and one of their reporters went with me. By then, I had joined the freak show. What

Leaving Paula Hamilton-Marshall's flat during the Profumo outcry.

Mandy and I arriving at the Old Bailey for Stephen's trial.

That's me with the Denning
Report and Paula Hamilton–
Marshall in 1964.

Reading the Denning Report –
the painting told a better story.

Lord Denning.

With photographer Ray Bellisario,
brought in by Mr Lyons, the lawyer,
to take lots of pictures of me.

A couple of shots from my famous fashion picture session with Lewis Morley – including the one with THAT chair.

The day I was released
from prison in June 1964.

That's me outside
Holloway Prison.

This is me in Southend visiting with my Aunt Pam – the smiling chap with me is an American actor called Manning Ross.

With Mike Nelson, the wild Australian who was always ready for romance or a laugh, 1967.

A life of twists and turns . . . me at Le Mans, in 1967.

With just-born Jimmy in 1966.   With Jimmy, aged three, in 1969.

With Seymour in 1976 at our flat in Earl's Court, London.

Getting the news about my story in 1968.

With the late, great, Screaming Lord Sutch. He fought for Profumo's parliamentary seat for his Screaming Loony Party after Jack resigned.

A rather mournful portrait taken by Ian Potter in 1983.

A recent portrait by Adrian Houston.

a circus it was with photographers and crowds trying to get a look at me. I marched from a taxi and through the crowds with the police making a way for me. And there at the top of the steps was Lucky Gordon. I almost fainted on the spot. Lucky went berserk: he kept screaming that he loved me. It took five policemen to control him and even then his arms were flying around and he was shouting: 'I love that girl.'

So much for a low profile. Fearful, I was relieved to be rushed into the court building which in the months ahead was to become so familiar to me. For now, my visit was brief and I was only fined forty pounds for not turning up for Johnnie's trial. If only everything else could have been so easy.

I was still furious with Stephen so when Detective Sergeant John Burrows telephoned me about another interview I told him what had happened and he quite sharply told me, 'Stay away from him. He is not your friend and don't sign anything with him.' It was a serious change in attitude from the police.

I was now a gypsy in London: I did not know where to go and I found that I was something of a social pariah. My mother was being supportive but I did not want to compromise her by staying with her. Paula Hamilton-Marshall agreed that I could go and live with her in Devonshire Street.

Sergeant Burrows turned up at Devonshire Street for his interview. With him was Chief Inspector Samuel Herbert who was to become my nemesis. 'It's a matter of security, Christine. We have to ask you a few questions,' explained Burrows. I thought: 'They know everything.'

Herbert said, 'There might be a Russian connection.'

Again, I thought, 'They know.'

They didn't. But I went with them to be questioned at Marylebone Police Station. It was a horrid little room. I was given a glass of water.

Their questions revealed that they knew little more than I had already told them. They wanted details of when Stephen asked me to get the information about the nuclear warheads from Jack. The questions were constant and repeated again and again, it seemed for ever. Finally, this session ended but they soon returned with detailed plans of Jack's house in Regent's Park. It looked like architect's drawings. They suggested I could have stolen papers when I was there with Jack. From where? Under the bed?

I had to repeat in detail my time at the house, my association with Jack and the times Jack and Eugene met. I never said anything to them about Stephen's spying or association with Hollis and Blunt.

But it became clear that Burrows and Herbert were after me. They had bought Stephen's story that I acted out of love for Eugene. Burrows said, 'About your relationship with Mr Profumo, we must be quite certain that you had no opportunity to go into his office. Now, tell me quite truthfully, did you on any occasion go into his office? We'll quite understand if you say yes. It won't necessarily mean you're in any trouble. These people have ways and means of forcing a person to do things against their will, and all this will be taken into consideration.'

I protested. I told the truth: I had not taken anything, I had been too busy dealing with Jack's sexual demands. They didn't like that; they wanted to know if someone had 'sent' me to Jack's. Why had we not made love at Stephen's place as usual? They wanted me to say Eugene had orchestrated the visit, planned it, but I did not play along. They changed tactic, asking if Jack had taken me into the War Office.

The questions went on for days; the two of them collected me at Paula's flat and then we went back to that little room with the numbing wooden chair. And the equally numbing questions continued: there was the gun to account for, and who had paid for me to run to Spain. I parried and only ever lied by omission; I didn't want other people involved.

That attitude landed me in gaol – after another encounter with Lucky Gordon. Stephen wanted me out of the way. Permanently. He told Lucky I was still in London. I was frightened and told Burrows. The police picked up Lucky saying he had to have psychological tests but Burrows told me: 'Don't forget, Christine, we can't hold him for more than a week.' In my frame of mind that seemed like a lifetime. It wasn't.

Interview number twelve with Burrows and Herbert came around. Burrows sat in his pinstripes, absorbing the questions and answers in silence. I felt that he was on my side, probably the only person in the world who was, but I hated Herbert with his full face, fair hair and darting eyes. He was always dressed in tweeds. Whatever, I knew I had to keep answering the questions. Now they wanted to know what I was going to do with my money – cash they supposed I had been paid by Eugene for spying. What they called 'large sums'. Herbert said: 'We know all about it.'

It was a bluff – I had not been paid. I was confident then, confident that I could get through these interrogations without letting anything go that I didn't want to. I could see their hand. Finally, they threw it in and there were a couple of days of just sleeping and thinking. When they came back I knew that the investigation had changed from Herbert's first question: 'When did you meet Bill Astor?'

I told him the truth about meeting Bill at Cliveden. He wanted to know if I had sex with Bill. Again, I told the truth and said no. Then they brought Mandy into it. I said I could not talk for her and they dropped a bombshell. They said they had been after Stephen for eleven years for using women. They wanted to know all about the men in my life since I had lived with Stephen. I did not lie but my answers were pretty much waffle. The next day these two, who by now I thought of as Laurel and Hardy, took me to see Commander Townsend of MI5.

The two policemen stayed in the room while I answered questions about having sex with Jack and Eugene. Townsend asked me about Stephen wanting me to find out about the bomb from Jack. Townsend then asked Burrows and Herbert to leave the room and said, 'I have some important questions to ask you, but it is very important that you never tell anyone what I have to say next. Not even the police. Nobody. Do you understand?'

He said they believed me when I said I had taken nothing from Jack's house and that it was Stephen who had asked me to get the bomb information from Jack. But his people had a report from Michael Eddowes about me being a Russian spy and also a report from the CIA about what Stephen had told them. The CIA were flapping, realizing that Stephen had put the blame on to me. They were terrified of security leaks and a sex scandal involving America. Stephen had sketched David Bruce, the American ambassador, and Bruce's assistant, Alfred Wells. When Douglas Fairbanks Junior was interviewed by the FBI he said half the House of Lords would be implicated by Stephen.

I told Townsend that Stephen had said that there was money to be made in spying. I also told him that I had *not* asked Jack about the bomb and that I would not have done so. He then asked if I thought Stephen was a spy and I said he was. So the security people knew the truth.

The commander then asked me who else I had told about Stephen's request to get the information from Jack and I told him Michael Eddowes and John Lewis, though I forgot to mention that Mandy had been present when I'd told Eddowes. The security people had been observing Stephen since he had set alarm bells off with his visit to Lord Arran on 27 October 1962 but he had been lying low after the Johnnie Edgecome shooting and his spying days were over. Still, he had to be manoeuvred out of the way. Townsend was building a dossier and he made it clear to me how much information he had gathered. He had my mother's statement about the visit from Eddowes when he had told her I was a spy and that she might be shot. He had elaborate details about John Lewis and the solicitor he had introduced me to. It was clear to me that Townsend had suspected a Labour plot, some 'dirty tricks' politics – something that Harold Wilson and George Wigg were beginning to get a reputation for. Townsend now decided that there had been no security leak and that Macmillan was safe. However, Lord Arran and Sir Godfrey Nicholson and Bill Astor knew better, as did the CIA.

I was politely shown out and Herbert and Burrows took me back to the station for more questions. It was all about my boyfriends. Who? Where? When? Peter Rachman's name was mentioned and all about him giving me money and clothes; how Stephen had introduced us, how I had lived with Mandy and how she had gone with Peter Rachman.

It's easy to see the scheme now but at the time I did not understand what they were doing. Why would I have? Stephen was a spy and I had just given the details to British security. They would arrest him for spying. What were all these questions about? But they persisted with them. Who visited Wimpole Mews? How many men? How often? Who paid the rent?

Finally, the questions stopped and I was back at Paula's when Stephen telephoned me asking me to go over and sign up for the book with him. I was exhausted with it all. I told him that I wasn't interested and that the police were after him. 'Don't be silly, little baby. What have I done that the police can be after me for?' I put the telephone down.

Stephen was still trying to keep control. He had bailed Lucky out of gaol and the night he phoned me he had been to the police station to report a robbery. This was to cover up his meeting with Lucky Gordon that same night when he gave Lucky a sketch he had drawn of me at the cottage at Cliveden and told Lucky I was staying at Paula's in Devonshire Street. He also reported the sketch stolen in the 'robbery'.

I'd thought Stephen was a beaten man; when I saw him that evening about the film, the resilience he had displayed in the early days of our relationship had gone. He seemed dissipated. Even his face looked as though it had fallen, with loss of sleep deeply marked all over it. His high-and-mighty society friends had deserted him. Maybe that was another reason he was so vengeful when he set Lucky loose on me. And the hounds after Jack. Resorting to blackmail, Stephen tried to do a deal to stop the police investigating him: unless the inquiries were called off he would go public about me and Jack, that Jack had lied to the Commons. Burrows and Herbert kept digging away. Stephen wrote letters including one to Harold Wilson who was obliged to send it on to Macmillan because of protocol about security matters.

Harold Macmillan shrugged off Wilson's anxieties saying a further security review had not shown Jack's association with me or Stephen. No wonder Wilson and George Wigg – who had been fed everything by John Lewis who had offered me £30,000 in a legal contract to live with him – said they would ask more questions in the Commons unless more inquiries were made. An investigation by the Lord Chancellor was announced to begin on 30 May and Jack was told he would be questioned the following week. It could not go on, there could be no more brinkmanship.

The game was up. I seemed to smell it in the London air. Jack and his wife went to his beloved Italy, to the calming waters of Venice: it was the last act of bravado. After he confessed all to Valerie, he returned and confessed to Macmillan's Private Secretary: 'I have to tell you that I did sleep with Miss Keeler and my statement in that effect was untrue.' He then wrote to Macmillan, on 4 June 1963, with his resignation:

> In my statement I said that there had been no impropriety
> in this association. To my very deep regret I have to admit
> that this was not true, and that I misled you, and my
> colleagues, and the House. I ask you to understand that I
> did this to protect, as I thought, my wife and family, who
> were equally misled, as were my professional advisers. I
> have come to realise that, by this deception, I have been
> guilty of a grave misdemeanour.

He got a 'Dear Profumo' letter back accepting his resignation with alacrity. The news broke the next day. To sum up the madness of it the leopard-skin-wearing rock star Screaming Lord Sutch, who died in 1999, announced he was standing for Jack's constituency as a candidate for the Monster Raving Loony Party. It seemed appropriate. At the same time all hell broke loose around me. There were two telephone threats and the police put a guard on us. We were told not to go out or open the door to anyone. The anonymous threats were made separately by a man and a woman who phoned a London newspaper earlier in the day. The woman said, 'We are going to destroy Christine.' The man said, 'Christine Keeler will be attacked this afternoon.'

I was window-shopping in Soho and the West End with Paula Hamilton-Marshall when the calls were made. We'd gone out to get some air, find some space for ourselves. When we got back to Paula's flat several plain-clothes police were already there and four uniformed men were patrolling the street. The detectives told me that if I went out to beware of people holding parcels or carrying mackintoshes which could conceal a weapon. They were taking it very seriously. Other calls warning the police that someone would try to kill me were made to Paddington police station and to the police station at Leyton in East London. We had no threats to the flat direct but we had a number of telephone calls where the caller hung up without saying anything.

I was not surprised that with all this pressure there would be more and, sure enough, Lucky Gordon appeared.

I'd had a row – it got quite physical – with Paula's brother John who was being a proper pain. To escape, Paula and I decided to go out with two West Indian guys, Rudolph 'Truello' Fenton and Clarence Commachio who had come around to visit her. As we left the flat, Lucky was in the street and I could tell he was at boiling point. He was acting alone but he would have taken on the world.

He went for me, crushing his body into me and shoving me back into the apartment building. He was screaming filth in my face and punching at me, short hard jabs in my breast. Paula raced to the flat to phone the police. Lucky did not seem to care: he punched and punched until I fell to the pavement then he kicked me all over, on the legs and in the ribs and chest. I was blinded by my own blood and my legs were pouring with blood. The two West Indian lads had watched all this, stunned by the sudden savagery of the moment. Finally, they acted and pulled Lucky off me and I was able to make it back into the flat. The housekeeper, Olive Booker, started trying to stop the blood pouring down my face. Paula, whose Cleopatra make-up was running in tears down her face, shouted that the police were coming.

Lucky had run off hearing the police were on their way and Fenton and Commachio came into the flat with my handbag. Inspector Samuel Herbert and Detective Sergeant John Burrows arrived to investigate the threatening phone calls. Fenton and Commachio were terrified. One of the guys was on bail and awaiting trial. The other was worried that if he got mixed up in any trouble he would lose his flat. He had six children and it wasn't worth the risk. The police might get nasty as he was black.

I felt sorry for them; they had literally got Lucky off my back. Paula told them to hide under the bed in her room. As they did so, Herbert and Burrows walked in the front door. They got a police doctor to examine my injuries and with this hard evidence against him Lucky was arrested the next day. They knew nothing about the men under the bed and I never said a word. It was a terrible mistake, another terrible error and again just because I wanted to help other people.

Herbert and Burrows were soon back at their double act quizzing me relentlessly about Stephen and girls, money and rent, who paid what and to whom. It seemed endless and at times intolerable. I found it brutal. Then someone from the past turned up to make the situation even worse.

He had sat in the car and watched me take Stephen's heavy packet of documents up to the front door of the Soviet Embassy and now Manu Jahambin, my Persian ex-boyfriend, came forward and informed the police that he had taken me there to deliver a letter to Eugene. The questions that resulted went on for hours. 'Why didn't you tell us that you delivered letters to the Russian Embassy?' Herbert asked angrily. 'How many letters, and how many times did you go there?' I told them a story about bridge arrangements and taking a letter cancelling them but it didn't sound very convincing. Then they dropped in another question about the gun Johnnie Edgecome had used. They had finally, all that time later, discovered that it was my gun. But I refused to tell them how I got it – why involve other people at that stage? There was no point but the implication was that if I did not give them the answers they wanted about Stephen then I could face at the very least gun charges. I wasn't going to stand for that sort of blackmail; I would sit out the questions no matter how long it took.

The constant, nagging questions began again about Stephen and his patients and this time they were almost directly saying I was servicing Stephen's patients including Bill Astor. They seemed to know a lot about Bill's sexual tastes. The question sessions sometimes went on for more than eight hours as they tried to get me to say what they wanted to hear. Like reporters, the police knew most of the story they wanted before they had my answers. The questions were all about Stephen and women. Herbert and Burrows were still relentless. I told them Nina Gadd had paid Stephen rent. And then I told them that Jack had given me twenty pounds for my mother. I could have said thirty pieces of silver for the effect it had on Herbert:

'Because you slept with him?'

'No. For my mother.'

'He gave it to you, though?'

'Yes.'

'After intercourse?'

'No. He wanted me to have something, I told him I didn't want anything. We had been talking about my family. They're only ordinary people you know, struggling along. So he left twenty pounds saying I could give it to my mother.'

'Did you?'

'Yes.'

Herbert noted: Mr Profumo gave Christine Keeler twenty pounds . . . 'for her mother'.

Herbert was now getting red in the face. The questions had gone on at Marylebone for hours and I had not even been given a glass of water. I could see he had the scent; I thought if I mentioned another name they would be satisfied. I told them about Major Jim. He wasn't my lover but I slept with him. As I talked I could see from their faces it was a mistake. They had triumph in their eyes. 'How much did he give you?'

'I can't remember.'

'You must remember.'

'I can't. He gave it to me quite often.'

'How often?'

'Over about two years.'

'So he came to the flat and slept with you, and gave you money?'

'Sometimes.'

'How much?'

'Twenty pounds.'

'How much did he give Ward?'

'Nothing, why should he?'

'Stephen introduced you to him?'

'No.'

'How did you meet him?'

'Through a friend of Mandy's.'

'And then you slept with him?'

'He took me out to the cinema or to dinner. Sometimes he slept with me. Sometimes he gave me money. Not always.'

'How much of the money received from him did you give to Stephen?'

'Why?'

'You tell me.'

'Sometimes I lent Stephen money if he hadn't got any, but it was I who always owed him.'

'Did Stephen ever ask you to meet someone who would give you money?'

'Yes.'

'Ah-ha! Now we're getting to the point, Christine, aren't we?' Herbert was happy.

'What do you mean?'

'Who was this person?'

'Charles.'

'What happened?'

'We were out of cash, so Stephen suggested I went round to this man to borrow some money.'

'And you had intercourse with him?'

'No.'

For nearly four decades people have written and said that 'Charles' was the property tycoon Charles Clore. I don't know how many times I have read that I slept with Clore for money. I didn't. I went to his house for dinner once with Stephen and that was it. No sex. Not for love. Or money. I hope that tears another nail out of the coffin of lies that I have been confined in for so many years. The next day my private Laurel and Hardy asked me the same old questions all over again. They stopped suddenly and there was a respite.

During those exhausting sessions I learned to think about all aspects of what was going on. The early sixties have remained fascinating because the events were vast, teeming dramas, with complex sub-plots that overlapped and intersected until it was almost impossible to say where one ended and another began. The *dramatis personae* were never cardboard characters. It was a golden age of characters. And, of course, scandal.

One of the characters I met at this time was Robin Drury, a friend of Stephen's who had been the personal manager to Lionel Bart the composer of *Oliver!* Times for him were not so good and he borrowed money from me. Now he approached me about writing a book. He turned up at Paula's and said he wanted to be my 'manager'. He seemed OK. It would be strictly business and I liked the idea of that. A lawyer called Walter Lyons was part of the deal with Robin. Even before Jack resigned they had been quietly talking to the *News of the World* about selling them my story. It was the heyday of cheque-book journalism with newspapers, especially the Sunday papers, fighting over the stories of those involved in big court cases and paying handsomely for their versions of events. It was a terrific deal – they were going to pay £23,000, a fortune in those days, maybe a quarter of a million pounds today. Robin produced a tape-recorder and we set about doing the book. He kept me talking, feeding me coffee, for hours. I talked and talked. I wouldn't shut up. The day after Jack's resignation, Robin came around to clinch the deal with the *News of the World*. Reporters were constantly asking more questions, then writing the answers in the first person, as though I had written the story. And the madness was set to continue for now I was going to be a movie star.

17

DANGEROUS DECEPTIONS

WHAT THE HELL IS GOING ON IN THIS COUNTRY?

Daily Mirror editorial, 6 June 1963

Walter Lyons made himself a busy man following Jack's resignation. I seemed to be on the front pages every day. Lyons turned me into a company called Millwarren. For him, it was to be a very profitable one. He and I were directors. I had ninety-nine shares and Lyons had one. I signed all the documents but I never read them. Lyons got all the money that came in and I was to be paid a salary by the company. My new legal representative advised me that I couldn't do anything to stop the film I had agreed to with Stephen, John Nash and Pelham as my signature on the back of an envelope was legal. He impressed me, however, for he had negotiated new agreements with them for me to play myself and he gave me a synopsis of the film. The world was interested in my story – and pictures.

Robin Drury had arranged for me to be photographed by Lewis Morley. Those memorable photographs will always be part of history for, in 1963, the year sexual intercourse began according to Philip Larkin, I became a symbol of the sexual revolution. I am always asked if I wore knickers for the shot astride the chair. I certainly did. But it had been a battle to keep them on.

Morley had wanted to photograph me without any clothes on but I used the chair to cover my bust and pulled up my white knickers around my waist. Although the illusion was that I was totally naked, I wasn't. I think Lewis captured in just twenty-nine frames every facial expression I have. That was it. And just as well: it was awkward sitting on a chair in a pose which threw all my weight forward. It was difficult but I have very good balance. I like the photographs. There is a mystery there, a mask on my face. I suppose that was because so much had happened and so much remained hidden, secret.

The picture has been used thousands of times world-wide but few people know who took it – many people attribute it to David Bailey as he is so associated with sixties photography. They also got it wrong about the chair which was meant to be by the modernist designer Arne Jacobson. It was a copy. The curve of the chair back, which so closely reflects the curve of a woman's body, was chance, an inspiration for a pose that has often been recreated. At times over the years I have hated it. It is always around and a constant reminder of those difficult days, but I do like it. I am now dealing fully with those times for I am not afraid of the fear any longer.

I was getting the movie-star treatment. John Nash took me to France for more photographs and a promotional film for the movie that was made a year later. Lyons arranged more photographs taken by another photographer, who had me posing playing a guitar and wearing a sombrero.

I also had a starring role in court as one court case seemed to lead straight into another. In the dock for the first case was Lucky Gordon. Then it was Stephen's turn. And finally mine. But I felt myself on trial in all three cases. I was in the spotlight all the time, still a rabbit in the headlines. It was a horrid, difficult time – events and people whizzed by – and it is important to set the record straight.

On the day Jack's resignation was announced, 5 June 1963, Lucky Gordon appeared in court charged with causing actual bodily harm to me. I was a witness along with Paula and Olive the housekeeper. Robin Drury, protective of his interests, came with me. Lucky had been in custody for some weeks and it was eerie knowing I was in the same building as him, even with all the police and security.

He pleaded not guilty, at which I had to smile for I could still feel his punches, the actual bodily harm. Surely he had to go to gaol, hadn't he? I had made a promise to Paula's two friends who had hauled Lucky off me that I would not implicate them so when I was asked whether I knew two men called Rudolph 'Truello' Fenton and Clarence Commachio I said I did not. I lied in court. I committed perjury.

On 6 June, while Jack and I were all over the world's front pages, Lucky dismissed his lawyers and told the judge he was going to conduct his own defence. In court he called me a prostitute and Stephen a pimp. He said he had caught venereal disease from me. I looked at the press bench and their shorthand pencils were blazing across their notebooks. I shouted that it was lies; I was almost hysterical trying to get the judge to stop Lucky from talking and the press from writing it all down. I was in tears when they escorted me out of court and Lucky carried on with his ravings, calling Stephen and me all sorts of names.

It didn't help him. He was sentenced to three years in gaol but as he was taken from court he sneered at me, 'I'll get you.' Walter Lyons was there and he got that remark put in the court record. In court, I approached Burrows and Herbert and said, 'About those people present I—'

Herbert stopped me in my tracks: 'Don't worry about that, Christine. Lucky is a very dangerous man.' He assured me that with the police records of Lucky's past attacks on me there was nothing for me to be concerned about. Lucky was on his way to gaol. I was, he assured me once again, completely safe. From Lucky – and the courts – if not from the headlines which trumpeted the case and Lucky's allegations.

At almost the same time as Lucky was going to the cells a conference was being arranged between Scotland Yard and their lawyers. Someone had tipped off Herbert and Burrows or their colleagues that Stephen was getting out of the country. They thought he was going to America where he still had friends and contacts from his time training as an osteopath. Given all the arrangements he had made and the travel documentation he had in Russian names, he was surely on his way to Moscow. What if?

There would have been another name to add to the runaway spies.

On 7 June, it was agreed that Stephen should be arrested and the next day, at the home of *News of the World* journalist Pelham Pound, he was. He was refused bail. The charges were of living off immoral earnings and that landed me seriously back in trouble.

Which was something I was already having with my 'manager' Robin Drury. He had brought in a friend called Alex to help me write my version of events and the two of them suddenly announced that Alex was to be paid fifteen thousand pounds for his efforts. It was absurd. I protested. Robin told me not to concern myself with such issues as money. I told him something that's always been my mantra: 'It's *my* life.'

Robin argued and said he was looking after me. I wanted to walk out with my rambling tapes but as a compromise Robin suggested that we burn them instead. I think he was surprised that I agreed to that but it was my life to control. The deal was done, a match struck, the tapes went up in flames and I walked out on Robin Drury. Lyons sacked him as my manager but he brought a wrongful dismissal lawsuit which was settled.

Lucky Gordon, with good legal reason, appealed against his sentence. On 11 June 1963, he said the two witnesses he wanted to call, Rudolph 'Truello' Fenton and Clarence Commachio, had not been present. I was relaxed about it for the two lads could only back up my story, tell what happened. They had seen Lucky attack me and pulled him off me. Paula and Olive Booker had also been witnesses to the attack so it was a situation I put as far back in my mind as I could. There was, after all, much else to worry about.

With Stephen under arrest, Michael Eddowes talked to the newspapers. He said I had told him Eugene had asked me to get secrets from Jack. He said he had given that information to Special Branch a week after Jack had denied in the Commons any 'impropriety' with me. Eddowes also said he had told Special Branch to talk to five people who had been 'intimately associated' with me. He didn't name the five but later said they were 'frightfully unimportant'. It meant nothing to me but more headlines. Eddowes said he had written to Harold Macmillan because the security people had 'ignored' him. He told the press: 'I was given to understand that the security police were watching both Profumo and Ivanov and had the matter in hand. This came from a source I had no reason to doubt.'

It all tumbled out in newsprint. I was not only sleeping with a Soviet spy, I was hopelessly in love with him and at his beck and call. It was nonsense. But not to 10 Downing Street. Harold Macmillan's private secretary, Harold Evans, contacted Lyons. There was one big question concentrating the prime minister's mind. Had I slept with another Tory minister? I hadn't and told Lyons the truth. He said he would negotiate with Harold Evans and see what could be done about Eddowes's statements. Macmillan called in Lord Denning the following day, 21 June 1963.

Stephen's trial was still about five weeks away and Herbert and Burrows turned up to tell me I might join him in the dock. They started off quizzing me about abortions – had I had one in London? Had Stephen arranged it? He was a doctor of sorts. It was the cat-and-mouse question game again and, as always, they returned to Stephen and girls. Had I got them for him? By now I was used to the routine – I had certainly done the training with these two. They talked to me thirty times, always cajoling and pressuring. In the end they talked to me in my bedroom at Paula's, wanting to find out if I had had an abortion in London.

I felt that they knew all the answers by then so there did not seem any point in lying. I knew they had interviewed all my friends, everyone I had ever known. They had questioned people from every place I had worked and even visited people from back home. This was one of the most thorough goings-over ever. Amongst the statements they had collected was one from Mandy saying that an abortion had been carried out at Wimpole Mews. It was true but Stephen had been trying to help the girl out. He had asked me and I called someone who contacted someone else and everything was taken care of safely. Stephen was not masterminding illegal abortions; he knew about it, that was all. The poor girl was neurotic: she didn't want the baby. She couldn't afford it. She had made a mistake. But Herbert made it clear that I would be charged with helping set up an illegal abortion if I did not sign a statement they had typed up. It was a reasonably accurate document and I signed.

The set-up was moving forward. Mandy wanted to get out of the country but ended up in Holloway Prison for a week on some trumped-up driving charge. That kept her in place and when she got out she was accused of stealing a television set and jailed again. This time she talked, about Emil Savundra 'the Indian doctor', and claimed to have been at the 'Man in the Mask' party, a story she had given to the *Sunday Pictorial* and repeated to the police. Sitting in a car in Hyde Park Square would not have earned her such big headlines.

Robin Drury then tried to get me in a corner. He was well aware that I had been paid £23,000 by the *News of the World*, and felt that he deserved some of it. I told him to get lost. I started to feel like it was open season on Christine Keeler.

Everyone wanted something from me. L'Hirondelle Restaurant in Swallow Street near Piccadilly Circus offered five thousand pounds a week for me to appear for twelve weeks in a 'satirical floor show', 'Turkish Delight'. I was to compère and introduce performers like Bob Newhart and Mort Sahl. But then Joseph Mourat who owned the club said that he was withdrawing his offer because of a threatened strike by the rest of the cast. Josephine Blake, who was the lead in the show, said she would walk out if I appeared. I felt sorry for Mourat; his hand was being forced by a very difficult person and Blake said she was supported by the club's dancers. I wrote them all off as small-minded but there were many like them without any grace or mercy. I was to find the vast majority of people only wanted to exploit my name for financial gain or simply to be associated with it for their personal vanity, their own warped gratification. There were offers to appear in cabaret in Las Vegas, to make films on the Continent and in Hollywood. Walter Lyons was looking after it all. There was even more interest when the *News of the World* published the story they had paid me £23,000 for. They illustrated it with one of Lewis Morley's photographs, one of me sitting on a car.

I was 'it'. The world was after me. In Pakistan, there was an outcry over a story that I had been sexually involved with President Ayub Khan. The Pakistan High Commission in London had to deny that the president's state visit to Britain was going to be cancelled. They said he had been alongside the pool at Cliveden – but not in the swimming pool with me. Which was true. It was just more flak. The police investigation was much more serious – they were going after me over the missing witnesses at Lucky Gordon's trial.

And then along came Clarence Commachio. I had to wonder at my luck. The sheer absurdity of chance still makes me smile. Why I didn't crack during up that summer of 1963, I will never know – other than putting it down to sheer bloody-mindedness.

John Hamilton-Marshall, Paula's troubled brother, was desperate for money. We had been rowing the day Lucky attacked me and John saw a profit in this. The newspapers offered him £500 for his story that he had hit me before Lucky arrived and went berserk. He also said his sister and I had committed perjury in court over the presence of Clarence Commachio and Rudolph 'Truello' Fenton that evening. The newspapers then got to Commachio. And he in turn got to me demanding money. I was furious at this attempt to blackmail me again, especially after I had risked so much to protect him and his friend Fenton who was also after money. They knew I was getting money from the *News of the World* and they wanted some of it.

I said I would meet Commachio and he said he had been promised £1,000 to sign the statement saying he was present at Paula's. He wanted me to match the newspaper money for him to stay silent. I said I wouldn't and he then mentioned the name of a policeman involved with Herbert and Burrows in the investigation of Stephen, Inspector James Axon. He had the detective's business card.

There was nothing I could do about it. I had received none of the *News of the World* money from Lyons and I was in no mood to pay anyone off. It was just as well. I did not know it then but the deck was stacked against me.

But not as much as it was against Stephen, who went on trial at the Old Bailey on 22 July 1963.

18

ROUGH JUSTICE

SCANDALOUS INFORMATION ABOUT WELL-KNOWN PEOPLE
HAS BECOME A MARKETABLE COMMODITY

Lord Denning, the 'Denning Report', 1963

Before the beginning of one of the greatest miscarriages of British justice ever, in early July 1963 I had to go to see Lord Denning at the government offices near Leicester Square. Denning had started hearing evidence on 24 June 1963, and interviewed Stephen three times and talked to Jack Profumo twice. He talked to lots of people – from the prime minister to newspaper owners and reporters, to six girls who knew Stephen.

I was not included in that half-dozen. I found myself a major player in the inquiry and had two interviews with Denning. I was allowed to have a legal representative and Walter Lyons went with me to the polished-wood-panelled offices Denning used. Denning was quietly spoken and asked me all the relevant questions, the ones I had expected. Questions like who had been present with Eugene and Stephen and where and when, and if I knew of any missiles. I answered him honestly. Denning had all the – well, all the ones they had given him – police, MI5 and CIA reports before him. He also had Sir Godfrey Nicholson's and Lord Arran's statements.

He knew that Stephen was a spy and that I knew too much. During my two sessions with him I told him all about Hollis and Blunt: how Stephen had politely introduced me and how I had said 'hello' and nodded when they visited. I told him all about Sir Godfrey's visit and how I had seen Sir Godfrey with Eugene. He asked me very precisely who had met Eugene and about the visitors to Wimpole Mews. He showed me a photograph of Hollis – it wasn't a sharp shot of him – and asked me to identify him. I told Denning this was the man who had visited Stephen. He showed me a photograph of Sir Godfrey and I also identified *him*. He did not show me a picture of Blunt for, I suspect, they already knew more than they wanted to know about Blunt. Denning was very gentle about it and I told him everything. This was the nice gentleman who was going to look after me. But I was ignored, side-lined – disparaged as a liar so that he could claim that there had been no security risk. It was the ultimate whitewash.

I told Denning that Stephen had wanted me dead because I could have betrayed them all. I told him I had been entrapped in Stephen's spy ring and had witnessed his meetings with double agents and Soviet spies. I told him I had taken sensitive material to the Russian Embassy. He ignored my evidence that Stephen Ward was a Russian spy and that one of the top men in British intelligence was a Moscow man. I was a young girl when I met Stephen Ward and not much more than a teenager when I was interviewed by Lord Denning. Like Stephen, he seemed a father figure.

I told him all about Stephen's spying activities and about high society decadence. Denning chose – as with everything in his flawed report – to ignore me for the national interest. I told him about Stephen saying John Kennedy was 'too dangerous' and would have to be 'put out of the picture'. That Kennedy was the main threat to world peace. A few months later Kennedy was killed in Dallas. I was told to be quiet or else. I was terrified.

Fearful about what secrets Stephen had sent to Moscow Centre, when he produced his report Denning had Eugene being introduced to Cliveden with Arran on 28 October 1962, and to Lord Ednam's home on 26 December 1962. He used dates and places to cover up all that happened and denied all the evidence he had from me and others. He wrote his report to have Mandy take over my life and had her living at Wimpole Mews on 31 October 1962. It was rubbish and it introduced her to people and events she knew nothing about. And Mandy made as much capital as she could from that.

It is clear to me now that Denning's agenda was set from the moment he was appointed. Why else would he have covered up, told such lies? He even wanted all his files, all the statements he took, destroyed, but they are locked away in a cabinet office and I hope future generations read them and understand the extent of his distortion of the truth. Three of the most important files are being censored until 'an unspecified date'; according to the civil service. When I asked a government official about them I was told they are 'too sensitive' to be released. Oh, really? Well you read it here first. All those years ago all Denning was required to do was to condemn me and have Stephen convicted as a ponce.

He had asked me if I had been present at the 'Man in the Mask' party and I told him the truth. But in his report he suggested I knew more than I did about that particular sex orgy and, in doing so, Denning deflected questions about Stephen's other espionage machinations and manipulations. The attitude was simply: let's blame Christine Keeler for everything.

I can tell now, for the first time, exactly what I did see at the 'Mask' party and also what Stephen Ward, who was present throughout, told me. But, first, a little more background about Mariella Novotny, notorious by then as the sex-queen hostess of London society, who had invited Stephen that Christmas time in 1961. Mariella called herself the government's 'Chief Whip'. She also hosted 'salons' gathering together important people for dinners which didn't end in sexual hysterics. People like the then Earl Spencer – Princess Diana's grandfather – would attend the demure dinners which were about gathering information rather than indulging the guests' peculiar peccadilloes. Stephen went to these too, the only difference being that he kept all his clothes on, not just his black socks.

When she was not hosting orgies Mariella was sleeping with important men like President Kennedy before he took over the White House, and his brother Bobby. One item that Mariella treasured was the black mask with slits for eyes and laces up the back which, over the years, has become infamous. Even Denning admitted he was told she had kept the mask. It was her memento from the party which was also known as the 'Feast of Peacocks', a lavish dinner in which this man wearing only the mask and a tiny apron – one like the waitresses wore in 1950s tearooms – asked to be whipped if people were not happy with his 'services'. He also got a lash or two as the guests arrived at Hyde Park Square.

One evening towards the Christmas of 1961 Stephen asked me to pick him up from a party – his Jaguar had engine trouble and was in the garage. My friends were banned from Stephen's and that included Mandy. But she had a car and was willing to go with me to pick up Stephen so he agreed to that. She did go with me to collect Stephen from the party being hosted by Mariella but she sat in the car as I went in. Later, she would muddy the already dirty waters with nonsense about her involvement. She knew nothing about what was really going on – about Stephen's devious thinking and plotting. I wasn't busy so I agreed to help, not knowing I was walking into one of the most talked-about gatherings of the past century.

When I arrived at the house to collect Stephen I could not find him outside where he was meant to be waiting for me so I went into Mariella's on my own to try to find him. I wandered into a bedroom and saw Mariella rolling about on the bed wearing a black corset which exposed her breasts and with the snap catch between her legs undone. There were five naked men on the bed with her, all of whom looked respectable – if nude men, some aroused, some satisfied, can be called respectable. They were certainly not a rough crowd but groomed, manicured men, the barrister-MP type but without their blue pin-striped suits. Mariella was certainly giving them what they wanted, pleasuring them every which way. None of them took a blind bit of notice of me, they were so intent on their fun. Hod Dibben was in the room, naked but just watching. So was Stephen.

Stephen seemed most amused by events. He said Mariella had served up roast peacocks and prairie oysters – bulls' testicles – but all everyone was interested in was the sex. Girls marched around in high heels and trashy lingerie; there were whips and handcuffs. There were girls giving oral sex to one man while being taken from behind by another. And they kept changing roles. When one man had come often enough another would take his place. There were girls going at it together as others watched and masturbated. Stephen was naked but got dressed quickly. He told me the story of the man in the mask and he even gave me his name. I hate to admit this but I've forgotten it. It was not a household name but, as I recall, from an aristocratic family. There were other things still to learn that I have not forgotten and they involved Mariella in more than sex. She was clever with her teasing and was revealing about everything but the truth. I was fascinated by how clever she was. She gave enough information about the 'salons' she hosted to be titillating but no more than that in an interview for the *Sunday Mirror* in 1977.

> When I was living in Hyde Park Square in the early sixties, I used to host frequent dinners, drinks and weekend parties. The parties were glittering affairs with eight-feet-high flower arrangements and the best silver for seven or eight courses. The 'Man in the Mask' was a frequent guest. In fact, he and I had a sexual relationship for some years, ended only by his death. One particular night at the flat there were about twenty-five guests. After dinner when the servants had been dismissed, guests were given to understand that they could let their hair down. Some guests took off their clothes and sexual intercourse began taking place in various rooms. Nobody bothered to keep anything secret from anyone else. If they had wanted to, they wouldn't have been invited in the first place. On this night the masked man was one of those who took off his clothes.
>
> He liked to be humiliated in front of people he considered his equals, and one of his quirks was to eat his dinner after the other guests. He would get down on all fours and eat from a dog's bowl. He ate scraps. This time he stripped off his evening clothes and donned a white apron and a black mask. He wore nothing else. I was his mistress and he wanted only to be under my domination.

He would do anything I told him. I would tell him to go and give pleasure to another female. He did so in public view. He loathed it and yet he loved it. He would only ever make love to me in private. The other guests never knew the identity of the man under the mask because it covered his whole face. He would always remain until they had gone. All sorts of things happened at my parties. They happened quite naturally as a certain atmosphere developed. I will never forget one when a well-known MP, leaning on the chimney-piece naked, went into one of his really hot political tirades as though he was addressing the House. The rest of the people were also naked.

It may sound today like the plot of some Channel 5 television series, but it shows the dangerous social lives some of the top people in Britain were indulging in and you can easily understand the American security services being 'wary about the Brits'. But for Stephen the sex was just a means to help his espionage activities.

There were all sorts of stories about who The Man in the Mask was but it was all to divert attention from the espionage muddle. I know that the Special Branch spread some of the more outrageous stories and others were 'filtered' by the security services. Denning said I talked to the press about who the naked man in the frilly apron was and I did mention Ernest Marples who was the Tory Minister of Transport but that was just flak, dirty tricks inspired by Stephen.

The Man in the Mask? The word was the man was a government minister or a Tory grandee, an aristocrat. Rumours have gone on for years. I can't clear it up. I don't think anyone will now with Stephen and others dead. Hod would have known but he banked his information, like Stephen, 'for a rainy day'.

Denning, in his report, also talked about another man – this one had no mask and no head. 'The Man without a Head' featured in a photograph in which Margaret, Duchess of Argyll, wearing only a string of pearls, is performing oral sex on a man whose head is not visible. The photograph was produced in evidence during the Argyll divorce case in Edinburgh in March 1963. One government minister was said to have shown his penis to Harold Macmillan to prove it was not him. In fact, Duncan Sandys, one of Macmillan's ministers and the son-in-law of Winston Churchill, felt obliged to give Denning a photograph of his penis to show it wasn't his distinctive organ the Duchess was performing on. My former bed companion Douglas Fairbanks Junior denied for years that it was him. He would. When he was asked in 1963 by a group of *Daily Express* reporters about his friendship with Stephen, he quickly replied: 'Well, Max Aitken knows him too.' Aitken owned the *Express* and the newspaper suddenly stopped all those inquiries. But Fairbanks was the ultimate sexual swordsman; he wanted it all the time and in the circles I moved in there was never any doubt that he was the man in the photograph being pleasured by the Duchess of Argyll who had a reputation for being a formidable practitioner of oral sex. And the pictures? When Fairbanks was in action a camera was never far away. There have always been stories that there were a lot more and that they are now in a vault in Edinburgh where the Argyll divorce case was heard in the Court of Session.

Certainly, the not-so-good and mighty provided enough distraction from the serious business of spying and contributed to the cover-up with the trial of Dr Stephen Ward.

19

THE TRIALS OF
CHRISTINE KEELER

IF YOU WANT TO BE REALLY SUCCESSFUL, RELIABILITY AND DETERMINATION
ARE WHAT YOU MUST HAVE.

Stephen Ward to Christine Keeler, 1961

British justice has not much changed in the twenty-first century.
The masters, those who pull the strings of all of us, are still in
command. I vote Conservative which, ironically, in the early part
of the millennium put me in the minority.

New Labour appeared to me to be a bunch of control freaks, just
more ardent, more determined to bring in rules and take away our
freedoms. What I have learned most is that those who would lead
have agendas rather than feelings or emotions. Power makes people
think they can do anything – with events and with people. Which
is why they fear and strike out at those who do not conform.
Where's the justice in Stephen Ward going on trial for living off
immoral earnings when he should have been arrested as a Russian
spy?

Where's the justice in Bill Astor – albeit that he only survived
until 1966 – not being brought to account for his indulgences, his
peccadilloes? Who lies wins? Who manipulates wins? Expedience is
the code of conduct?

Anthony Blunt was discovered to be a spy in 1964 in the aftermath of the Profumo affair. From my researches and those of others
it would appear that the security services were aware of that as early
as 1951. Nothing was done for many, many years. And then only

when the government's hand was forced. Sir Anthony Blunt was not unmasked until 1979 when Margaret Thatcher had no choice but to admit it. A book was published all but naming him as the Fourth Man. He was stripped of his knighthood but that was it. He ran away and lived abroad in relative luxury until he died in 1983. Justice? Certainly, English-style.

Blunt was educated at Marlborough and, acting for King George VI, he was responsible for smuggling sensitive Hanoverian documents and other effects out of Germany in 1945 and placing them in a safe at Windsor Castle. He was an expert on the seventeenth-century artist Nicolas Poussin and owned one of Poussin's last works, 'Rebecca at the Well', which hung in his flat at the Courtauld. I never found him a pleasant man. At least Hollis would smile a 'hello'. Blunt was the opposite, aloof and awfully arrogant. He certainly thought nothing of me; he was condescending.

He was also a spy who was allowed to live a lie as surveyor of the Queen's pictures for sixteen years from when we know for certain he was discovered to be a Moscow agent. Why was he not exposed? Embarrassment? Whose wonderful idea was it to leave him alone? Here was a man trying with Stephen Ward and Roger Hollis to get nuclear secrets to Moscow – a man cleared by one inquiry after another.

What the hell was going on in the secret world that we still do not know about? And what is going on now?

While most people must have smiled a little at the story of the 'granny spy', Melita Norwood, in 2000, it made me consider again all that had gone on during the early sixties. It came out that MI5 had not told the Home Secretary or the Attorney General that Norwood, who was then eighty-seven, had been unmasked as a KGB agent in 1992. She escaped prosecution and was living a chocolate-box country life in Kent. Her name and those of others were revealed in 1992 when Vasili Mitrokhin of the KGB defected, bringing his files with him to the West.

Without telling any government officials or the Crown Prosecution Service, MI5 decided it would not be worth arresting Norwood; the argument was that Mitrokhin's evidence could not be used in court.

They also said it could jeopardize ongoing investigations. And I thought the Cold War had ended.

When the Mitrokhin archive was published in September 1999, all hell broke loose with Norwood and others being named, including a university lecturer and a former policeman who was a 'Romeo' agent who went around seducing staff at embassies.

Reports were commissioned by the Home Secretary, Jack Straw. What a surprise that the investigators recommended the strengthening of procedures monitoring the security and intelligence services so that government ministers are kept fully informed of any breach of national security. Nothing changes but the personnel. As ever, 'national security' is the blanket excuse for all those who operate in the twilight zone. They are people without shadows.

Stephen Ward's trial in June 1963 was a farce orchestrated by those from an invisible constituency. One question that was never answered was who instigated the police case against Stephen? And we all played our part. Mandy and I were brought into it but lined up with hardened prostitutes. The whole case was weighted against Stephen: he was a pimp and we were supposedly all his girls, his 'popsies' as the police termed it.

To arrive at a case against Stephen all sorts of lies and half-truths, sprinkled with circumstantial evidence, were employed by a number of parties whose interests were involved. The *Daily Telegraph* called it the 'most lurid *cause célèbre* since Oscar Wilde'.

I knew the public hated me. It was obvious from the force with which they were throwing eggs at me – and screaming at me – their shouts coming out as one, synchronized into a piercing howl. There was a scrum when I arrived for the trial with policemen being shoved around by people trying to get a look at me.

Finally, they brought me into the courts through the judges' private car park. I did not want to be there, to be part of the set-up, but I was in the witness box for two hours and thirty-eight minutes as my character and those of most of the others in court were shredded. They had given me sedatives and I felt woozy but when I looked over at Stephen who wore a tight smile but frightened eyes as he sat in the dock, I made myself be strong, be resilient.

It was not easy. It was like sitting with Herbert and Burrows again – the questions kept coming at me. The same old questions but never in context. Sex. Money. Who? Where? How many times? I had been coerced into signing my statement, which was in some ways the truth, but the way it was being presented and interpreted in court was nothing like the reality. Stephen had never had to live off women. There may have been money handed around but it was never as though he was running a brothel. It was no sex-for-rent operation.

Stephen used girls to gain influence, not cash. This was something that was tritely glazed over at the Old Bailey where in Court Number One it was standing-room only for the eight days of the trial. I've often read about big court cases being tagged the 'Trial of the Century' by the newspapers but this was more the 'Mistrial of the Century' and one that did indeed affect the second half of the twentieth century arguably more than any other.

The lifestyle of the nation's rich and famous was on trial along with Stephen.

I didn't know how I was going to live with any of it. I had seen Stephen briefly when he was on bail following a preliminary hearing and he had looked worn out. Now, in the dock, he seemed overwhelmed by it all.

The judge, Sir Archibald Marshall, was clearly ready to hear it *all*. And it came spilling out: from Diana Dors' former husband's two-way mirrors, to my relationship with Peter Rachman and, very damagingly, Mandy's sex games with Emil Savundra. There was the twenty pounds that Jack had given me for my mother and there was Major Jim, the only one of these so-called 'clients' who appeared in court. Bill Astor and the others were never invited to appear. My involvement with Major Jim was damaging for Stephen although in two years he only had one chance meeting with him.

In the witness box I gave evidence about meeting Stephen at Murray's and it seemed to go on from there; every meeting or man was another raised eyebrow from Judge Marshall or the prosecutor, Mervyn Griffith-Jones. How I hated those evil men going about their bad business in those toffee-voiced tones. This was dog-eat-dog for Stephen was one of them. Griffith-Jones tried to establish that Stephen had been in the flat with Jack or Eugene – he wanted me to testify that Stephen had been standing round the corner, as it were, waiting for me to hand over money. It was so wrong what they were being allowed to do.

Stephen's barrister was the Rumpolesque James Burge and he was a welcome face in front of the witness box but he troubled me by asking, although I expected it, about Lucky Gordon and the missing witnesses. I said again – in court, again – that they had not been there when Lucky attacked me.

I was deeply hurt at having to give such evidence against Stephen. I had not wanted to do that despite everything. It was such a carve-up. And it continued after I left the witness box.

Sally Nowells who I had introduced to Stephen gave evidence only identified as Miss X. She said she had liked Stephen and had had an affair with him because she wanted to. The second girl, from the dress shop opposite the Kenco, was called Miss Y and she said she had an enjoyable affair with Stephen.

Mandy was on next. She was dressed up and in full make-up, full warpaint. We were having our hair done every day for the trial, trying to look our best, at Vidal Sassoon's in Bond Street.

Griffith-Jones implied that Mandy had been established in a prostitution business by Stephen. He tried to make out that Bill Astor had paid a cheque for our rent in return for sex. Mandy explained that the cheque had been given two years before she had sex with Bill Astor, and that the sex had been for fun. Bill had denied the sex but he would, wouldn't he? When Mandy was asked about Savundra she admitted that he had given her money after sex. But she never said she gave Stephen any of the money – he was always complaining about her running up enormous telephone accounts. But Miss X agreed that Stephen had mentioned performing in front of two-way mirrors so voyeurs could enjoy themselves. The damage was done before she could point out it had been said as a joke.

Inspector Herbert's friend Ronna Riccardo had lied at the preliminary hearing about having sex for money that she then gave to Stephen. Herbert had forced the statement from her by threats against her family. She retracted it at the trial but it made no difference; no one paid any attention to what Ronna 'the Lash' Riccardo had to say. I listened and watched it all, in disbelief, I want to say, but by then I did not expect any better treatment for anyone in the front line of this court case.

The police had produced from somewhere a girl called Vickie Barrett who, after the case in 1963, vanished off the face of the earth. Since helping to hammer the nails in Stephen's coffin, she has never to my knowledge been seen again. I suspect she was spirited out of the country, given a new identity, a new life.

Stephen must have known Vickie but I had never seen her before. She told her story: she was a prostitute and when she was stopped and questioned by the police in Notting Hill it was discovered that she had met Stephen. Herbert got involved then in his usual rounds of the cesspits. Vickie told the all-ears Judge Marshall that Stephen had picked her up in Oxford Street and taken her home to have sex with his friends. She didn't seem to know who these friends were, but they were apparently always to be found on freezing cold winter nights, lying naked on Stephen's bed, waiting to be whipped into satisfied shape by Vickie. She said Stephen had been paid by these friends and kept the money for her in a little drawer until it piled up. She described Stephen handing out horsewhips, canes, contraceptives and coffee and how, having collected her weapons, she had treated the waiting clients. It sounded, and was, nonsense. I had lived with Stephen and never seen any evidence of anything like that.

When they put Herbert in the witness box and he was asked whether there had been any suggestion to the witnesses that they would be in trouble if they didn't sign the statements, he replied: 'I cannot recall so doing.'

What an epitaph that is for the Stephen Ward trial. The policeman would not even deny nobbling the witnesses.

Then, Judge Marshall did exactly that to the jury. He might have shouted 'Guilty' rather than bothering to instruct them. Only half of his summing-up was complete when the court adjourned on 30

July 1963, but it was travesty enough. I could see the hopelessness all over Stephen's face. There had to be a guilty verdict. Everyone, including Stephen, knew that. With him in gaol for probably three years or more what else would be found out? Better to destroy all the evidence, better to destroy himself?

Stephen was fifty-one then. He was staying with the man I had always wanted, Noel Howard-Jones, who had stood by him during the trial along with others like the reporter Pelham Pound. It was only in 1999 that I found out all the details of Stephen's suicide via Pelham's son Stephen.

Stephen Pound became the Labour MP for Ealing North when New Labour were elected in 1997. As a fifteen-year-old lad he had run errands for his dad during Stephen's trial but it was only all these years later that he produced an answer to something that had always puzzled me. Where did Stephen get the drugs to kill himself for he was no longer at his own place or going to his treatment rooms? Pelham Pound had resigned from the *News of the World* and styled himself Stephen's literary agent. He also put up the bail for him – Stephen was arrested at Pelham's home. During the trial young Stephen Pound and his father used to take Stephen home in a taxi at 4.30. The last night they were driving past Harrods when Pelham asked his son, 'Can you pop out and get this prescription?' Neither he nor his father had any idea that Stephen was contemplating suicide. The prescription was for Nembutal.

That was the drug Stephen used to kill himself after writing some notes, one of which said: 'It is really more than I can stand, the horror, day after day at the court and in the streets. I am sorry to disappoint the vultures.'

I was devastated by it all. I couldn't breathe properly. It was a sort of asthma but so acute I thought I would die. Stephen was taken to, of all places, St Stephen's Hospital. As he lay dying in agony – it took seventy-nine hours – Judge Marshall again instructed the jury. They found Stephen guilty of living off the immoral earnings of Mandy and myself. Stephen did not survive to hear the verdict.

I have survived and never cried so deeply since then. I've had tears but never the emotional bursts I had after Stephen's death. It was as much for me as for Stephen. I had been robbed of the truth. I had told it to the police and to Denning but this is what it had resulted in. There seemed no one in the world I could trust. Except Walter Lyons. He was like a father-figure to me but I was crazy for a time.

One day I was so angry I nearly committed murder. I was in the car and, as they walked past, I heard some complete strangers putting Stephen down, calling him dirty names. My hatred was violent and complete. As they were crossing the road I took my foot off the clutch. I put my foot down on the accelerator and drove straight towards them. I hated them: why should they live so they could sneer at Stephen and call me a prostitute? I drove on and on towards them. At the very last moment, I hooted and they managed to jump clear of me.

Lucky Gordon was freed on appeal at the beginning of August because of the missing witnesses, Rudolph 'Truello' Fenton and Clarence Commachio. I was expected to fly to Copenhagen to make *The Christine Keeler Story*. Mr Lyons, who was selling my story around the world, advised me to go, to get out of the country and avoid being arrested. But I cancelled the flight plans and stayed at Paula Hamilton-Marshall's flat in Marylebone. Mandy was also being asked about a film the day after Stephen died and Bill Astor went racing at Goodwood. For some, life would go on as normal. It had been a hiccup in the routine. There were also trivial repercussions. Although I was a regular, a good client for about two years at Vidal Sassoon's in Mayfair, I was banned because society women objected to sitting near me. The so-called VIPs included a European princess, the Duchess of Bedford, Lady Listowel, Lady Rendlesham, Lady Moorea Wyatt and actresses like Margaret Leighton, Dorothy Tutin and Georgia Brown. Vidal got around it by offering to send his stylists to me. I didn't really care.

They weren't going to be styling my hair in Holloway Prison.

The courts now had Robin Drury's tapes in which I talked about the two guys being at the flat and about Paula's brother getting physical with me. They also had statements from Commachio and Fenton that they had been present. I was in the bath at the flat in Devonshire Street when they arrested me for perjury. Olive Booker and Paula were also charged with telling lies at Lucky's trial at the Old Bailey. When we left Paula's I told the detectives the quickest way to Marylebone Police Station; it had been my home from home for weeks. The police were unhelpful as I tried to get Mr Lyons to free me and when he first asked for bail that night it was refused. And what a cast the prosecution had for the preliminary hearing: Robin Drury with his terrible tapes, Lucky Gordon with his crazy love and John Hamilton-Marshall. They also called Burrows. Lucky was my only break: he admitted he had hit me outside Paula's flat.

I was facing charges which carried a long prison sentence, but finally I went home on three thousand pounds bail. When I was arrested I was finalizing plans to buy my mother and stepfather a house in the country, a hideaway from all the publicity and trouble. Then, when the trial began, my real father appeared. Lyons tried to warn me off but we had a good talk – I loved him, even though we had not met since 1946. Colin King was now fifty-six years old. He seemed bright and intelligent and I felt so close to him.

With the *News of the World* money I had bought a house for £13,000 in Linhope Street in Marylebone; it was close to where Jenny Harvey lived and it felt good having an old friend nearby. My real father came around to the house for us to talk during the trial. He said I hadn't changed but what did he know? He hadn't seen me since I was four. He came to court every day during the trial and the court officials were kind to him giving him a seat near the police box, just a few yards away from me in dock. I could see my features in him, which I found reassuring. Here, surely, was unconditional love when I needed it most.

It was clear the prosecution would do a deal. If I pleaded guilty at the trial proper to conspiracy to obstruct the course of justice and to perjury, charges of wrongfully accusing Lucky of assault and Commachio of blackmail would be dropped. My legal advice was to go for it – asking for the court's pardon and with mitigation I would get a six-month prison term. It did not sound too terrible – certainly not after what had happened. It would also stop Lucky from suing for wrongful arrest – and getting any of my *News of the World* money. Without the deal, Lyons said I would be convicted of all the charges.

I pleaded guilty and got nine months, not six. Paula was gaoled for six months. Olive, a kind woman, got off with a year's probation and I was glad about that and sorry for Paula. I was not sorry for myself. Or not too sorry. Lyons would look after my affairs for me. He, of course, was taking over my life, writing articles as me which were being sold with photographs around the world for a healthy revenue.

I soon found myself in Holloway being tested for venereal disease, fingerprinted and having my 'mug shot' taken. I was inside. There was nothing dignified about that world; it was cold in every sense; the food and most of the people were unpleasant. They set a psychiatrist on me and I eventually took an IQ test – 141. I then took Spanish lessons twice a week with Joan Bakewell, the broadcaster, who was doing social work in prisons. The other prisoners didn't mean much to me and mostly kept to themselves. The routine gave me an inner freedom. Everything was organized in prison: I did not need to think, just keep out of trouble. By doing that I was released early from Holloway after six months and two weeks.

I made a good friend in prison, Libby Crawley, who was in for helping her burglar husband. While I was in Holloway threatening letters were sent: there were people outside those walls that wanted me dead. I was terrified. Lyons arranged with the police and the prison governor a safe way for my release. He had also arranged two photographers to take pictures of me that he could sell. One photo session was in the country with my mother and the other at Linhope Street.

Lyons warned me that my real father was trying to sell his story to the newspapers and I refused to see him. Et tu, Daddy? At the same time Lucky Gordon contacted Lyons and through him, for one hundred pounds, sold me the sketch Stephen had drawn of me at the cottage at Cliveden. Lyons wrote a first-person story about my prison life. It suited me as I just wanted to be left alone by the press. I trusted Lyons and genuinely believed he cared for me. I signed everything that he put in front of me.

I had considered and reconsidered everything. I thought of all that had happened and could happen to me. I thought of the dangers and decided to keep my own counsel over much that had occurred.

I was twenty-two and just wanted to get on with my own life. This was supposedly the new beginning, starting with spend, spend, spend. I bought a mink jacket and a car as I wanted something faster than my Mini but Lyons didn't allow me a high-powered car. He had the bank accounts, he was paying the bills.

Suddenly, Harry, the body-building Greek, appeared at my front door with all his suitcases. He said he was going to look after me. He fixed a plane to take me out of the country but too much had happened since the days when he used to carry me up the stairs for exercise. I wanted to move on; I had to start my life again somehow now that Stephen had gone.

My father came to see me but without any reporters. Despite Lyons' warning, I allowed him to stay with me for a few days and we patched things up; blood *is* thicker. I knew Billy Butlin and he helped me by arranging to get my father a job as a photographer at Butlin's camp at Clacton. My mother was furious that he had been staying with me and I didn't want to upset her so I asked him to go. I wish I had never done that.

Kim Proctor, who was staying at the Linhope Street house with me, brought around John Rudd who seemed a nice enough sort of person. He had been imprisoned in South Africa for having an affair with a black woman and he told me how he'd felt drawn to me because of that. He certainly was not my type but good fun; he had a fancy history for his grandfather had founded the de Beers diamond business with Oppenheimer. He was a bit of a snob and bragged that the company would not function without a Rudd in it. Linhope Street became something of a salon. I would have bridge parties and the Mexican actor Cantinflas who everyone loved in

Around the World in Eighty Days was once my card partner. He was a great player. Peter Lewin's crowd came around; they were a good bunch. Libby, my prison friend, also visited and I helped her to get on her feet.

I had been seeing a man called Mark Warman who had introduced me to the Ad Lib Club which was one of Britains' first popular discos. It was run by Brian Morris, a nephew of Al Bennet who owned the Stork Room and the Pigalle. Mark and I were not right for romance but he remained a close friend for many years and I started dating another friend of Kim Proctor's, Dr Carley Pricopi. He was a white Russian, dark and handsome, and we started an affair. Carley didn't approve of Lyons.

'Why don't you look after your own affairs, Christine?' 'Oh, I trust Lyons,' I said. 'Don't trust anyone, you silly girl.' But I defended Lyons: 'Carley, I know I can trust him. He really does care for me.' Carley was a kind man and he gave me an enormous religious painting which he told me had been in his family for generations. His family had managed to get out of Russia during the revolution. He wanted to get to know about Lyons and when he spoke to him about the painting, he asked about my business situation. Lyons did not like him and put the telephone down. It was the first indication that he did not want anyone else interesting themselves in my financial arrangements. Carley and I fell out but not about Lyons and our affair ended.

Kim had also brought around Anthony Edgar who was the heir to the H. Samuel jewellery chain. His father had made him join the army as a regular soldier and Anthony hated it. He was rather feminine and he got a lot of stick but he certainly was not gay. Far from it: he loved women. He was very handsome with a good physique but not my type. But he made me laugh as he was so inhibited, so uptight. He was like a big kid and never took anything seriously in those days. He became friendly with John Rudd.

Men were becoming a habit – they were around me all the time. I did not mind the attention; after all I had been through, I wanted people close to me, around me. The problem was what was attracting these men. They wanted me, wanted to *have* Christine Keeler. They did not want to be involved with me in a romantic relationship. As a sexual scalp, I was a trophy to boast to the boys about but not take home to Mummy.

20

LUST AND MARRIAGE

CAN'T YOU JUST SEE ME AS FIRST LADY?

Marilyn Monroe to her best friend
Jeanne Carmen, 1962

I have not lived with a man since 1978. I find it impossible. Ever since the Profumo Affair, I have never known if a man was capable of loving me for me and not for being Christine Keeler. It's like being an heiress except I had inherited the flotsam of folly rather than a fortune. It meant I never had to buy a drink at the Ad Lib Club which became the centre of my social life. It was loud and popular and everybody seemed to be someone or was trying to be. Although I was emotionally confused I had the confidence to deal with all the attention, with the men, but I have to admit that sometimes my relationships got a little complicated.

I had lost my driving licence on speeding charges and was driving on a provisional licence so I needed someone to sit next to me to keep it all legal. I didn't want any more problems. The man who took the passenger's seat was Billy Meak who was buying the Mini through the company, Millwarren, on the never-never, hire purchase. He was a bit of a cliché, the cheerful Cockney always willing to help and one day he turned up with, Freddy, a young man I was instantly attracted to. Freddy's uncle by marriage was Charlie Kray, the older brother of the notorious twins. Charlie worked in his brothers' clubs often arranging entertainment so he knew lots of 'names' like Judy Garland, Muhammad Ali then Cassius Clay, and Sonny Liston. Freddy loved all the glamour.

I met everyone at the Ad Lib but my heart, or so it seemed to me, belonged to Freddy. I had money and paid for the two of us to take off to Spain. Lyons wanted a writer to tag along for he had some deal going on a story about me and could fix something with Spanish taxes. It was all rather vague and I said I wanted the sun, sand and Freddy and nobody else – except Billy Meak who was going to help drive my new Triumph down to Marbella. Spain was a joy, so relaxing. We walked on the sand and messed around in the fishing villages but I think it was too far away from the city lights for Freddy. He got increasingly irritable. After a spectacular row in a local restaurant, I stormed off and walked back to the villa we had rented. Freddy was furious: he started driving after me and he was going to run me over. His driving was so bad, so dangerous the villagers wanted to lynch him. We had to hide from them as Billy calmed them down. The holiday was over, as was my honeymoon with Freddy.

Lyons was not happy with me taking off for Spain, spending money without his knowledge. He came around for a meeting and created quite a scene: 'You know that I look after your affairs. You are like the daughter that I could never have.' He was almost in tears. Olivier would have applauded.

'I know that, Mr Lyons, and I'm very grateful,' I assured him.

'You arranged to take your holiday with Freddy and Billy without even consulting me and you know I take care of your affairs.'

'Don't worry Mr Lyons, you can handle everything next time,' I said, wanting to keep him happy, and he seemed satisfied with that. I thought the money would simply keep arriving if I kept Lyons on my side. So I kept him even happier by agreeing to his demands to be photographed topless for *Nova* magazine.

I wasn't so keen to keep Freddy happy, I was getting bored with him. His idea of glamour was pubs smothered in clouds of blue cigarette smoke and echoing with loud talk. He had a key but I would throw him out for a few weeks then take him back. I kept going to the Ad Lib and one night ended up dancing with Ringo Starr. The Fab Four were the biggest thing in the world and we were great curiosities on the dance floor. Which is why we ended up in bed together the next morning, the morning Freddy turned up unexpectedly for a reconciliation.

If it had been anyone else but a Beatle I think he might have bashed Ringo about. As it was, he was so taken aback when he saw it was Ringo in bed with me that he did nothing, just stood there gawping. Ringo made a break for it – and broke my banister as he went. He got married for the first time a week later.

The money did not keep rolling in. In fact, there was a dramatic shortage. Lyons told me that I would have to sell my house and move into something smaller and in February 1965 I took a three-year lease on a place at Elm Park Mansions in Barnes. I hated it, a one-bedroomed arrangement that looked more like a council flat. I sold Linhope Street, which had been my refuge, and gave Anthony Edgar my mink jacket to look after for me. Barnes seemed like the Outer Hebrides and I stayed mostly at John Rudd's flat just off Bond Street as he was abroad most of the time on business. Tony Hancock lived in the flat below.

An admirer it would hurt too much to name came to visit me but the outside door was closed. Determined to get in, he went up the fire escape and climbed into Hancock's bedroom. Hancock was in bed at the time and my friend just walked through his bedroom, through the flat and out the front door. Hancock never said a word. I would see him sometimes and he would just stare at me. I found it funnier than 'The Blood Donor'. I'm not sure he did.

Of all the famous people of the time that I met I think I was most fond of George Peppard. He had just made *Breakfast at Tiffany's* with Audrey Hepburn and was a Hollywood leading man on the way up. He was kind to me and we had a long romance which only faded because of the Atlantic.

We kept in touch even when he became a popular television star as the insurance investigator in *Banacek* and in the 1980s with *The A-Team*. Others wanted only one thing, but often they said another. The Austrian actor Maximilian Schell said he was doing research for a film and took me to dinner at the Dorchester but it went no further than that. He was a strange one who looked at me all the time as though I was a newspaper puzzle.

For me, it was clear from the start that Warren Beatty could do anything he wanted. He was gorgeous and fun and talked all the time: he certainly talked me into bed. The freedom was marvellous but I wondered as much about my capability for monogamous love as that of the men I was dating. We were all terribly young and the diktat of the time was to forget inhibitions, focus on fun and love. It was hedonistic and so thoroughly selfish, so typically youthful.

Lyons, through Millwarren, exchanged the Mini and the Triumph for a Sprite in a further economy move but my social whirl continued with an eclectic bunch of people. John Rudd introduced me to Hugh and Hanja Bebb who had arrived from South Africa and introduced me to Sean Morrisey and his wife Shirley. Sean was considered the best sculptor of his time. A chap called Denis Evans, who was a chemist, rented a room from them.

When they invited me to stay the night, I was shown into a room where they hung Sean's pornographic paintings. Denis was the ugliest man I had ever met and was taking heroin at the time. I was terrified of him; with those paintings hanging all round and Denis in the next room I was afraid to stay the night. I didn't mind wild times but this was too weird.

Hanja and I went on holiday to the South of France where we ended up at a party hosted by Gunther Sachs in the days before he married Brigitte Bardot. He offered to put me a film. Everyone, even multimillionaires, wanted a piece of me, a piece of the action. But John Rudd had flown down and we had business back in London. I was going international. I had no idea of the extent of the money that Lyons was making through the use of my name worldwide. I was being marketed like a Hollywood movie is today. They were stamping my name and image on anything they thought they could sell. Especially sex stories, photos, serializations and films about me that didn't appear in Britain and I could have no knowledge of.

Lyons had set up Zimbabwe Gemstones with John Rudd. It was an offshore shadow company and all my dealings with Millwarren were transferred to it. Companies I had dealt with and percentage due were shown by the vowels, which represented numbers, in the company name. It was set up to avoid the attention of the tax authorities. And me.

Slowly, ever so slowly, I was getting disillusioned with London nightlife and even more so with the people in it. There seemed no depth. Only one thing seemed important to so many people I met – themselves.

John Rudd loaned me his Mercedes and I decided to visit my mother at the bungalow I had bought her in Wokingham with some of the *News of the World* money. I don't know exactly what happened but a tyre burst on the way and I crashed. I remember seeing the trees going round and round as I lay on the seat but I was unhurt; not a bruise on me but the car was a write-off.

Was it an omen? I thought I would be better off in the country and I bought a bungalow near my mother. It was the beginning of my attempts to escape from being Christine Keeler. Lyons arranged the deal on the purchase of the bungalow and kept the deeds.

And that was when Jim Levermore arrived in my life, at a time when I wanted to be nothing other than 'normal'. Jim was a rugged man, a working man; he was straightforward and said what he thought. His agenda did not follow him in the door. He had dated my old friend from Wraysbury, Jackie White, and when I was visiting my mother she introduced us. At that precise moment in my life he was Prince Charming, just what I wanted.

He was a strapping six feet tall and looked and talked nothing but stability. He worked for a company of civil engineering contractors. He had lived close to me, near Staines in Middlesex, when I was growing up in Wraysbury.

We had a quiet romance and I really wanted to get married, to become someone else, to be Mrs James Levermore. I honestly believed we could make a go of a marriage: he seemed able to love me just because of who I was. But as I was nervous I changed my hairstyle to get away from the publicity. I didn't want anyone to know me as Christine Keeler in future, just plain Mrs Levermore.

Lyons was a witness and he helped me to keep the marriage, by special licence at Wokingham district register office in Reading, reasonably quiet. The special licence meant we only had to give three days' notice of intent to marry and they keep the details in a notice book which can only be looked at on application.

Lyons was there with my mother and stepfather and local friends, about eighteen of us. I wore a green two-piece corduroy suit; I did not want to look too flash, too London. I remember having to brush back the fringe of my new hairstyle.

I wanted to start a fresh life, as an ordinary woman, an ordinary housewife. I desperately wanted to forget the past and prayed at night that I would be allowed to live in peace and quiet. The neighbours had no idea who I was and I wanted to get to know them, to make them my friends, for them to think of me as just another housewife. I wanted to keep my married name out of the newspapers – I didn't want any more pointing fingers in the street.

I didn't want Jim to suffer from my notoriety. He was twenty-four years old and we had all to live for. We had almost got married a couple of months earlier but I was concerned what might happen to him. He had to convince me he would never be Mr Christine Keeler as that would have happened to many men. He was the strong, silent type and if I did have any doubts about him it was that he did not talk enough.

I began to live as Mrs Levermore. I sold my Sprite and bought an Austin Cambridge – in my own name, not Millwarren. We were comfortable and life seemed good, seemed 'normal'. Then we had a Peeping Tom. One night I went into the bedroom and noticed a face looking through the window. I'd just got out of the bath and I was only in a towel. I pretended not to notice him and walked as normally as possible out of the room. I rushed into the sitting-room to Jim: 'There's a man looking in the bedroom window. I'm calling the police.'

Jim wanted to go outside before the police arrived but I wouldn't let him. The police brought tracker dogs round as they found semen outside the window but the man had escaped. Then a few days later someone entered the bungalow and left semen in my bath. It was all very nasty and didn't help my marriage much. I agonized about whether I could ever be normal. First the spies, now the freaks seemed to be after me.

I told John Rudd of our problems and he visited and brought me an Alsatian dog which became a friend for the one I had already bought for protection.

For a young couple we had plenty of separations, the first just two weeks after the wedding. We argued about money and even about who to buy Christmas presents for. We were both immature but marriage was what I wanted. I think Jim did too but neither of us realized how much was involved. Also, I started getting suspicious of Jim with other women. I don't know if it was just jealousy. Jim and I split up about three or four times with Walter Lyons announcing it each time to the press – it made more stories, more pictures. By now I was pregnant and expecting our baby in July 1966. The last time we separated, before our son was born, we both went home to our mothers. The bungalow, which I had bought for £5,000, was locked up.

Whenever we broke up, I'd go to London. One night Hugh and Hanja and I went to the Ad Lib where we met Victor Lownes. He was young and handsome and lived in Montpelier Square. He was opening the Playboy Club in London for Hugh Hefner. When I was six months pregnant, Hugh, Hanja and I went to a party at Victor's. Roman Polanski and the American actor Stuart Whitman were there. Someone spiked the drinks with LSD and when I drove home I could hardly keep the car on the road. I asked Lyons to find out if the drug could harm the baby and if so what I could do but he said it was harmless.

We got back together after our son Jimmy was born but it didn't last long as he sold a story about our marriage to *Stern* magazine. While he was in Germany he fell for a girl over there. But Lyons got him back because he had arranged for the *People* to interview both of us. From those interviews which he secretly taped, Lyons wrote and sold his own stories abroad. As always, he just accounted to me for a photograph published in Britain.

Lyons preferred my life on a roller-coaster, a little unsettled, because it gave him more control. He showed me another story in *Stern* with Jim confessing his love for the German blonde and I finally ended with Jim on a permanent basis. The cruelty of that situation was that it left baby Jimmy in the middle of our problems. And when the *People* published our story their readers wrote in to protest. How dare I be happy? How dare I have a baby? What horrible people. David Frost, who had crucified Emil Savundra on television, supported me, hoping that I would enjoy my new life with Jimmy.

My mother helped look after Jimmy and I would take time to visit Anthony Edgar and my mink in London. He had a home near Victor Lownes just off Montpelier Square and I stayed there while Anthony was at his country place in Hampshire. I was trying to sort my life out and was looking for modelling work to help support myself and Jimmy. I joined the English Boy model agency run in Chelsea by Sir Mark Palmer. He was in his mid-twenties and an Old Etonian. He wanted his agency to represent me not just in photographic modelling but in films and television but nothing developed. When Anthony Edgar came to London we went out a lot.

He took me to the Star Tavern in Belgravia and the owner Paddy Kennedy recognized me as I had been there years before with Stephen. Paddy was a lion of a man and his word was law. He told me that he never believed in violence but he used it often enough if someone came into the pub who he didn't like; he'd throw them out bodily. I felt safe at the Star for he protected me; I could go there and be left alone. It was a pub full of familiar faces, actors and aristocrats – and names from the past like Eddowes except this was John, Michael Eddowes' son. He was one of the crowd I went to Dublin with for a rugby international. Paddy became a good friend, a protector.

I rented a furnished flat in Weymouth Street, got Jimmy back from my mother's and employed a good American girl, Maureen, to look after him. I also found a good home for my two dogs and sold my car. I was trying to base myself back in London and build a home for Jimmy too.

The Arethusa had taken over from the Ad Lib as *the* nightclub and we'd go straight there from Paddy's. I also ate at Alvaro's which had become popular at the same time as flower power arrived. An American called Steve Abrams was the head of the hippy movement in England and because I never saw the harm in cannabis and enjoyed a joint now and then, I was interested in meeting him. I got on well with Steve, and still do. Steve always spoke openly about pot in front of anyone. He introduced me to Jonathan Aitken who was then a reporter on the *Evening Standard*, not a convicted criminal.

Jonathan had a crush on Caroline Coon who was the co-founder of Release, which was set up to help youngsters arrested on drug charges. She helped to organize the London 'pot rally' in 1968 and thirty years later supported a pro-cannabis demonstration through the city. Steve Abrams' wife Jane Firbank was editor of *Forum*, the sexual advice magazine. Sex, drugs and rock 'n' roll – it was all covered.

And it all seemed so innocent. There was no harm in anyone. They wanted to float along and love the world. It seemed very reasonable to me, at the time. But I was to find that my world was to become more and more bizarre.

At Paddy's I met Mike Nelson, a handsome New Zealander who swept me off my feet. We soon became a team. Michael introduced me to Shirley Abicair who was a wonderful character. We became good friends over the years. She had travelled to Britain to study philosophy but showbusiness gradually took over and she appeared on children's shows. She was very popular with stories about Tumdbarumba, the Aborigine boy, and songs with a zither accompaniment.

On the surface, innocent days indeed. Shirley had a flat in Fulham which she bought with a twenty-one-year lease. I went to see her in her one-woman show. It was directed by Victor Spinetti who directed the play of John Lennon's books, *In His Own Write* and *Spaniard in the Works*, at the Old Vic. She was one of the first high-profile folk singers in Britain and a total anglophile: she joined the Queen's Club in West Kensington to play tennis.

Shirley was a delight and so was Mike Nelson. He just was not as innocent as Shirley's children's songs. He had some odd friends and was into sex-swap parties, which not was not my scene at all but I liked him enough to hope it would work out and we went motor racing in France. On our return, I found out my mother was seriously ill.

She had cancer of the womb and Mike and I went to visit her in hospital. She was upset with me as I had not been around before her operation. She told me that they had removed everything inside her and that they wouldn't know for a year if she was clear of cancer. Mum was very upset and she kept on about Jimmy. 'I wish I could have him, Chris'.

I could never have seen the future then. And what she said made sense. It was better to have his grandmother caring for him. Maureen understood and said she would be on standby to help if she could. She loved Jimmy. I know exactly what I said to my mother and it was casual. The words still haunt me every day: 'All right, Mum, you can have Jimmy back for a while.'

I let my mother take care of Jimmy for her own happiness as she said she only had a year to live.

Mike Nelson and I booked berths on a boat for New Zealand to marry out there but I changed my mind at the last minute – I couldn't trust him. But we were still going out and went off to the cinema to see *The Sound of Music*. He disappeared half-way through the film. Film critics might not blame him, but I did. Not least because I think he went round to seduce the girl who lived next door to me. New Zealand was out of the question. Permanently.

Hugh Bebb had left Hanja and was telling me he loved me. I was always faithful to my girlfriends about their husbands or lovers, but Hanja blamed me which was hurtful. I then started seeing Hugh and he took me to meet Sara Heath, the daughter of Harold Macmillan. He had no great motive and was not playing games: he liked Sara and he liked me. He thought we would get on and I don't think he gave a thought to the politics of it all. Sara was a marvellous person. If anyone naked had called on her, the response would have been: 'James, get a coat.' She was a true lady. As Stephen had always taught me, the right people are able to talk to anyone.

I met Laria Knights at Sara's. Laria was the intelligent, down-to-earth type. She stirred me with questions on matters of interest to me. We got on well and it was a good time for both of us. We even gained the reputation of being the first angry women among our friends. She was good at English and I wanted to write my own story for a newspaper or magazine. Laria was good at anything she attempted. I wanted to get back into London to work with her so I sold the bungalow in Wokingham and had my furniture put into store. I rented a one-bedroom unfurnished flat in Grosvenor Crescent Mews and Laria came to stay with me. She introduced me to Alexander Mosley whose father, Sir Oswald, had been in Stephen's rooms when Lucky Gordon had been making his threatening calls. Macmillan? Mosley? The past, unlike the future, you cannot change. No matter how much you want or try to. I cannot have regrets for if I did I would not have survived. I had to learn and to move on and to hope.

Alexander 'Ali' Mosely was not like his father in attitude but he had the same strong jaw and look about him. Richard Johnson, the actor, lived opposite and was handy if we ran out of sugar; a delightful man. Ali took me to dinner with a cousin of his, Henrietta Guinness, who was just about to run off with her lover, an Italian waiter, much against her family's wishes. Ali told her to follow her heart but she killed herself jumping off an Italian bridge.

We mixed with lots of writers and started going to Tramp's which had just opened and was attracting the London glitterati. I met David Bailey who wanted to photograph me for a book. I signed his release for it and there was hell to pay when I told Lyons. He wrote to Bailey threatening to sue if he dared to use any of the photographs.

Lyons took control of the book and had it edited. He also set up yet another company, this time offshore in the Cayman Islands, under my service agreement with Millwarren which, at the same time, I happily renewed for a further five years. He told me it was another 'tax efficient' scheme which he would still fully control. While my lawyer took care of business I continued to meet astonishing characters. Through Steve Abrams I met Barry Lowe who looked like the dormouse in *Alice in Wonderland* and always carried a black, eight-foot-high crossbow around with him. Barry had a disorder which caused him to fall asleep in the middle of a sentence. I would be talking to him when suddenly he would yawn and go to sleep. He had rented a beautiful house in extensive grounds with a tennis court and croquet lawn just outside East Grinstead. I drove down there with him in his Bentley. Laria moved in there too.

The story I had worked on with her was bought, through Lyons, by the *News of the World* for £21,000 although it was only a sketch of events. Nevertheless, Rupert Murdoch had just bought the paper and wanted a big launch with my story. It was the start of the Murdoch revolution in Fleet Street – journalism that was altogether different. I was perfect. My affair with Jack and the awful aftermath was still an open wound to the Establishment; Murdoch enjoyed that as much as anything about the enterprise and made much of it. His instincts were correct – the *News of the World* got their money back in publicity – and circulation. There were snags: Black & Decker, the power tool company, cancelled more than one million pounds of advertising with the newspaper. The Independent Television Authority (ITA) banned an advertisement for the series and said they would only broadcast adverts for the paper if they were about other features in that Sunday's edition.

The BBC got in on the act by cancelling my appearance on 24 *Hours* which was then a very popular current affairs programme. I had been invited to discuss the *News of the World* serialization but shortly before the BBC 1 programme was screened they told me it was off. They said it was for 'editorial reasons'. The night before they had talked to Murdoch on air about my story and run the commercial banned by the ITA.

The controversy rumbled on. Why was there such a fuss? Who was worried? I was due to appear on a David Frost interview with Murdoch for ITV, the plan being that I would sit in the studio audience so the cameras could spotlight me. The ITA ruled that Murdoch could only be interviewed if the discussion did not centre on Jack Profumo and I was not in the studio. I just couldn't believe all the fuss and said so. There had to be someone, somewhere, putting on the pressure.

And I had more direct pressure over the story from Laria as she demanded £50,000 as settlement for her involvement. I was livid and got Lyons involved. Of course, I did not know that more money was being made around the world. Lyons arranged for a photographic session at Barry Lowe's house with me dressed as the goddess Diana, the huntress.

Despite the censorship, I did appear on television in an interview with Bernard Braden. We spoke at the Mayfair Hotel and I tried to present my side of the story – something that, as usual, had vanished, this time in the debate over the rights of the *News of the World*. I wrote to *The Times* to put my case.

But I was still being censored – for no reason. The film, *The Christine Keeler Story*, had been put forward for a viewing certificate from the British Board of Film Censors. They banned the movie but not for anything that took place on the screen. John Trevelyan, who was then secretary of the board, said the movie created no censorship problems, either visual or verbal, under their policies but they were afraid of the public reaction. It was the first time they had ever turned a film down on those grounds. My only contribution was to introduce the film, which they had made in Denmark with actors and actresses playing me and Jack and the others. David Conyers, who financially backed the first rock musical *Hair*, was involved and he later applied to the Greater London Council for a licence but again I was too hot to handle, even in central London and nearly a decade after the movie was made. After all this happened, I had met David Pelham's film colleague John Nash at Paddy's. I explained to Paddy that I had received nothing from Nash for *The Christine Keeler Story*. Paddy had a few words with him and then Lyons called me. Lyons had always told me that he received nothing from Nash so I settled with Nash for the film. This was all fodder to Lyons: he demanded more photographs, this time with Jimmy, and got Ray Bellisario, who was the crackerjack photographer of the day, to take family and general photographs of me.

There was so much going on I didn't think anything else extraordinary could happen. Then, out of the blue, Sara Heath turned up at Barry Lowe's place asking me to go and meet her father. She insisted Harold Macmillan was expecting me for afternoon tea. It's been said that I went. I didn't. I don't know why but maybe because I didn't want to be the salt in his wounds and I had no idea what game Sara might have been playing. She was so frail and, sadly, died. I had been to visit her in hospital not long before that and she had given up all hope. She said I cheered her up and I was happy for that. It made me think more of family and I did so much miss my son Jimmy. I moved from Grosvenor Crescent Mews to a rented three-bedroomed house in Shawfield Street, off the King's Road in Chelsea. I was able to get an au pair so that I could have Jimmy back to live with me.

Finally, Laria agreed to take £7,000 in settlement for her work. I was unaware that Lyons had also negotiated 75 per cent of world-wide serialization rights. I still did not realize that I had to take total control. I was in a whirl of Old Etonians like Sir John Whitmore who I met at Tramp's and visiting Americans like the tobacco heir Robert Gallagher. I also went out for a long time with Prince Merid Bayeme. I was surrounded by wealth and, silly, stupid girl, thought nothing of protecting my own interests. I should have.

21

TAXING TIMES

ONE, PERHAPS, TWO, CONCEIVABLY, BUT EIGHT – I JUST CAN'T BELIEVE IT.

Harold Macmillan on being officially told that eight High Court judges
had been involved in an orgy in a public park in London

The chattering classes believed I had stories to tell but they were
about spies not sex and I stayed quiet. Macmillan and his men had
stayed silent and, through fear for my life, I did too. The public,
even years later, would always wonder: if all those titillating tales of
High Court judges and sado-masochistic sex and the other lurid
tales were untrue, why had the prime minister of the day asked Lord
Denning to investigate 'rumours affecting the honour and integrity
of public life'?

The *Daily Mirror* published the story of Lord Boothby and the
Krays with the headline: 'Peer and Gangster: Yard Inquiry'. All the
essential ingredients were present and correct – 'prominent public
men', 'Mayfair parties', homosexual orgies in Brighton, allegations of
blackmail. Even though Boothby was not named in the story, he
wrote to *The Times*. 'I am not a homosexual,' he insisted. 'I have not
been to a Mayfair party of any kind for more than twenty years. I
have met the man alleged to be the "King of the Underworld" only
three times on business matters . . . in short, the whole affair is a tissue
of atrocious lies.' It was Boothby who lied. And even got paid for it.
The truth seems to outlive them all. I wanted to be around when it
was fully told because you get to an age when the truth seems all-
important. Other than my sons, that is all that matters to me.

Until about the time I arrived in London, public life in Britain
was run by a cabal of men who had known one another since Eton

or Oxford, married into one another's families and spent their weekends in one another's country houses. Just think of Bill Astor's Cliveden and his weekly guest list. They thought they could behave as badly as they wanted, confident that well-connected friends would shield them from exposure. When the MP Tom Driberg was tried at the Old Bailey for sexually molesting two Scottish coalminers, no mention of the case appeared in the newspapers: Lord Beaverbrook, Driberg's mentor, persuaded the other newspaper owners to stay quiet.

It was not a matter of not scaring the horses – the intention was not to scare the voters. Tony Blair tried that with Ken Livingstone running for London mayor and it did not work. He failed to frighten the voters about Ken and it was good to see that people cannot be totally manipulated. Maybe, maybe, maybe, things have changed. I would love to believe that we are no longer victims of our master's voice. You cannot fool all the people all of the time. As they found out in the sixties. The major trap in that old-school-tie protection society was that when scandal did break free from Establishment controls it caused an almighty stink. Everybody, to a degree, was involved and running for cover.

I was still trying to find modelling work but I felt my figure could do with a boost. My breasts had never really recovered from being bound up following my first abortion so, in 1967, I had one of the first breast implants. I was a silicon pioneer. They were checked early in 2000 and I am glad to report everything is well and where it should be. I don't know if my enhanced appearance helped to get me more work modelling but it certainly gave me confidence. And maybe that is why the modelling work became less and less fulfilling. I felt strong enough in myself to do other things and I became interested in trying to prevent young people going to prison for smoking drugs which I thought were harmless. I knew about Release and went to work for them with the help of Caroline Coon. I was proud of myself being a counsellor to others but it wasn't long before I needed it myself.

By 1967 I was in love again. His name was David Curry and he seemed so strong and brave and in control of the expensive lifestyle in which he lived. We met at a party in Kensington and there was an instant attraction. I thought our love could stand anything. We'd meet every lunchtime at Bill Bentley's restaurant in Kensington. We adored each other and went on holiday together to Spain. We had an argument on Lord Pearson's yacht where Patrick Lichfield photographed me. I left David in Spain and flew back to London. Then we spoke over the telephone and patched things up so I flew back to Spain and to him the next day. It was going to be a bumpy ride but I was willing to fasten my seat belt for him. He introduced me to his grandmother but she didn't approve of me. I tried to explain to her about my work for Release but she frowned on that. David's family paid for a pheasant shoot for David to go on the following week and I was invited but one of David's former girlfriends was to make up the numbers for dinner. I was so hurt that I threatened to leave him if he went. He did. I decided to look for another man and found my second husband at the Arethusa club.

Anthony Platt seemed like a dream after the nightmare. I had it the wrong way around. Anthony loved good food and the theatre. He styled himself company director and he had as much money as charm. He was a director of a north London metal factory. I adored him and on 18 February 1971, with Lyons and his wife as witnesses, we married at St Pancras Register Office. It was only eight months after my divorce from Jim Levermore became final. We had our wedding lunch at the White House restaurant. It was all new to me, to be an intimate of this social circle with trips to the opera and smart dinner parties, although the dinners we hosted were always catered as the menus stretched my culinary talents.

John and Ann Rudd became our good friends. Anthony, who was thirty-one when we married, wanted to have children but I was not too keen. We had one of those silly fights with him hiding my birth control pills and then us ending up in bed to make up. Once pregnant, I yearned to have Jimmy back to complete the family and, against all my mother's protests, he did live with us. I desperately wanted us to be a big, normal, and most of all happy, family. Jimmy was lovely and seemed pleased to be with us. We decided to take him on holiday to Spain and, to keep the peace, took my mother and stepfather Ted Huish with us. It was a disaster. My mother was upset about me wanting to have Jimmy, she felt that she was his 'proper' mother. It hurt so much for I did have guilt. I had allowed her to care for Jimmy while I lived my life. But I wanted my boy so badly that it felt like a physical pain.

The trip ended in a terrible row with my mother and stepfather walking down a mountain from a beauty spot we had visited and taking a taxi to the airport. They were off. I had always believed in the unconditional love of my mother. Now, there were conditions.

There was more pressure from within my marriage. Anthony had a foul, violent temper: we seemed to spend all the time shouting at each other. But there were also good times – and extraordinary incidents. We were living in Fulham, in Seymour Place, and would spend time in the local pubs which were a very lively social scene. We were friendly with the socialite Vicki Hodge and her lover John Bindon who lived only two doors away from us. I liked John whom we all called Biffo because he was so bear-like. He would always say to me: 'Christine, we are not the people they think we are. They are wrong. But we can never run away from our reputations. We can't escape.'

John wanted to be a serious actor but he was always cast as this terrible tough guy in shows like *Softly, Softly* and *Hazel*. And tough he was but always very protective of me. Vicki and I used to have long chats. She was the daughter of Sir John Hodge, a baronet's girl, but in love with this London hard-man who I'd first met through Billy Meak when I was going out with Freddy.

Biffo's party trick was to balance five half-pints of beer on his penis. It attracted much attention. He went to Mustique with Vicki and Princess Margaret chuckled at his cockney rhyming slang. I don't know if the Princess's parties on Mustique were ever wild enough for him to display that skill. I used to meet him at the Star Tavern when he had parted from Vicki and was living in Chesham Mews in Belgravia. It was tragic when he died of cancer in 1983. He was a real Jack-the-Lad. Once when we were neighbours in Fulham, Vicki appeared hammering on my front door with a gun in her hand and wildly hysterical: she had just shot John. She had arrived home and walked in on him going all out on another girl. His bottom was dancing in the air so Vicki got the gun they kept in the house and shot him. In the backside. I made her a cup of tea and calmed her down.

John shrugged it all off; they got a doctor on the quiet and no one ever heard about it. Whenever I saw John after that he always winked at me and patted his rear end. There was something quite compelling about him. He was a very likeable man. Vicki made no bones about her infatuation with him. She talked of the most outstanding sexual moments; they had a truly lusty, rollicking romance and she always said she would attack any other women who showed a physical interest in him. He would tell us how Princess Margaret was fascinated with his background, as the son of a London taxi driver. He was always amused to watch her swimming with her cigarette holder still in her mouth. He was a cheeky chappie, a unique character.

I thought about him a lot when I got a writing job as an agony aunt for *Men Only* magazine. Paul Raymond hired me to advise readers on their sexual problems. Of course it was a gimmick, but it was writing work and I really thought I could help people as I had at Release. I was also trying to establish a regular income for myself and my unborn baby, Seymour, who was soon to be the only man in my life for my second marriage was clearly over. Any love between us had gone. It was another mistake and this one broke up the family: Jimmy went back to my mother and I got a flat in Belgravia. All my mother wanted was Jimmy and my stepfather around, no one else. When I was three months pregnant Anthony came round and we talked and talked and went to a marriage counsellor. We tried again but I knew deep inside that it was pointless. Shirley Abicair helped me in my down moments. She could always cheer me up. I let her have my car as Anthony was working from home and I used his Jaguar. A friend of hers visited her and a gun fell out of his sock. He was used to strapping it to his ankle as he had just returned from Vietnam. It scared me. I had changed. I'd become a bit of a shrinking violet.

Seymour was born in a private maternity clinic in London. The nuns who ran St Teresa's Hospital, Wimbledon, were wonderful to me: it was not an easy birth and there was little support from Anthony. He and I went to Italy. When we ran out of money, I had to arrange with Lyons for my company, Millwarren, to send money to me. Anthony's money problems did not help the marriage and I left Anthony for good in March 1972, when Seymour was three months old. I stayed at Shirley Abicair's until I rented a small house off the King's Road. Shirley introduced me to rock group the Grateful Dead, and a nasty piece appeared in *Private Eye* calling me an ageing groupie. Within three weeks of my leaving him, Anthony made Seymour a Ward of Court. For the next two years there were court hearings and I was never certain if I would be allowed to keep him. I had lost one son and was not about to lose another. My son was everything to me. Here was someone I could give all my love to. I was absolutely devoted to Seymour; it would have broken me completely to part with him. I pawned everything I had from mink jacket to handbags because I knew it was going to be an expensive legal fight in the High Court.

We went before Mr Justice Ormerod and he heard evidence in private for a day and a half. Anthony's accusations were horrible, deplorable. He thought he could say anything about me because of my name, my notoriety. Kim Proctor was so astonished by it that she helped me get affidavits from women my husband had had sex with while I was in hospital giving birth to Seymour. Everybody could see I was in the right and Anthony's barrister offered a reconciliation as the way out for all of us. I refused – he had been cheating on me from the moment we met. Kim had known but had not wanted to hurt me; she had hoped the marriage would survive for Seymour's sake. Seymour's father was ordered to pay six pounds a week to me but did not give up the fight.

We were back and forward to court over Seymour until I made Anthony bankrupt and he left the country. I didn't feel a bit sorry for him. He talked of 'this woman on my back' but that was not me but his first wife, Joan, who had constantly pestered him for financial support. I had only two questions for Anthony in court:

'Were you ordered to pay six pounds a week for your son in June 1973?'

'Yes.'

'And you failed in paying this?'

'Yes.'

I had already claimed £2,400 in arrears under a maintenance order. Anthony ran off to avoid appearing in court for his public examination and sent a letter to the court saying the first Mrs Platt was 'hounding' him for money. I found out his business details in court: in 1970 he had been worth at least £320,000 but seven years later he was more than £40,000 in debt. When he divorced in 1970, he was told to pay £12,000 in a lump sum and £7,000 a year, less tax, to Joan. And two years later I was awarded £2,500 a year. But it was not until years later that a decree nisi was finally granted.

And it was my sons, not money, that mattered. During my quarrels with Anthony he sided with my mother and gave Jimmy back to her. One moment Jimmy was with me and then he was gone and was back living with my mother.

My mother wasn't even talking to me; she simply wouldn't communicate. I could do nothing because from 1972 to 1974 I was involved in the custody struggle over Seymour and if I had lost a court battle against my mother I could have lost them both. The cruelty of that situation made me a fighter again. More than twenty-five years later, my mother and I still do not see each other or speak. I last had proper contact with her in 1986. I do not know if my stepfather, Ted Huish, is alive or dead. I have not seen Jimmy for years. I send them a Christmas card every year and Jimmy a birthday card, signed from myself and Seymour. Seymour sent his e-mail address to them but we get no cards or word in return. I have just had to accept how impotent I am in this situation and hope that one day Jimmy will want to contact me. It makes me even more glad that I was able to keep Seymour.

While the court hearings over Seymour were going on I got a reminder of my misadventures of the early sixties. The stories about the cousin of my old boyfriend Michael Lambton were all over the newspapers for days. Lord Lambton was another Tory government minister whose career was ruined by sex. The scandal involving Norma Levy lost Lord Lambton his position as Under-Secretary of State for Defence in 1973. Lambton resigned from Edward Heath's government after nude photographs of him having a jolly time with Norma turned up in Fleet Street and then with Scotland Yard. The Lord Privy Seal, Lord Jellicoe, left Ted Heath's lot shortly afterwards after admitting he also had a fling with Norma, whose speciality was sado-masochism and bondage. She named a third minister and there was a lot of gossip but no other resignations.

I was still working, when I could, for Release and would do shifts in the office. I became friendly with Rufus Harris who was a legal expert there. He was a real mentor and cared for people; he stayed with me and helped me understand the legal difficulties in helping people who had been arrested on drug charges. It was seen as such a subversive thing that I should not have been surprised when my old friends the FBI appeared on the scene. Rufus knew all about them as they were investigating the drug trade and were monitoring people who had contacted Release for help. However, we were temporarily caught off-guard when, in a remarkable meta-morphosis, the FBI turned up in the shape of Ty Hardin, the tall, blond American actor who had made his name in the Western television series *Bronco*. I had also seen him in a movie called *The Chapman Report* which was a risqué film in its day, 1962, but in reality was a melodramatic potboiler; you get more insight into life listening to *The Archers*. Hardin was pleasant enough to Rufus and me but our suspicions were aroused when he started to ask about people we knew who smoked cannabis. He then got me involved in sending a parcel which contained oil of cannabis to Ireland and made sure that my fingerprints were on the parcel, but Rufus stopped me having anything to do with it. He had a contact at the Home Office and discovered that our new friend had FBI con-nections and was bad news. We stayed away from him but it was a warning to be aware. Something I should have been for a long time.

It was also Rufus who finally made me see the truth about Walter Lyons. He found a Japanese translation of my story and staring out from the covers from beneath a sombrero was me. It was the story

I had stopped publication of when I married Anthony Platt. Lyons had sold it worldwide though, of course, he denied all knowledge. Release, through their lawyer Dennis Muirhead, helped me to start an investigation into Lyons – and then proof arrived with a tax demand. The Inland Revenue wanted £33,000 going back to the year 1969/1970. Lyons had received the money, not me, but how did I explain that to the tax man?

Lyons held the best hand: he had a lot of the paperwork and also claimed to control my rights to photographs and writings. It was going to be a struggle: I was facing huge bills over Seymour's custody case. Lyons was taking his charges out of property deals that had been done by Millwarren. Nothing appeared to belong to me. I proved to the tax people by working with them over the years that I was guilty of nothing – and my tax bill was reduced to virtually nil. It was a mess but I had Seymour. We moved into the World's End housing estate in London and the name tells you everything. It was an infamous council block but I had little choice because Lyons had left me with debts. I went on social security and it was a low, low point for me. I telephoned his office one day and found out he had died. He had five heart attacks, one after the other. His secretary said I killed him by putting all the pressure on him. I like to think it was his conscience taking revenge.

It was a terrible time for me and my son. We would be left alone for a time and then someone would tell this or that story and I would be a headline again; there was no running away from being Christine Keeler. I often feel disorientated by that, *lost*, if you know what I mean. I had changed my surname by deed poll but I am still easily recognized. It is difficult for me as a woman who takes pride in her appearance to dress down the way I do. I do not want attention and woolly jumpers and jeans work as a disguise. People think of me as all heels and cleavage not someone who looks like a founder member of the Ramblers' Association. I let my hair grow and then get fed up with it and cut it all off. I no longer fuss about it. But still people know me. Sometimes in my few low moments I think that lost feeling will never really end. My first marriage lasted a year and it was just an attempt to escape. My second marriage only lasted the same amount of time. I have my two sons, one from each marriage, whom I cherish and love. I did not fight my mother to get Jimmy back, as how could I take him away from my bungalow in the country to come and live with Seymour and me on a London council estate? I became a full-time mother to Seymour and began to research and study everything that had happened, going to libraries and scrutinizing the newspapers all the time.

Then, one day in October 1977, there staring out at me from the pages of the *Daily Mail* was Mariella Novotny. Except that she was calling herself Henrietta Chapman and giving her age as twenty-two. And saying she was Hod Chapman-Dibben's daughter rather than his wife. But it was Mariella, all right. She had been living in a flat in London's Fulham Road belonging to the then Lord Burghersh, an Old Etonian and heir to the 15th Earl of Westmorland. Lord Burghersh had had to go to the High Court to try and win back possession of his flat. Mariella said she was a stripper but was using the flat as a base for research into a book on international politics and crime. In court she said that her research involved interviews and discussions at the flat with representatives of heads of state and international companies; during the last three months of 1976 she was meeting at least six people a week there as she worked on the book *Power, Politics and Pleasure*. Lord Burghersh won his case, but not before his lawyer, Derek Wood, had revealed that Henrietta Chapman, twenty-two, was also Mariella Novotny, thirty-five.

In court, Mr Wood pointed out that Mariella had been a friend of Stephen Ward and named me as well. Hod tried to say he had two daughters and it was the other one who was Mariella and living in California. He also said that he and Mariella had given evidence to Lord Denning. However, he refused to identify as Mariella a woman shown in a *News of the World* photograph serving dinner to a naked man in a mask. Lord Burghersh won his flat and costs but the Deputy Judge, Simon Goldstein, had the last word: 'Looking at her, I find it very difficult to accept that she is the thirty-five-year-old Mariella Novotny that she is supposed to be.' But she was, of course. British jurisprudence? Well . . .

Mariella, who lived for sex and intelligence gossip, died in February 1983. In bed. She was only forty-one years old. The Westminster Coroner, Dr Paul Knapman, called it misadventure. Along with people in Moscow, I still think it was murder. A central figure in the strangest days of my life always believed Mariella would be killed by American or British agents, most probably by the CIA. And Britain's Secret Intelligence Service, MI6, would have known. It would be extraordinary if they did not because she was one of their contacts. Of course, there was and will always be total denial for even in the twenty-first century we live in a UK obsessed with 'official secrecy', which so often means versions of events which have a beginning, a muddle and no end.

Mariella had choked on her own vomit while lying on her bed face-down eating jelly at her place in Tonbridge, Kent, which was just one of her homes. At the time she was talking about publishing an expanded version of her 'memoirs'. She kept files on her lifetime of encounters in Kent and also at the place she and Hod had in Dancer Road, Fulham. She always talked about a 'little black book' but it wasn't a euphemism. She had a small black address book which included the names of political leaders in America, Britain, France and other countries that she had been involved with. There was even a diplomatic list – almost like the official one. The other names were businessmen, many of them in New York. The little black book was never found after her death. Maybe Hod took it but it was never seen again so I have to suspect some dirty tricks department. I believe Mariella was pivotal to the events because of all she knew and the power of blackmail.

What has also always intrigued me is what evidence Mariella and Hod Dibben gave to Denning. Why was it kept out of the report? Was it quietly censored as my testimony was? Why has Hod never said a word? How did Denning ensure his silence? Mariella certainly knew more than has ever been said about the sex and blackmail of high society. And she could have been me, played my role in Stephen's scheme of things.

22

SUCH A SCANDAL

A PLACE WHERE THEY PAY YOU 50,000 DOLLARS FOR A KISS
AND 50 CENTS FOR YOUR SOUL.

Marilyn Monroe on Hollywood 1959

The world is a cruel place – and so is the school playground. From an early age, I told Seymour about what had happened. I wanted to prepare him to face the taunts of the other children when they discovered who his mother was. As they would and did.

He regards me as straight and moral for that is how I have brought him up to be. I have always said that the truth is everything. You can make mistakes, make a fool of yourself but you must never lose your integrity. That is who you are and who you must always fight for. I told him I was wild and naughty. I was. And there was a price. Seymour has accepted it all over the years and has found his place in life. We are friends as well as mother and son. He gets annoyed with me when I mess up on the computer and most mornings I drive him to the station to see him off to work.

That's when I pick up my copy of *The Times*. I am addicted to the cryptic crossword. It relaxes me to sit over a cup of coffee and have only the puzzle to be concerned about. All my life there seems to have been something to worry about. I tried to keep my identity a secret when I sat on a jury at Knightsbridge Crown Court in 1986, wearing a conservative green two-piece suit. We had to decide on a drugs case. It took two days and before it was over there was a story, reported with some shock, that I was sitting in judgment on others. I was upset for a few days about that.

But in the 1980s the main worry was getting myself and Seymour out of the ever more depressing World's End Estate. I was eventually able to with the help of John Profumo – and Hollywood. In the early 1980s producers had bought some of my rights and those of others to various versions of the Profumo Affair and they were concocted into a screenplay for the movie *Scandal*. The British actress Joanne Whalley-Kilmer played me and Bridget Fonda, niece of Jane, granddaughter of Henry and daughter of Peter, was Mandy. That crumpled-looking actor John Hurt played Stephen.

Hurt was supercilious. In his strange manner the first thing he said to me – in front of other people – was that he recalled *me* being thrown out of the gaming club in the incident with Lord Kimberley. I protested, but he was not interested in hearing what I had to say. Nobody connected with that movie was. They had their own version of events and even then after all the years I think there was government pressure to present a certain point of view. I pointed out some things to them but it was like talking to Lord Denning – a waste of breath. They, as he did, had their minds made up about what had happened. As far as that movie is concerned, *Star Wars* is closer to fact.

Sir Roger Hollis was identified as a player for the Russians in *Spycatcher*, the 1987 memoirs of former spy Peter Wright. But no one followed up on it to any great extent. It was best, it seemed, that Hollis should remain quiet in his grave, having died in 1972. And, as Margaret Thatcher famously told the House of Commons in 1981, when she was quizzed about Hollis, it was impossible to prove the negative. There was no proof. My eyes proved it to me. Hollis was exonerated yet again, having been investigated four times. There was certainly no mention of him in *Scandal*.

I hated that film, which skipped over events and motivations and imagined others which never happened. It came nowhere near the truth but I went to the 1987 London premiere because I was paid five thousand pounds to watch it. I would not have gone near had I not needed the money. Nevertheless, *Scandal* brought me attention again, some of which was welcome. The film resulted in an eclectic mix of offers. There was to be a Christine Keeler perfume called *Scandal* and I was to have my own talk show in America.

People, as always, skipped into my life with ideas and then vanished.

I find it safer now to control my own income if I can. I found work in telephone sales, first in Regent Street and then in Fulham, selling advertising space for magazines. It was high-pressure selling but I enjoyed the work and the targets they set. But I was always looking for something closer to home – I didn't want handouts, I like to make my own way in the world. I didn't care what it was: I just wanted to earn a wage to help get things for Seymour. I found a nice couple in Battersea who ran a dry-cleaning business. They wanted someone for reception and to work the till and I ended up doing everything from wrapping and presenting the clothes to operating the ironing equipment. They were long hours but the couple were fair about what they paid and I felt happy with it. Sadly, the dry-cleaning business got into difficulties and closed down. It might help to understand if I tell this next story for it is what has made me tell the truth at last. It was an event that made me go off in the 1990s to the south coast of England and re-evaluate my life and everything in it, now and in the past.

I was lucky to find another job in the area at Norton School. I was working in the pupils' canteen serving food and clearing up – a dinner lady. I worked hard and the supervisor was always saying how good I was. I got on with the kids and the rest of the staff and it was fun. The money was fine and in the evenings I could do my reading and research and writing. One day the supervisor came up and said I was sacked. I was astonished. She said it was the head-master's decision and nothing to do with her, she liked my work immensely. So what was wrong?

She looked like an undertaker at that moment and said, 'Someone told the headmaster you are Christine Keeler.'

EPILOGUE

HINDSIGHT

WE DO NOT SIMPLY WISH TO HONOUR AGE;
WE MAY ALSO PROFIT FROM IT.

The Archbishop of Canterbury, Dr George Carey,
at the service of thanksgiving for the Queen Mother
at St Paul's Cathedral, 11 July 2000

I feel a little bewildered for it doesn't seem that long since all this began. At times I feel I have lived through a fog, that life went spinning past in a blur. I see it all clearly now and it is unsettling but, if it is not too contradictory, I also feel content that finally everything has been said.

What would Stephen have thought about what happened to us all, to the world he was so intent on protecting from itself? He was a Soviet agent and ran his 'cell' in the middle of the Cold War which is now supposedly all over although, after what I have seen, I am not totally convinced. Especially with a KGB man, Vladimir Putin, in the Kremlin. Yes, the Berlin Wall has gone – more publicly than it was built. MI6 and the Americans didn't know for forty-eight hours that it was going up. But Stephen did. On that point he knew more than John Kennedy, President of the United States, and Harold Macmillan, Prime Minister of the UK.

It is all an essential piece of history now. There are incidents, happenings, accidents, simple moments in time, that never leave the public imagination. I went to see the big *Titanic* movie recently and loved the Kate Winslet character – my sort of heroine, plucky and never-give-up. I didn't like the boy too much. It was only later, reading the reviews in the newspaper, that the significance of the date of the *Titanic* disaster struck me. Stephen Ward was born in the same year; he was a Libra, born on 19 October 1912. Stephen was always delighted that I remembered his birthday. We would have tea and cake to celebrate. As the sixties song says, there's always something there to remind you. Birthdays. And deaths.

One moment my thoughts will be on the crossword or what I am cooking for dinner – nothing special for I have never mastered that art – and the radio or television news will transport me back. In 1990, it was the death of British agent, Greville Wynne, who had been subjected to a show trial in Moscow alongside the Russian defector, Colonel Oleg Vladimirovich Penkovsky. Having supplied vital intelligence to the West at the height of the Cold War Penkovsky was trapped by Moscow, tried and then executed by firing squad on 16 May 1963. Wynne, sentenced to eight years in a Soviet prison, returned to Britain a broken man after only eleven months, having been exchanged for KGB officer Gordon Lonsdale who was gaoled in the UK in 1961.

Wynne returned to Britain bitter and disillusioned. By contrast, when Eugene Ivanov escaped home to Moscow after being tipped off by Stephen, he was given the Order of Lenin. He had – on Stephen's orders – compromised the British government in such a way that Macmillan resigned in October 1963. Sir Alec Douglas-Home kept the Tories hobbling along until Harold Wilson and Labour took over in 1964. For Eugene it was a triumph. The *Daily Express* wanted to set up a reunion so I went to see him in Moscow in 1993 and he met me with a kiss and hug and a box of Russian chocolates. He took me around Red Square and we walked outside the KGB headquarters. He was sixty-seven then but he still liked his vodka – and could hold it. But he was pale with a shock of thick, grey hair and not that big, powerful bear of a man who took me home to Wimpole Mews from Cliveden. The strange thing about meeting Eugene again – and this was a man who had played such a part in my life – was that I realized I hardly knew him. Or he me. It was only in Red Square, after all the years, that he was finally able to look me in the eye.

He admitted to me that he had felt guilty about sleeping with me and betraying his wife. He had always looked that way to me at

Stephen's – embarrassed, ashamed. When his wife heard about him sleeping with me she left him in an instant and he never remarried. Eugene complained to me that it was unfair that he should lose his wife but that Jack could keep his. He was a sad figure and lived alone in a flat in Moscow but was nervous about showing it to me. He said it was too 'poor'. The world he had spied for was gone – as was that handsome Soviet agent in a naval uniform. But his country was true to him at the end. He died a year after I saw him, in January 1994. He was sixty-eight, another birthday had past, and according to the obituaries they gave him an honourable funeral.

Jack finally lost his wife too. When Valerie Hobson died in 1999 she was eighty-one years old. How cruel had it all been for her? Denning said that when Jack confessed to her what he had done over a quiet dinner, she told him: 'Oh, darling, we must go home now as soon as we can and face up to it.' I thought of that, of the class she had shown, and my mind tumbled over it all again, when they said on television that she had died. I, of course, was mentioned too. She was a leading lady in the British cinema but what everyone recalled was her husband's affair with me. She retired from show business at the age of thirty-seven after her greatest success in 1953, as Anna, the governess, in the first London production of *The King and I*. She married Jack a year later and they had a son, David Profumo, who is a writer. And until it all went mad, she led a charmed life. I think her appearance of aloofness helped her image at the time; she seemed so above it all and that came from movies like *Kind Hearts and Coronets* in 1949. Jack used to say he was a close friend of Alec Guinness who was in that movie with Valerie. With their wives they went on Italian holidays together. I saw her as Estella in the great David Lean version of *Great Expectations* and thought she was horrid to poor Pip. A real heart-breaker.

In our small world, she had also starred with Douglas Fairbanks Junior in 1937 in a film entitled *Jump for Glory*. A couple of years later she married the now Sir Anthony Havelock-Allan, who was ninety-six in 2000 and they had two sons. That marriage ended two years before she married Jack. After Jack left the spotlight to do charity work in the East End she got involved with good deeds as well, working for mentally handicapped children and for Lepra, a leprosy relief organization. In 1975 she accompanied him to Buckingham Palace when he received a CBE for his work.

Then, on 12 July 2000, there was Jack among the guests at St Paul's Cathedral for the tribute to the Queen Mother on her upcoming one hundredth birthday. I watched it on television and didn't see Jack but read in the papers that he attended in his smart morning suit. He would have enjoyed the protocol and pomp. I wonder if he will ever talk about what happened. He has his personal notes on the affair in a bank vault near his home in Upton Grey, Basingstoke, Hampshire. It has been his discreet approach to the whole affair and his charity work over the years which have kept his place in the proper circles, but he will always be Jack-the-Lad to me. And others, as Shirley Abicair's experience testified. I read in the summer of 2000 that he was seeing Thelma King-Fretts who was fifty-two and the former wife of a Lt-Col. Paddy King-Fretts. Jack was eighty-five then but described as having a 'spring in his step' because of 'walking out' with Thelma. He always got on with the ladies. Margaret Thatcher invited him to join the celebrations of her seventieth birthday in 1995, when she said, 'He is one of our national heroes. His has been a very good life. It's time to forget the Keeler business.'

Perhaps for Margaret Thatcher. But, despite me, Jack has remained on the guest list for events like the Queen Mother's centenary celebrations. Also present at them, of course, was Stephen Ward's old acquaintance, Prince Philip, looking immaculate as he walked from the cathedral behind the Queen Mother who was being helped by Prince Charles. It made me think again of those men from the past who, on the surface, always shone with propriety. As we have found out, the polish was often a thin veneer. Many of the men of the Macmillan era were of the old school in look and manner but they have nearly all gone.

Sir Colin Coote, who edited the *Daily Telegraph* from 1954 to 1964, died in 1979 at the age of eighty-five. Sir Godfrey Nicholson was eighty-nine when he passed away in 1991. Lord George Wigg, who was the first person in the Commons to suggest that my affair with Jack was a threat to national security, died in 1983. He has left a legacy – his private diaries. He said they were 'red hot' and bequeathed them to the London School of Economics but with strict orders that they could not be opened until a decade after he died. I am still waiting. Have these papers vanished too? As the Paymaster General he had a special role to liaise with the security services but found himself on the wrong end of the law in 1976 when he was charged and then cleared of kerb crawling in Park Lane. Wigg, who was said to have approached six women, maintained that he was merely looking for 'an early edition of the *Daily Express*'. To use that most famous of phrases: he would, wouldn't he?

And where is she now? Well, Mandy was fifty-six and a grandmother in 2000, living with her third husband, Ken Foreman, a retired British businessman ten years her senior. She's done well. They have three homes: one in Miami, another in the Bahamas and one in Surrey. She's had cosmetic surgery but underneath I feel she's still the same old Mandy, telling people what they think they want to hear.

Which is what Lord Denning did too. He died on 6 March 1999, at the age of 100 and many of his obituaries called him the greatest judge of the twentieth century. I could not agree but, obviously, others would for he did what was asked: he pulled a shroud over all that had happened. He lied for his country.

I am telling the whole truth for history. And, I admit, for myself. I shudder to think of it now. I always thought of myself as a loyal Englishwoman. Whatever I have done wrong in my life I never thought I could be called a traitor. Until now, as I said, I have always shut out the fact that I was a spy. But I was a totally manipulated one. As were others who were caught in Stephen's net. I want to finally clear the decks. I want to get on with my life properly for the first time.

Only in 2000 did I find out I had half-brothers and -sisters and I hope to meet them all. We don't know each other, yet we have the same blood. It is a slow, trusting process we are going through, but the confidence is building. I even went to a school reunion as part of trying to understand where I came from. There were no nasty words or sneers and people were kind to me.

But, yes, I did feel like a curiosity. I always will. When people look at me I can see them reading the headlines in their minds. Add their imaginations to that and it creates quite a picture for them. Maybe now it will finally change and there will be understanding, but that will depend on the power of the truth. I have survived and possibly I should not hope for more than that.

AFTERMATH

When *The Truth At Last* was published in hardback in 2001, I felt I could deal with people on an even footing for the first time in decades. I had told my story in full for the first time and it removed an enormous burden from me. Oh, how I wish I had found the courage to tell it earlier. From the moment of publication my life became so much easier. Friends were astonished at what had happened to me and what I had kept to myself for so many years. So many told me I had grown in stature in their eyes. Some said they had always thought of me as a victim of circumstances and were amazed at the reality of the web of intrigue and cover up I had been enveloped in. And now I was able to talk openly to them.

People I met for the first time who had read the book were sympathetic and, if anything, wanted to know more. They encouraged me to elaborate, but I said I had written only what I knew about and I did not want to speculate. I believe writers and commentators will do that in a few years when others who played roles in the Profumo Affair – and in that particular period of history – no longer need to be protected. I was encouraged by the book's reception, most significantly by the eminent critics who studied what I had to say. I took my share of chattering classes' sneers as well, but I have endured that sort of treatment for most of my life.

I was heartened by the analysis of Chapman Pincher, who in the early 1960s reported the story for the *Daily Express* and remains one of our most respected commentators on the Cold War and other secret intelligence issues. He suggested, and made a strong case, that Stephen was working for the GRU, the military arm of the Soviet intelligence service. Eugene Ivanov was also with the GRU rather than the KGB. But Chapman Pincher also offered another connection between Stephen and Roger Hollis, the head of MI6, who I said was a Moscow spy. He wrote in his review: 'All the evidence suggests that if Hollis was a spy, he too was recruited by the GRU while living in Shanghai after leaving Oxford prematurely in 1926.' Later he pointed out that Hollis did not 'leave' Oxford early but was sent down – shortly after the government learned of a communist cell at Oxford and ordered the university authorities to eradicate it. He wrote: 'Christine Keeler makes two claims which cannot be ignored by serious students of Cold War espionage.'

What I had been able to do with this book was encourage others to study the evidence and not just accept the myth which had grown around my story since the Denning Report was published in September 1963.

But happy as I am that the truth is finally out in the open, I am still careful and wary of people – I have had to be for too many years to change – but it is fabulous to see the difference in other people now they know my side of the story.

I received scores of letters after the original publication of this book, many praising me for finding the bravery to speak out. Another avalanche of letters arrived after the screening of *Christine Keeler: Sex Bomb* on ITV in February 2001, which scored remarkable ratings for a late-evening documentary. Certainly, Yorkshire Television, which made the programme, was delighted. The producer and director, Andrew Sheldon, and his number two, Rick Goodwin, were very kind to me during the filming. It was quite a journey they made me take.

In the book I wrote about Murray's Club and Cliveden and the Soho of the sixties, of the moments of peril and of pleasure. It is another matter to revisit your past – literally. I was filmed at Cliveden and at Spring Cottage where I went that first weekend with Stephen. The camera crew were setting up their equipment and as I gazed around I could imagine it all as if it were yesterday, but in some ghostly way. I could see Stephen and Bill Astor, hear the clink of glasses and people shouting by the swimming pool. When I blinked, the film people were looking at me: I had, for a moment, vanished into that past. We walked around the pool where I first encountered Jack Profumo and around the elegant grounds. It remains a magnificent place although, for me, the memories are not as majestic.

We filmed at what was Murray's Club and, for the cameras, I could not resist getting onstage and doing a little twirl, part of the routine from all those years ago. I felt a little light-hearted as I did the steps, surprised I suppose that I could remember them and perform then without tripping over. I was lighter on my feet than I could ever have expected to be. We went to the National Portrait Gallery in London where my portrait by Stephen remains on display. That was eerie.

For the television documentary, I watched some vintage film footage of myself when I did a screen test in 1963. Sitting in the dark as the projector flashed the images on the screen close ahead of me, it was like watching a different person. Yes, it was me but it was also someone who had not endured so much. Today I can see that pain in my face every morning. On the screen I looked without fear or care. It was disquieting to understand again what Harold Macmillan dismissed as 'events' had done to me physically as well as emotionally.

The power of television in getting massive, instant responses was demonstrated to me by the letters I received arguing points about the Cold War and about the people who populate *The Truth At Last*. There were a few 'strange' letters but the majority were serious and made strong points, if not always convincing to me.

What was gratifying was being able to take part in such debates without always watching what I said or wrote. I had told the whole story and now I was happy to discuss the black and white and even the grey areas of the events that I had lived through and been so much a part of.

It was the same for me at book signings: in London I did one at Harrods in Knightsbridge and at Selfridges on Oxford Street.

I know many people came out of curiosity – 'let's have a look at Christine Keeler today' – but I was surprised that so many people took the trouble on a Saturday afternoon to buy the book and meet and talk to me about it. My son Seymour came to Selfridges with me and I think he was taken aback and impressed by the reaction. I don't think I was: I feel people want to know the truth and if you are offering them that, they will at the very least listen to what you have to say and, if they are reasonable, then make up their minds.

Selfridges has a massive book department which I felt I could happily get lost in for days, just browsing among the shelves. I was at a display table signing my books when a pleasant man approached me. We talked about the book and he then announced, 'I'm Major Jim's son.'

It shook me. Major Jim Eynan, you will remember, was a regular lover of mine who was with me when Jack Profumo turned up at Stephen's flat unexpectedly. I was always fond of Major Jim. His son said he had died, but that his mother was still alive. I looked at him, 'Does she know you're here?'

He just smiled at me and said, 'Oh, she forgave you and my father a long, long time ago. She's looking forward to reading the book.'

I was lost for words for a moment and muttered, 'I hope she enjoys it.' And I hope she did, for her husband was a remarkable man who, throughout the years after Stephen's trial, never uttered a word about what happened between us and what he witnessed when Jack visited the day he was present at Wimpole Mews.

I thought my life would settle back into a routine after this book was published but it seemed to have intrigued many, many people. What had once been accepted no longer was, and I was visited by journalists from a German magazine, my story was told in a national publication in India and, also, in an abridged form, over ten pages of America's *Vanity Fair* magazine. From that came enquiries from television companies in America. Everyone, if seemed, wanted to be told the new truth.

It was heartening to be given the chance to do so for I was not just being dismissed, played to the rules of the trap that Denning had set nearly four decades earlier. In writing this book I had only ever wanted to set out the facts of the Profumo Affair as I know and lived them. That people have been so open-minded as to read them in such numbers and to discuss my story and its place in modern history is more rewarding than I cold hope to explain.

Publication also raised my profile above the barricades once again but that was a risk I was prepared to take. As I said, I got some stick and, strangely, mostly from female writers. One girl from the *Independent* wanted me to play the role of a sad old bat with a mad cat, so she wrote me up that way. A man in the *Times* had me living on the south coast with a husband. The television critic of the *Times*, though, was kind enough to suggest that if the Profumo Affair happened in 2001 I would be given my own TV series and a recording contract. More seriously, and I agree with him, he argued that you should never bet against the establishment – even today.

But for all the good reactions and the positive reading and understanding of this book there are just some preconceptions about that will never change; not now and not after I'm gone.

I was approached by the Saatchi and Saatchi advertising agency to make a television commercial for the *Sunday Business*, and I agreed. They prepared a script and I was to read from it sitting in that famous chair. I was consulted over wardrobe and told a selection of clothes was being brought to the film shoot.

On the day of filming – it was all rush, rush, rush – I turned up at the studio. They were all smiles and kindness and offering me cups of tea, glasses of water. It was all set up, they said, and I was just to make myself comfortable in the chair.

'What outfit do you want me to wear?' I asked.

The young man looked aghast. 'Didn't they tell you? We want you to do it naked.'

I'm smiling about it now but at that moment I was outraged. Didn't they understand? There was a flurry of activity and I completed my assignment – with my clothes on. The television commercial was a great success.

Just as I plan my life to be from now on.

APPENDIX

THE CHRISTINE KEELER FILES

These are just a few of the documents I was able to get under the American freedom of Information Act. They give some idea of the frenzied speculation and misinformation that surrounded the Profumo Affair.

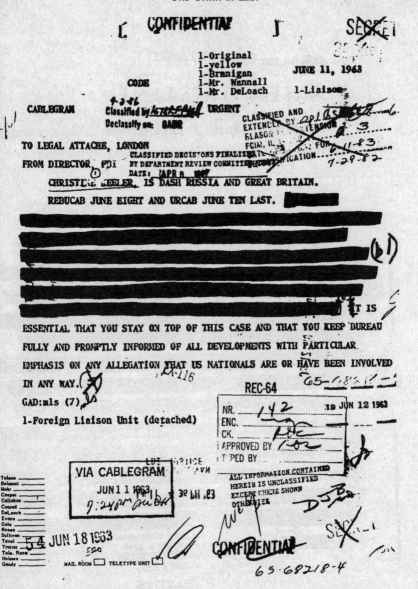

CONFIDENTIAL

SECRET

1-Original
1-yellow
1-Branigan   JUNE 11, 1963
1-Mr. Wannall
1-Mr. DeLoach   1-Liaison

CODE

CABLEGRAM   Classified by   URGENT

CLASSIFIED AND
EXTENDED BY

Declassify on:

CLASSIFIED DECISIONS FINALIZED
TO LEGAL ATTACHE, LONDON

FROM DIRECTOR FBI   BY DEPARTMENT REVIEW COMMITTEE
DATE: APR 8

CHRISTINE KEELER IS DASH RUSSIA AND GREAT BRITAIN.

REBUCAB JUNE EIGHT AND URCAB JUNE TEN LAST.

IT IS

ESSENTIAL THAT YOU STAY ON TOP OF THIS CASE AND THAT YOU KEEP BUREAU

FULLY AND PROMPTLY INFORMED OF ALL DEVELOPMENTS WITH PARTICULAR

EMPHASIS ON ANY ALLEGATION THAT US NATIONALS ARE OR HAVE BEEN INVOLVED

IN ANY WAY.

GAD:mls (7)

1-Foreign Liaison Unit (detached)

REC-64

NR. 142   19 JUN 12 1963
ENC.
CK.
APPROVED BY
TYPED BY

VIA CABLEGRAM
JUN 1 1 1963

ALL INFORMATION CONTAINED
HEREIN IS UNCLASSIFIED
EXCEPT WHERE SHOWN
OTHERWISE

Tolson
Belmont
Mohr
Casper
Callahan
Conrad
DeLoach
Evans
Gale
Rosen
Sullivan
Tavel
Trotter
Tele. Room
Holmes
Gandy

JUN 18 1963

MAIL ROOM ☐ TELETYPE UNIT ☐

CONFIDENTIAL

65-68218-4

Appendix

RADIOGRAM TO NEW YORK
         LOS ANGELES
         BALTIMORE
RE: CHRISTINE KEELER; JOHN PROFUMO

LORD ASTOR OF ENGLAND ON WHOSE CLIVEDEN ESTATE SEX ORGIES
REPORTEDLY OCCURED. IT WAS HERE THAT PROFUMO FIRST MET
KEELER.

DOUGLAS FAIRBANKS, JUNIOR, MOVIE ACTOR; EARL FELTON,
AMERICAN SCREEN WRITER; AND MANY OTHERS ALSO INVOLVED.

(S)

FEDERAL BUREAU OF INVESTIGATION
U. S. DEPARTMENT OF JUSTICE
COMMUNICATIONS SECTION
JUN 22 196
TELETYPE

269

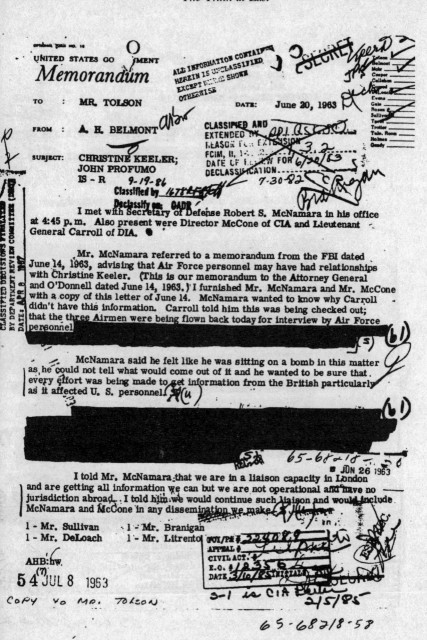

UNITED STATES GO ᴼ MENT

Memorandum

ALL INFORMATION CONTAINED
HEREIN IS UNCLASSIFIED
EXCEPT WHERE SHOWN
OTHERWISE

TO : MR. TOLSON   DATE: June 20, 1963

FROM : A. H. BELMONT

SUBJECT: CHRISTINE KEELER;
JOHN PROFUMO
IS - R

CLASSIFIED AND
EXTENDED BY
REASON FOR EXTENSION
FCIM, II,
DATE OF REVIEW FOR
DECLASSIFICATION

Classified by
Declassify on OADR

I met with Secretary of Defense Robert S. McNamara in his office at 4:45 p.m. Also present were Director McCone of CIA and Lieutenant General Carroll of DIA.

Mr. McNamara referred to a memorandum from the FBI dated June 14, 1963, advising that Air Force personnel may have had relationships with Christine Keeler. (This is our memorandum to the Attorney General and O'Donnell dated June 14, 1963.) I furnished Mr. McNamara and Mr. McCone with a copy of this letter of June 14. McNamara wanted to know why Carroll didn't have this information. Carroll told him this was being checked out; that the three Airmen were being flown back today for interview by Air Force personnel

McNamara said he felt like he was sitting on a bomb in this matter as he could not tell what would come out of it and he wanted to be sure that every effort was being made to get information from the British particularly as it affected U. S. personnel.

65-68218

JUN 26 1963

I told Mr. McNamara that we are in a liaison capacity in London and are getting all information we can but we are not operational and have no jurisdiction abroad. I told him we would continue such liaison and would include McNamara and McCone in any dissemination we make.

1 - Mr. Sullivan   1 - Mr. Branigan
1 - Mr. DeLoach   1 - Mr. Litrento

AHB:hw.

54   JUL 8 1963

COPY TO MR. TOLSON

65-68218-58

270

Appendix

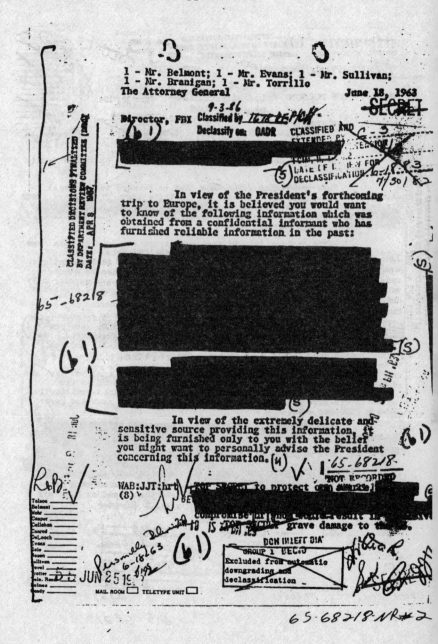

1 - Mr. Belmont; 1 - Mr. Evans; 1 - Mr. Sullivan;
1 - Mr. Branigan; 1 - Mr. Torrillo

The Attorney General   June 18, 1963

Director, FBI

In view of the President's forthcoming
trip to Europe, it is believed you would want
to know of the following information which was
obtained from a confidential informant who has
furnished reliable information in the past:

In view of the extremely delicate and
sensitive source providing this information, it
is being furnished only to you with the belief
you might want to personally advise the President
concerning this information.

65-68218

WAB:JJT:hrt
(8)

Excluded from automatic
downgrading and
declassification

65-68218-NR#2

271

UNITED STATES GOVERNMENT

Memorandum

ALL INFORMATION CONTAINED
HEREIN IS UNCLASSIFIED EXCE..
WHERE SHOWN OTHERWISE.

1 - Belmont
- Mohr
- Evans

TO : W. C. Sullivan (WC)   DATE: 7/11/63

FROM : W. A. Branigan Classified by   1 - DeLoach
Declassify on: OADR   1 - Sullivan
1 - Liaison
1 - Branigan
1 - Lee

SUBJECT: BOWTIE
INTERNAL SECURITY - RUSSIA - GREAT BRITAIN

Bowtie is the code name for case involving Christine Keeler and John Profumo.

This memorandum recommends that we forward to the Legal Attache, London, copies of reports in the White Slave Traffic Act (WSTA) investigation of Marie Novotny and ███████████████████ the signed statement given by Novotny in New York admitting prostitution activities.

Marie Novotny is a British prostitute involved in this case. She is known to Dr. Stephen Ward, procurer for Christine Keeler. Novotny is currently married to one Horace Dibben, an alleged antique dealer, and it was at their home in London that the infamous dinner party occurred at which a titled Englishman served dinner wearing only a mask. Their home has also been mentioned as the scene of perverted and sadistic activity.

Novotny, at the request of Harry Towers, British television producer, came to the United States 12/14/60 and lived in New York until 23/3/61, when she was arrested on a charge of prostitution. We filed a WSTA complaint against Towers on 3/7/61. In April and May, 1961, Towers and Novotny fled from the United States.

In a signed statement dated 3/7/61 Novotny admitted that she had sexual relations with Towers in England before coming to the United States. She further admitted that she entertained prostitution dates in New York regularly and earned about $400 per week and gave Towers $300 per week.

███
███
███

(S) Bates has also requested that he be furnished with copies of pertinent reports in that case for his own information.

65-68218

JPL:pm (9)

XEROX

JUL 17 1963

ST-115

REC-136 65-68218-263

L5-68218-263

INDEX

Index

Index

Index